MILD TO WILD

ADVENTURES & ACTIVITIES IN SOUTHERN AFRICA

Fiona McIntosh

Contents

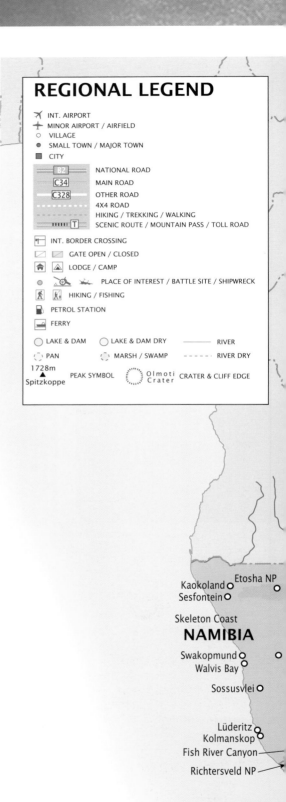

REGIONAL LEGEND

✈ INT. AIRPORT
✦ MINOR AIRPORT / AIRFIELD
○ VILLAGE
● SMALL TOWN / MAJOR TOWN
■ CITY

B2 NATIONAL ROAD
C34 MAIN ROAD
C328 OTHER ROAD
4X4 ROAD
HIKING / TREKKING / WALKING
T SCENIC ROUTE / MOUNTAIN PASS / TOLL ROAD

INT. BORDER CROSSING
GATE OPEN / CLOSED
LODGE / CAMP
PLACE OF INTEREST / BATTLE SITE / SHIPWRECK
HIKING / FISHING
PETROL STATION
FERRY

○ LAKE & DAM   ○ LAKE & DAM DRY   ——— RIVER
PAN   MARSH / SWAMP   - - - - RIVER DRY
1728m
▲ PEAK SYMBOL   Olmoti Crater   CRATER & CLIFF EDGE
Spitzkoppe

Etosha NP
Kaokoland ○
Sesfontein ○
Skeleton Coast
NAMIBIA
Swakopmund ○   ○
Walvis Bay
Sossusvlei ○
Lüderitz ○
Kolmanskop ○
Fish River Canyon —
Richtersveld NP —
Clanwilliam —

UGANDA
Murchison Falls
Lake Albert
Queen Elizabeth NP
Lake Edward
KAMPALA
Lake Victoria
RWANDA
Virunga NP
Lake Kivu **KIGALI**
Nyungwe Forest Reserve
BUJUMBURA
BURUNDI
Lake Tanganyika
Lake Mweru

KENYA
Lake Turkana
Marsabit NR
Aberdare NP
Losai NR
Buffalo Springs NR
Masai Mara NP
Mt Kenya NP
NAIROBI
Nairobi NP
Serengeti NP
Tsavo NP
Lamu
Amboseli NP
Ngorongoro Crater
Malindi
Kilimanjaro
Mombasa
Tarangire NP
Arusha NP
Pemba Island
DODOMA
Zanzibar
TANZANIA
DAR ES SALAAM
Mafia Island
Selous GR

Shiwa Ngandu
Nyika NP
Lake Malawi
Kasungu NP
Luangwa NP
LILONGWE
ZAMBIA
Kafue NP
LUSAKA
Cahora Bassa
Monkey Bay
Liwonde NP
Mozambique Island
Lake Kariba
Mana Pools NP
MALAWI
Zambezi Kariba
Zambezi
MOZAMBIQUE
Kavango River
Chobe NP
Livingstone
Victoria Falls
HARARE
Khaudum NP
Hwange
Mutare
Gorongosa NP
Tsodilo Hills
Maun
ZIMBABWE
Beira
Okavango Delta
Makgadikgadi Pans
Great Zimbabwe
WINDHOEK
BOTSWANA
Bazaruto Archipelago
Kruger NP
SWAZILAND
Kgalagadi TP
GABORONE
Pilgrim's Rest
Inhambane
Keetmanshoop
PRETORIA
Mpumalanga
MAPUTO
Cradle of Humankind
Mbombela
Augrabies Falls NP
MBABANE
iMfolozi GR
Zululand
Orange
Upington
Dundee
St Lucia
LESOTHO
Ladysmith
Battlefields
Springbok
MASERU
SOUTH AFRICA
Durban
Cederberg
Karoo NP
Sani Pass
Port Edward
Karoo
Beaufort West
Wild Coast
Cape Winelands
Knysna
East London
CAPE TOWN
Garden Route
Addo Elephant NP
Mossel Bay
Port Elizabeth

SEYCHELLES
Praslin Island
Mahé Island
COMOROS
Aldabra Islands
Montagne d'Ambre NP
Ankarana SR
MAURITIUS
ANTANANARIVO
Rodrigues Island
MADAGASCAR
RÉUNION (FRANCE)

COUNTRIES COVERED BY THIS ATLAS
○ CITIES, TOWNS, REGIONS & SITES

South Africa (includes Lesotho and Swaziland)

IN THIS CHAPTER

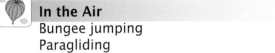
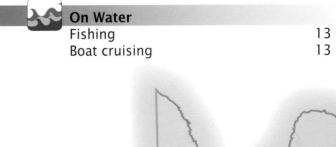

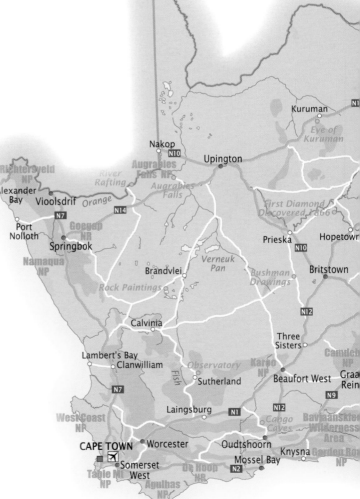

A herd of zebras grazing.

QUICK FACTS

Capital: Pretoria, Cape Town, Bloemfontein
Area: 1,221,040km² / 471,446mi²
Population: 48,8 million
Main ethnic groups:
· Black (75%)
· White (14%)
· Coloured (9%)
· Asian (2%)
Main languages:
· English
· Afrikaans
· 9 other indigenous black languages
Main religions:
· Protestant (55%)
· Catholic (9%)
· Hindu (1%)
· Muslim (1%)
Currency: Rand (100 cents)

Sterkfontein Caves.

Activities in Swaziland:

On Land
Adventure caving	14
Hiking	14
Climbing	14
Mountain biking	14
Horse riding	14
Rhino and elephant tracking	14
Cultural immersion	14
Quad biking	15
Game viewing	15

On Water
Rafting	15
Houseboating and cruising	15
Kayaking	15

In the Air
Canopy tour	15

South Africa

10 TOP ADVENTURES

1. Sandboarding
2. 4x4ing
3. Abseiling
4. Game viewing
5. Rock climbing
6. Hiking
7. Steam train trips
8. Shark cage diving
9. Bungee jumping
10. Paragliding

Sandboarding.

One-stop shop
SANParks
www.sanparks.org
+27 12 428 9111 or
+27 82 233 9111
Ezemvelo KZN Wildlife
www.kznwildlife.com
+27 33 845 1000
CapeNature
www.capenature.co.za
+27 21 483 0190
South African Tourism
www.southafrica.net
Nightjar Travel
www.nightjartravel.com

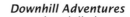 ## ON LAND

 WILD

Sandboarding

Sandboarding, South Africa's answer to snowboarding, requires the same skills and offers the same adrenalin rush. The hotspots are the white sands of the Atlantis and Betty's Bay dune fields near Cape Town, but if you want something a bit tamer, head to the golden dunes near Port Alfred. Sign up, wax your board, strap it onto your feet and carve your way down.

Downhill Adventures
www.downhilladventures.com
+27 21 422 0388

Outdoor Focus
www.outdoorfocus.co.za
+27 46 624 4432

MILD

4x4ing

There are endless 4x4 routes criss-crossing the country, but if you're looking for a real wilderness adventure, head to the Richtersveld, in the northwest corner of the Northern Cape where South Africa rubs shoulders with the arid mountain ranges of southern Namibia. Self-guided trails start at Sendelingsdrif and follow a network of gravel tracks and sandy stretches between the camp sites along the Orange River. This is the only place in the world where 'half-mens' trees (*Pachypodium namaquanum*) grow naturally, so keep your eyes peeled for the rare succulents.

SANParks
www.sanparks.org
+27 12 428 9111

WILD

Abseiling

The ultimate abseil is from the top of Table Mountain. Hold your breath, step over the edge and slowly descend 112m, enjoying the breath-taking scenery. Abseiling also offers a different perspective of the Garden Route's Knysna Heads, Oribi Gorge in KwaZulu-Natal and the Sabie River Valley in Mpumalanga.

Abseil Africa
www.abseilafrica.co.za
+27 21 424 4760
Garden Route Adventure Centre
www.gardenrouteadventures.com
+27 44 691 3182

Wild 5 Adventures
www.wild5adventures.co.za
+27 82 566 7424
Induna Adventures
www.indunaadventures.com
+27 13 737 8308

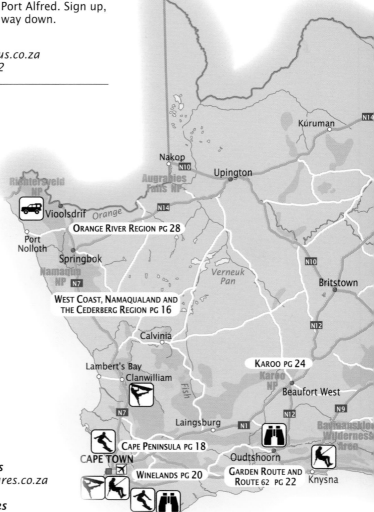

Lion spotted on a game drive, Mpumalanga.

Game viewing

MILD

South Africa's most famous park is the Kruger NP, but the country boasts several other fine reserves. Most game viewing is done from a vehicle, but there are many other exciting options that take you into the heart of the bush. iSimangaliso Wetland Park (a UNESCO World Heritage Site) offers game viewing on foot, on horseback and from a kayak as well as, from November to February, turtle tours on which loggerheads and leatherbacks can be seen dragging themselves up the beaches to lay their eggs. You can walk with intriguing little meerkats near Oudtshoorn, take a scenic whale-watching flight over Hermanus or, in the Cape of Good Hope Section of Table Mountain National Park and De Hoop Nature Reserve, cycle past herds of plains game.

Umfolozi Wilderness Trail
www.kznwildlife.com
+27 33 845 1000

Meerkat Adventures
www.meerkat
adventures.co.za
+27 84 772 9678

iSimangaliso Wetland Park
www.isimangaliso.com
+27 35 590 1633

Extreme Nature Tours
www.extremenature
tours.co.za
+27 82 257 5612

Jacana Collection
www.jacanacollection.
co.za
+27 12 803 9109

Downhill Adventures
www.downhill.com
+27 21 422 0388

De Hoop Collection
www.dehoopcollection.
com
+27 21 422 4522 or
+27 86 133 4667

St Lucia Kayak Safaris
www.kayaksafaris.
co.za
+27 35 590 1233

Rock climbing

WILD

South Africa is a rock climber's paradise, with spectacular routes on fantastic quality rock. The environments are pristine and it's almost unknown to have to queue for a route. The premier sites are Emgwenya (Waterval-Boven), Table Mountain, the Cederberg and uKhahlamba Drakensberg – where you can also ice climb in winter. Rocklands, in the Cederberg, is one of the world's premier bouldering venues.

Mountain Club of South Africa
www.mcsacapetown.
co.za
+27 21 465 3412

Peak High Mountaineering
http://peakhigh.co.za
+27 33 343 3168

Rock n Rope
www.rocrope.com
+27 13 257 0363

Climb ZA
www.climbza.com

Blue Mountain Adventures
www.samountain
sport.co.za
+27 82 550 6819

Venture Forth
www.ctsm.co.za
+27 21 554 3225

High Adventure Africa
www.highadventure.
co.za
+27 21 689 1234

Map labels:

Musina
Tom Burke
N1
N11
Thohoyandou
Polokwane
Kruger NP
Madikwe GR
Pilanesberg GR
N4
Sun City/Lost City
N11
PRETORIA
Mbombela
N4
Komatipoort
Mahikeng
JOHANNESBURG
N12
Middelburg
MBABANE
N17
SWAZILAND
N12
N2
Tembe Elephant GR
Piet Retief
Vaal
N11
Wilge
Newcastle
N3
Golela
iSimangaliso (St Lucia) Wetland Park
N1
N5
St Lucia
Richards Bay
N8
BLOEMFONTEIN
MASERU
Katse Dam
Estcourt
N2
KwaDukuza
LESOTHO
uKhahlamba Drakensberg Park (WHS)
Pietermaritzburg
Durban
Garieb NR
Oribi Gorge NR
Aliwal North
Port Shepstone
N6
N2
Mkambati NR
Mthatha
Mountain Zebra NP
Queenstown
N10
Bhisho
East London
Addo Elephant NP
N2
Port Alfred
Port Elizabeth

Rock climbing at Rocklands, Cederberg.

South Africa

ON LAND

Hiking

South Africa has a myriad marked trails, from easy strolls to multi-day treks. Some of the best, and most popular, take you through the forests and fynbos of Table Mountain, the Garden Route and Eastern Cape, to unusual rock formations in the Cederberg and Magaliesberg and to the high peaks of the Drakensberg. Slackpacking options cater for those wanting a good hike and overnight comfort without the hassle of lugging a pack.

SANParks
www.sanparks.org
+27 12 428 9111
Cape Nature
www.capenature.co.za
+27 21 483 0190
Ezemvelo KZN Wildlife
www.kznwildlife.com
+27 33 845 1000

Jacana Collection
www.jacanacollection.co.za
+27 86 152 2262
Wild Coast Holiday Reservations
www.wildcoastholidays.co.za
+27 43 743 6181
Spanafrican Adventures
www.spanafrican-adventures.co.za
+27 33 330 6125

Steam train trips

A trip with Rovos Rail, billed as the world's most luxurious train trip, is a first-class journey. Other notable excursions are on the Blue Train and the Atlantic Rail. Friends of the Rail run trips around the Tshwane, Pretoria, Midrand and Johannesburg areas.

Rovos Rail
www.rovos.com
+27 12 315 8242
The Blue Train
www.bluetrain.co.za
+27 12 334 8459

Friends of the Rail
www.friendsoftherail.com
+27 12 548 4090
Atlantic Rail
www.atlanticrail.co.za
+27 21 556 1012

ON WATER

Shark cage diving

The cage diving industry put the southern Cape town of Gansbaai firmly on the world adventure map, but, in winter, you can also go out to Seal Island, off the Cape Peninsula, with Apex Shark Expeditions. If lady luck smiles you'll catch great whites breaching and hunting for seals, then don dive gear and hop in the cage in the hope of getting up close and personal with 'Jaws'. Further up the coast, Mossel Bay has viewing areas 10 minutes from the launch site, and the adrenalin-pumping activity is now also offered at Scottburgh in KwaZulu-Natal.

Gansbaai Tourism
www.gansbaaiinfo.com
+27 28 384 1439
Apex Predators
www.apexpredators.com
+27 79 051 8558

Electrodive
www.electrodive.co.za
+27 82 561 1259
The Shark Diving Company
www.sharkcagediving kzn.com
+27 82 373 5950

Shark cage diving, Gansbaai.

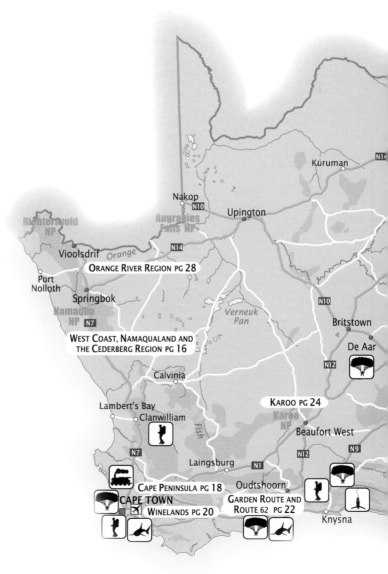

Kuruman

Nakop

Upington

Richtersveld NP

Vioolsdrif · Orange

Port Nolloth

Augrabies Falls NP

ORANGE RIVER REGION PG 28

Springbok

Namaqua NP

Verneuk Pan

Britstown

WEST COAST, NAMAQUALAND AND THE CEDERBERG REGION PG 16

De Aar

Calvinia

Karoo NP

KAROO PG 24

Lambert's Bay

Clanwilliam

Fish

Beaufort West

Laingsburg

CAPE PENINSULA PG 18

Oudtshoorn

CAPE TOWN

WINELANDS PG 20

GARDEN ROUTE AND ROUTE 62 PG 22

Knysna

Bungee jumping off Bloukrans bridge.

IN THE AIR

Bungee jumping
At a whopping 216m, the bungee jump off the Bloukrans bridge is the world record holder – a double trump since Bloukrans is the highest bridge in Africa. The 100m leap from the brightly decorated Orlando Towers offers an exciting detour on a visit to Soweto.

WILD

Face Adrenalin
www.faceadrenalin.com
+27 42 281 1458
Orlando Towers Bungee
www.orlandotowers.co.za
+27 71 674 4343

Paragliding
There are few things as exhilarating as flying. If you want to feel the thrill of free flight, take a tandem flight off Lion's Head or venture up the coast to the Map of Africa in Wilderness. De Aar in the Karoo is another top spot, and the feather in its cap is that several world cross-country paragliding records have been set in its skies.

MILD

Para-Pax
www.parapax.com
+27 82 881 4724
Cloudbase Paragliding
www.cloudbase-paragliding.co.za
+27 44 877 1414
Fly De Aar
www.flydeaar.co.za
+27 53 631 1555

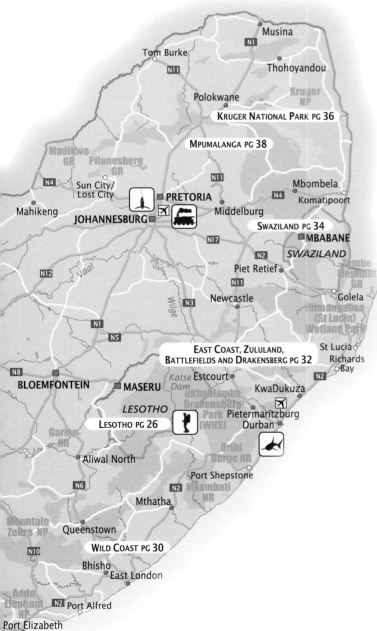

Paragliding at the Map of Africa, Wilderness.

OTHER ADVENTURES

1. Mountain biking
2. Caving
3. Horse riding
4. Stand-up paddle boarding
5. Diving
6. Sea kayaking

 ON LAND

The Cape Epic Challenge.

Mountain biking

Cycling is one of the finest ways to explore the country's vast and unique landscapes. The Karoo, KwaZulu-Natal Midlands and West Coast are top spots for freewheeling, while the Richtersveld MTB Trail in the Northern Cape and the annual Cape Epic are aimed at hard-core riders.

Tony Cook Adventures
www.tonycookadventures.co.za
+27 82 783 8392

Active Escapes
www.active-escapes.co.za
+27 33 330 6131

Wheels of Time
www.capebiosphere.co.za
+27 861 TRAILS (872 457)

Knysna Cycleworks
www.knysnacycles.co.za
+27 44 382 5153

Day Trippers
www.daytrippers.co.za
+27 21 511 4766

SANParks
www.sanparks.org.za
+27 27 831 1506

Bike & Saddle
www.bikeandsaddle.com
+27 21 813 6433

Cape Epic
www.cape-epic.com

Caving

Exploring the belly of the Cango Caves or following in the footsteps of early humans at the Cradle of Humankind top the charts for caving in South Africa.

Cango Caves
www.cangocaves.co.za
+27 44 272 7410

Wild Cave Adventures
www.wildcaves.co.za
+27 11 956 6197

Horse riding

Horseback adventures are a great way to explore the country. You can ride with the Big Five, canter along empty beaches or even go wine tasting without worrying about drinking and driving. And if saddling up is not your thing – or you've had one tipple too many and might topple – you can always take a carriage ride around the vineyards.

Bhangazi Horse Safaris
www.horsesafari.co.za
+27 83 792 7899

Wine Valley Horse Trails
www.horsetrails-sa.co.za
+27 21 869 8687

Wait A Little
www.africanhorsesafari.com
+27 83 273 9788

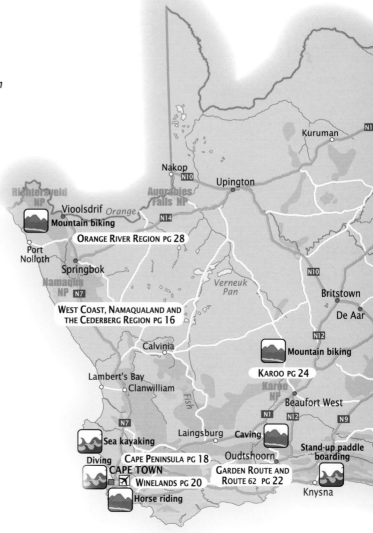

ON WATER

Stand-up paddle boarding
SUP is making waves across the country. Easy to learn and a great way to get fit, it's open to anyone, on almost any body of water. Hotspots include Surfer's Corner in Muizenberg, Langebaan and Knysna.

Tony Cook Adventures
www.kitesurfingafrica.co.za
+27 82 783 8392
Cape Sports Center
www.capesport.co.za
+27 22 772 1114

Diving
South Africa has a massive variety of diving on offer. Sodwana Bay is the Mecca, with its outstanding coral reefs. Diving with tiger and hammerhead sharks is a big attraction of the KwaZulu-Natal coast, while the kelp forests in the colder waters of the Western Cape are spectacular to explore. Try to catch the Sardine Run which takes place along the Wild Coast and south coast of KwaZulu-Natal in June/July.

Reefteach
www.reefteach.co.za
+27 35 571 0231
Adventure Mania
www.adventuremania.co.za
+27 82 653 7824
Sodwana Bay Lodge
www.sodwanabaylodge.com
+27 35 571 0117
African Watersports
www.africanwatersports.co.za
+27 39 973 2505
Blue Wilderness Safaris
www.bluewilderness.co.za
+27 83 303 1515
Pisces Divers
www.piscesdivers.co.za
+27 21 782 7205
Bubble Blowers
www.bubbleblowers.co.za
+27 21 554 3817
African Dive Adventures
www.afridive.com
+27 82 456 7885

Sea kayaking
Langebaan, on the West Coast, offers stunning kayaking on the protected, turquoise waters of the lagoon. You can also paddle out to find whales in Walker Bay or dolphins in Plettenberg Bay.

Cape Sports Center
www.capesport.co.za
+27 22 772 1114
Walker Bay Adventures
www.walkerbayadventures.co.za
+27 82 739 0159
Dolphin Adventures
www.dolphinadventures.co.za
+27 83 590 3405

Sea kayaking, Garden Route.

Lesotho

10 TOP ADVENTURES

1. Horse riding
2. Abseiling
3. Fossil viewing
4. Hiking
5. Mountain biking
6. Skiing
7. 4x4ing, quad and off-road biking
8. Rallying
9. Fishing
10. Boat cruises

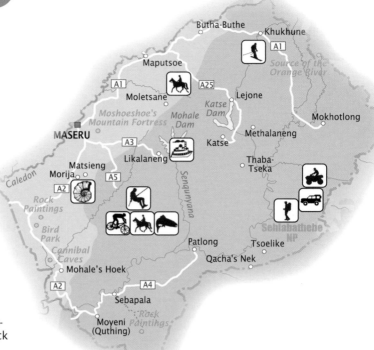

ON LAND

Horse riding

 MILD

This is the classic Lesotho adventure, with pony treks lasting from a couple of hours to a week. It's rugged scenery but the little Basotho steeds are sure-footed and mild tempered, and there is no better way to explore the country and enjoy the traditional hospitality of its people. Alternatively, hijack a donkey from Semonkong Lodge and go on a pub crawl to the local bars and shebeens!

Semonkong Lodge
www.placeofsmoke.co.ls
+266 27 006 037 or
+266 62 021 021
Malealea Lodge & Pony Trek Centre
www.malealea.co.ls
+27 82 552 4215
Phasemane Pony Treks and Adventures
www.tradingpost.co.za
+266 22 340 202

Khohlo Ntso Pony Trekking
www.geocities.ws/
katseponytreks/
aboutus.htm
+266 58 997 419
Maliba Lodge
http://maliba-lodge.com
+266 62 625 422

Abseiling

 WILD

At 204m, the precipitous Maletsunyane Waterfall abseil holds the Guinness World Record for the highest commercially run abseil in the world.

Semonkong Lodge
www.placeofsmoke.co.ls
+266 27 006 037

Fossil viewing

 TO DO

Lesotho is a real-life Jurassic Park, with some of the best deposits of dinosaur fossils and fossilised prints in the world. Dinosaur footprints may be found at a couple of locations, including on a great sandstone slab at Morija.

Morija Guest Houses
www.morijaguesthouses.com
+266 22 360 306

Hiking

 MILD

There are few marked trails in Lesotho, but, given that there are no fences and people seem fairly relaxed about where you walk, the country is ideal for guided and self-sufficient hikers. All the lodges will organise pack animals and guides, and you can take off for as long as you like along the pony-trekking routes, enjoying the hospitality of local villages. The Sehlabathebe National Park is a great wilderness trekking destination.

Sani Mountain Lodge
www.sanimountain.co.za
+27 78 634 7496

Mountain biking

 MILD

The Mountain Kingdom is the perfect place to explore on a bike. Bring your own steed and get a map and advice from the lodges, or sign up for one of the challenging multi-day rides. Be prepared for high altitude and some serious climbs.

The Lesotho Sky
www.lesothosky.com
+266 58 559 399
Tour de Lesotho
www.freedomchallenge.
org.za
+27 84 567 4152
Big Sky Ride
www.nicwhite.co.za
+27 82 855 3578
Semonkong Lodge
www.placeofsmoke.co.ls
+266 27 006 037

Morija Guest Houses
www.morijaguesthouses.
com
+266 22 360 306
Malealea Lodge & Pony Trek Centre
www.malealea.co.ls
+27 82 552 4215
Bike & Saddle
www.bikeandsaddle.com
+27 21 813 6433

ON LAND

Skiing
Afri-Ski, high in the Mahlasela valley of the Maluti Mountains, has downhill skiing in winter and a range of summer activities including river rafting, horse riding, quad biking and 4x4 adventures to amuse. When conditions are good, snow-skiing is also possible on the slopes below the Mahlasela Pass – rent skis and boots from New Oxbow Lodge.

Afri-Ski
www.afriski.net
+27 861 AFRISKI (+27 861 237 4754)
New Oxbow Lodge
www.oxbow.co.za
+27 51 933 2247

**One-stop shop
Lesotho Tourist Board**
http://visitlesotho.travel
+266 22 313 760 or
+266 22 312 238

4x4ing, quad and off-road biking
The Maluti Mountains are a massive unfenced region where, if you have a 4x4 or a quad or off-road bike, you can go exploring more or less at will. But if you really want to get a feel for the country, try the classic Lesotho 4x4 Trail which starts in Himeville, in KwaZulu-Natal, takes you up the Sani Pass and ends 400km later in Fouriesburg in the Free State.

Sani Pass Tours
www.sanitours.co.za
+27 33 701 1064
Major Adventures
www.majoradventures.co.za
+27 33 701 1628

The Trading Post Lodge
www.tradingpost.co.za
+266 22 340 202
Maliba Lodge
http://maliba-lodge.com
+266 62 625 422

Rallying
The famous three-day Roof of Africa Rally, often described as the 'mother of all hard enduro events', is open to participants in rally cars and on motorcycles and ATVs. The course, centred around the capital, Maseru, is a real test of a driver's skills, offering up all that a die-hard off-roader could ever ask for.

Roof of Africa Rally
www.roofofafrica.org.ls
+266 22 322 772

ON WATER

Fishing
There are few more pristine places to cast a fly. Most of the lodges will whisper the location of their secret spots and set you up with the necessary permits.

Semonkong Lodge
www.placeofsmoke.co.ls
+266 27 006 037
Malealea Lodge & Pony Trek Centre
www.malealea.co.ls
+27 82 552 4215
The Trading Post Lodge
www.tradingpost.co.za
+266 22 340 202

Boat cruises
Daily sunset, sunrise and champagne cruises are a great way to take in the highland atmosphere of the Mohale Dam.

Mohale Boating
www.ltdc.org.ls
+266 22 936 432

OTHER ADVENTURES

1. Mountaineering
   Sani Mountain Lodge
   www.sanimountain.co.za
   +27 78 634 7496
2. Morija Arts and Cultural Festival
   www.morijafest.com
   +266 22 360 308
3. Rock and ice climbing
   Semonkong Lodge
   www.placeofsmoke.co.ls
   +266 27 006 037
   Morija Guest Houses
   www.morijaguesthouses.com
   +266 22 360 306
   New Oxbow Lodge
   www.oxbow.co.za
   +27 51 933 2247
4. Horse racing
   Semonkong Lodge
   www.placeofsmoke.co.ls
   +266 27 006 037 or 62 021 021

Pony trekking.

4x4ing up Sani Pass.

Swaziland

10 TOP ADVENTURES

1. Adventure caving
2. Hiking
3. Climbing
4. Mountain biking
5. Horse riding
6. Rhino and elephant tracking
7. Cultural immersion
8. Rafting
9. Houseboating and cruising
10. Canopy tour

Caving.

 ## ON LAND

 ### Adventure Caving

Climbing, crawling and wriggling through a maze of passages in what may by the world's largest granite cave makes a visit to the Gobholo Caves a hard-core adventure.

 WILD

Swazi Trails
www.swazitrails.co.sz
+268 24 162 180

 ### Hiking

Swaziland has plenty of peaks to climb and game reserves to hike in, but don't miss out on the outstanding scenery of the Malolotja Nature Reserve in the northwest. Rolling montane grassland full of small game, tumbling waterfalls and clear pools make this a perfect place to escape for a short walk or multi-day expedition.

MILD

Malolotja Nature Reserve
www.sntc.org.sz/reserves/malolotja.asp
+268 24 443 241

 ### Climbing

Scrambling up the extreme, sheer granite face of Sibebe Rock is almost gravity defying, so you'll be glad of your experienced guide.

WILD

Swazi Trails
www.swazitrails.co.sz
+268 24 162 180

 ### Mountain biking

There's plenty to challenge on Swazi's hectic dirt and the country is ideal for journeying through on your own bike. The best cut trails are at Mlilwane Wildlife Sanctuary. Hire bikes from the Mlilwane Camp or nearby Swazi Trails.

 MILD

Swazi Trails
www.swazitrails.co.sz
+268 24 162 180
Mlilwane
www.biggameparks.org
+268 25 283 943/4

One-stop shop
Swazi Trails
www.swazitrails.co.sz
+268 24 162 180
Swaziland Tourism Authority
www.welcometoswaziland.com

 ### Horse riding

Rugged Swaziland is ideal riding country and the perfect size for a cross-country trail. Hawane Trails offer hourly rides in the northwest, while Chubeka Trails offer short and multi-day trails from Mlilwane Wildlife Sanctuary. One of the best is the overnight trail where you sleep in a cave with a view of the breathtaking 'Valley of Heaven'.

MILD

Hawane Resort
www.hawane.co.sz
+268 24 441 744

Chubeka Trails
www.biggameparks.org/
chubeka/
+268 25 283 943/4

 ### Rhino and elephant tracking

Mkhaya Game Reserve is one of the few places in Africa where, in the company of professional guides, you can track black rhino, white rhino and other endangered species on foot. Take a day tour or stay overnight in the all-inclusive bush camp.

 WILD

Big Game Parks
www.biggameparks.org
+268 25 283 943/4

 ### Cultural immersion

Get a feel for what it's like to live in a rural African community. Shewula Mountain Camp is one of Southern Africa's most successful community-run tourism projects. Enjoy walks through the community and extensive views from the Lubombo Mountains while soaking up the natural hospitality and friendliness of your hosts.

TO DO

Shewula Mountain Camp
www.shewulacamp.com
+268 76 051 160

ON WATER

Rafting

WILD

The Great Usutu is a Southern African gem and though water levels change, it's runnable all year. Exciting but relatively straightforward, it is usually run in two-person 'croc rafts' by Swazi Trails, who also keep eight-seater rafts for high-water season. Unusually for rafting companies, they guarantee departures for even a two-person booking. Combined days of rafting, tubing and abseiling alongside the Holomi Waterfall are available in the winter months.

Swazi Trails
www.swazitrails.co.sz
+268 24 162 180

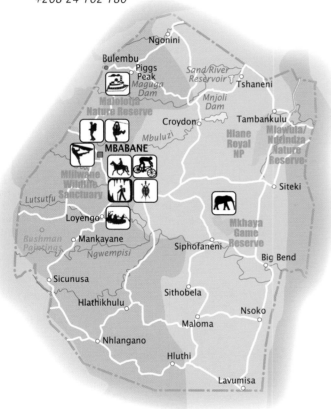

Houseboating and cruising

Renting a houseboat for a day on the magnificent Maguga Dam is a wonderful way to chill out and enjoy the scenery and bird life, or to indulge in a bit of bass fishing. For the ultimate 'no sweat' activity, take a relaxed late afternoon boat cruise across the scenic Maguga Dam aboard the 16-seater *Shosholoza* – a great way to celebrate the end of any day.

TO DO

Hawane Resort
www.hawane.co.sz
+268 24 441 744

Maguga Lodge
www.magugalodge.com
+268 24 373 975/6

Rafting.

IN THE AIR

Canopy Tour

MILD

Whizz through the trees above the otherwise inaccessible Majolomba River Gorge in the Malolotja NR. Consisting of 11 elevated forest platforms, 10 slides and a 50m-long suspension bridge over the river, this is one of the most exciting canopy tours in Africa.

Malolotja Canopy Tour
www.malolotjacanopytour.com
+268 76 975 704

OTHER ADVENTURES

1. Quad biking
   Swazi Trails
   www.swazitrails.co.sz
   +268 24 162 180
   Nkonyeni
   www.nkonyeni.com
   +268 25 400 023
2. Game viewing
   Big Game Parks
   www.biggameparks.org
   +268 25 283 943/4
3. Kayaking
   Swazi Trails
   www.swazitrails.co.sz
   +268 24 162 180

Climbing.

THE FLOWER ROUTE
The official flower route covers vast distances and can take several days to complete, but visitors often need travel no further than the Postberg Section of the West Coast National Park (an hour north of Cape Town) to enjoy the spring display. Species (4000 at the last count) range from gazanias, neon daisies and mesembryanthemums to hardy succulents and geophytes like irises and bulbinellas. Best viewed Aug–Oct, flowers open with the sun, so cloudy days are no good. Blooms are best between 11:00 and 16:00; ensure that you drive with the sun behind you so that the petals face you.

THE WEST COAST

The wild, rocky nature of the West Coast, coupled with almost desert-like conditions inland, creates a forbidding picture. But that's not taking into account two major rivers: the Orange in the north and the Olifants that snakes into Clanwilliam Dam, both of which have been harnessed to irrigate vast citrus orchards, wheatfields and vineyards. The N7 highway forges a route up the West Coast and connects Malmesbury (centre of the region's wheat industry) with Citrusdal, Clanwilliam and Vanrhynsdorp's spectacular spring flower displays.

LANGEBAAN

The lagoon is what draws crowds to the sleepy town of Langebaan: hobie sailers, windsurfers and parasailers consider this their playground. Part of the West Coast National Park and an important wetland for bird life, the 16km (10-mile) lagoon is also a paradise for bird-watchers. Ibis, flamingos, Hartlaub's gulls, herons, white pelicans and curlews are among the species that can be seen.

ELAND'S BAY

Eland's Bay is popular with crayfish divers in the open season, but dates can change and permits are required, so be sure to check with the local authorities. The terrain around here is great for off-roading; the local tourist information centre will supply you with a map of the best 4x4 trails.

MALMESBURY HISTORIC WALK
The local tourist bureau's 'historic route' brochure can be downloaded from www.malmesburytourism.co.za for free.

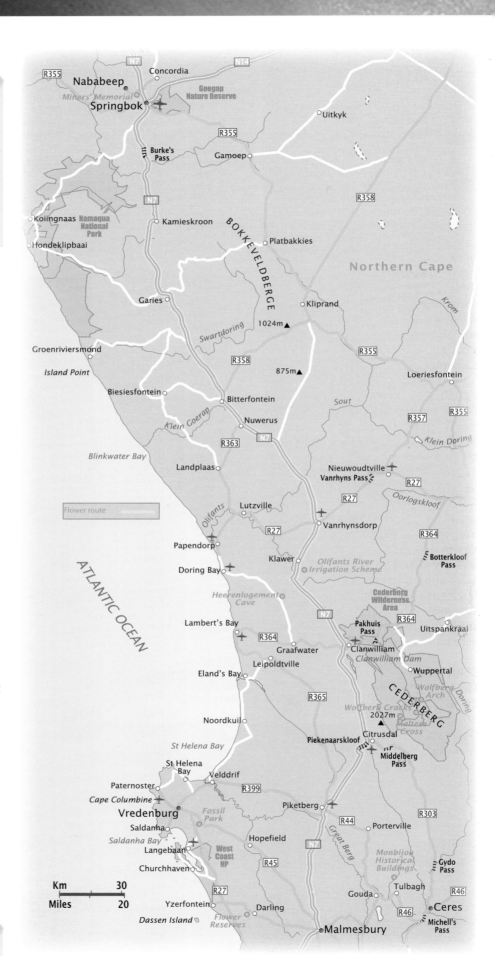

LAMBERT'S BAY

Bird Island is the main reason for a visit. It can be accessed via a breakwater-cum-harbour wall and you'll smell the guano before you get to see the thousands of African penguins, cormorants and Cape gannets, all of whom you can spy on from a viewing tower.

PATERNOSTER AND ST HELENA BAY

Paternoster, reputedly named for the Lord's Prayer after Portuguese sailors survived a shipwreck here, is a charming village with traditional, thatched fishermen's cottages. Around the promontory, St Helena Bay is another village on a pretty bay popular with scuba divers. Crayfishing does require a permit, so be sure to check with the authorities.

CEDERBERG HIKING

The Cederberg range has been eroded into fantastic shapes and is favoured by walkers and hikers. The 20m-high (65ft) Maltese Cross is a day hike from Dwarsrivier, the 30m-high (98ft) Wolfberg Arch less than half a day, and the Wolfberg Cracks closer still, though the latter is not for the faint-hearted. Views from all of the sites are stupendous. Nearby, the Tafelberg and Sneeuberg, where the snow protea grows, can also be climbed. And don't miss out on the fascinating San paintings in caves with evocative names like Amphitheatre and Stadsaal (city hall). Visitors need permits to see them.

CLANWILLIAM

The 18km (11-mile) stretch of lake at the foot of the gnarled Cederberg range is heaven for boaters and water-skiers. On its shore are holiday homes and an idyllically placed camp site. The dam, fed by the Olifants River, irrigates surrounding farmlands, and water can often be seen bursting through its sluice gates.

CITRUSDAL

A great base for day trips into the Cederberg, Citrusdal has a good information centre and accommodation (mostly out of town). It also has a little local history museum. Mountain-biking trips in the area are popular as are skydiving excursions (tandem, free fall and training for beginners) at Modderfontein farm. Around Citrusdal there is bass fishing and freshwater angling in the Olifants River, several hiking trails, 4x4 routes, scenic drives, sightseeing (from rock art to wildflowers) and wine tasting at Citrusdal Cellars.

TANKWA KAROO NATIONAL PARK

The 80,000-hectare (197,600-acre) park is in one of the most arid regions of the Karoo, where rainfall of 80mm (3.1 in) a year means that the gentlest shower produces a dazzling display of flowering succulents. The park offers solitude and spectacular views.

WHAT NOT TO DO IN THE CEDERBERG

· Don't touch or deface rock art.
· Don't bolt the rock without permission.
· Don't interfere with plants or wildlife.
· Don't litter (this includes toilet paper!) and remember to take home all the litter you bring in or create.
· Don't discard cigarette butts.
· Don't make fires anywhere other than in designated areas.
· Don't use soap or detergents in or near rivers and mountain streams.
· Don't bring pets unless they are allowed where you are staying.
· Don't forget the necessary permits.
· Don't damage the sensitive vegetation by walking off hiking paths.
· Don't remove or disturb fossils – they are protected as part of a heritage site.

CEDERBERG IN A NUTSHELL

Requirements: Permits are required for hiking and camping.
Risk factor: Hiking boots and thick socks prevent insect and animal bites.
Facilities: A number of basic camp sites cater for hikers. There are also several resorts with chalet accommodation, as well as a number of B&Bs.

Top to bottom: fishing boats in Paternoster; Namaqualand flowers; the Maltese Cross, Cederberg.

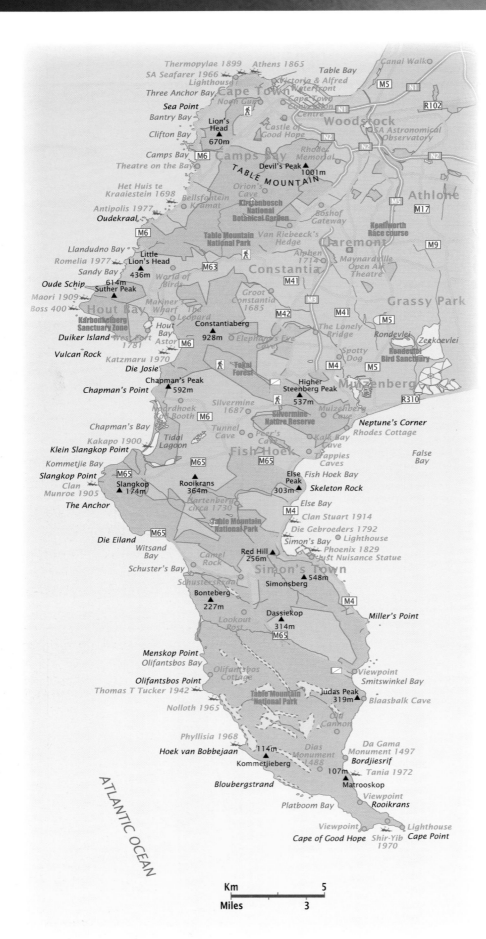

TABLE MOUNTAIN

The greatest natural asset in the Cape Peninsula, Table Mountain was carved over hundreds of millions of years as a result of dramatic geological movements and climatic changes, varying from ice ages to periods of low sea level and even volcanic disturbances. It is South Africa's most recognisable icon, the most photogenic of structures, and without it Capetonians would be lost (they navigate around the city with the aid of the mountain as a reference point).

KRAMATS AND THE CIRCLE OF ISLAM

Kramats (Mazaars), the holy shrines of Islam, mark the graves of holy men of the Muslim faith who have died at the Cape. There are more than 20 recognised kramats in the Cape Peninsula area, with at least another three in the outlying districts of Faure, Caledon, Rawsonville and Bain's Kloof. Locals and foreigners visit these special places to seek help with personal and physical problems as well as purely to practise their faith.

KIRSTENBOSCH GARDEN

Many of South Africa's finest floral treasures are on display in the easily accessible Kirstenbosch National Botanical Garden, nestled under Table Mountain. Numerous art and craft exhibitions (as well as flower shows and sales) occur throughout the year, as do music concerts and the incredibly popular Carols by Candlelight over the Christmas period.

CAPE POINT

Cape Point offers a varied experience of fynbos, topped off with rocky outcrops and intriguing stretches of beach. A nature reserve since 1938, its 7750ha (19,150 acres) of rich and varied flora and fauna and 40km (24.8 miles) of coastline provide a fitting 'ending' for the African continent. The mythical Adamastor was said to have been sent to the point to guard sailors rounding the Peninsula.

JUST NUISANCE

Just Nuisance, born on April Fool's Day in 1937, was a Great Dane that became a legend for looking after drunken sailors during WWII. Friendly, much loved and terribly spoiled, Nuisance became the first and only dog to be officially enlisted into the British Royal Navy. A much-visited statue at Jubilee Square (Main Road, Simon's Town) commemorates this fine hound's life.

HOUT BAY AND CHAPMAN'S PEAK

On a big rock below the start of the recently revamped Chapman's Peak Drive (one of the world's most wanted views) is a statue of a leopard. The iron effigy is a lasting tribute to the wild animals that used to roam Hout Bay (leopards used to wander around the village). Today, Hout Bay is popular with artists and crafters, has a lovely family and walking beach, and is also frequented by surfers and kayakers. The nearby World of Birds sanctuary is another well-loved destination.

SUPER SCUBA

Coastal conditions are generally good year-round for diving (with a wet suit!) off the Cape Peninsula. The Peninsula offers fantastic kelp diving for all abilities in depths usually not greater than 15m, and you can embark on shore diving from just about anywhere on the coast. Not for the faint-hearted or inexperienced, boat diving provides as good a wreck- and rock-diving experience as you could wish for anywhere in the world.

BOULDERS BEACH

Boulders Beach's spectacular rounded granite boulders offer unique, sheltered bathing coves. The boulders were shaped through a combination of fracturing, erosion and sea-level fluctuation – they did NOT roll down the mountain! Boulders is a vital conservation ground to save the African penguin for future generations (there is an entrance fee). There were just two breeding pairs of penguins in 1982, but 3600 penguins currently waddle around Boulders. Boulders Beach was rated one of the five best beaches to visit before you die by none other than the BBC!

GETTING WRECKED
High winds and a wicked coastline play havoc with much of Southern Africa's shores, and Cape Town is famous for its many shipwrecks, some of which provide excellent wreck-diving opportunities.
· *Kakapo* (1900)
· *Thomas T Tucker* (1942)
· *Athens* (1865)
· *Antipolis* (1977)
· *Romelia* (1977)
· *Nolloth* (1965)
· *Phyllisia* (1968)
· *Clan Stuart* (1914)

BAD NEWS FOR SAILORS
Shipwrecks aren't the only reasons for a coastline to be described as treacherous … piracy and general warfare also cause ships to sink without trace. Lovers of shipwrecks will be drawn to the following coastlines:
· Namibia's Skeleton Coast
· France's Bay of Villefranche sur Mer
· Argentina's Tierra del Fuega
· Mexico's Matagorda Bay
· Australia's Queensland and New South Wales
· The Caribbean
· The Spanish Azores
· Israel's Red Sea

Top to bottom: view of Cape Town and Table Mountain from Signal Hill; Fourth Beach and Lion's Head; the Thomas T Tucker *shipwreck (1942) at Cape Point.*

THE CAPE WINELANDS

How do you compete with towering jagged mountains, one range giving way to another, and many carrying whimsical names like Hex (witch), Drakenstein (dragon stone) and Riviersonderend (river without end)? At the foot of these great mountain ranges lie neatly manicured vine terraces whose crowning glory are the gracefully curved and moulded gables of historical manor houses, an enduring heritage of the early Dutch settlers. Passes forged through this mountain barrier to the east made it a gateway to the rest of the country – this region was, early on, baptised the 'overberg', meaning 'over (or across) the mountains'.

The Western Cape winelands are the main reason for South Africa's plum position as seventh-largest wine producer in the world, with a growing number of estates, co-operatives and private cellars. The wineland areas are accessed via two major national routes, the N1 and N2, with multiple connecting and well-signposted principal roads.

CONSTANTIA

The official Constantia Wine Route was once limited to five estates, but now consists of eight – Groot Constantia, Buitenverwachting, Constantia Glen, Constantia Uitsig, Eagles Nest, High Constantia, Klein Constantia and Steenberg. Leafy oaks, whitewashed gables, vine terraces and soaring mountains create an amazing backdrop to the source of some stunning wines. Buitenverwachting, Groot Constantia, Klein Constantia and Constantia Uitsig all once formed part of a farm granted to Simon van der Stel in 1685.

DURBANVILLE WINE ROUTE

Settled into undulating hills and mountains, the surrounding slopes decked in vines, Durbanville's vineyards are producing very respectable grapes that are being pressed into highly quaffable wines. Durbanville Hills winery waves its magic wand with some very fine lemon-butter chardonnays and grassy-nosed sauvignon blancs ('chard' and 'sav blanc' to the wine toff). The

Diemersdal, Nitida, Meerendal and Altydgedacht estates don't do too badly either on all lip-smacking scores of both red and white wines.

THE TOP WINE COUNTRIES			
Wine Producers		**Wine Drinkers**	
1	Italy	1	Luxembourg
2	France	2	France
3	Spain	3	Portugal
4	USA	4	Italy
5	Argentina	5	Switzerland
6	Germany	6	Argentina
7	South Africa	7	Greece
8	Australia	8	Spain
9	Chile	9	Uruguay
10	Romania	10	Austria

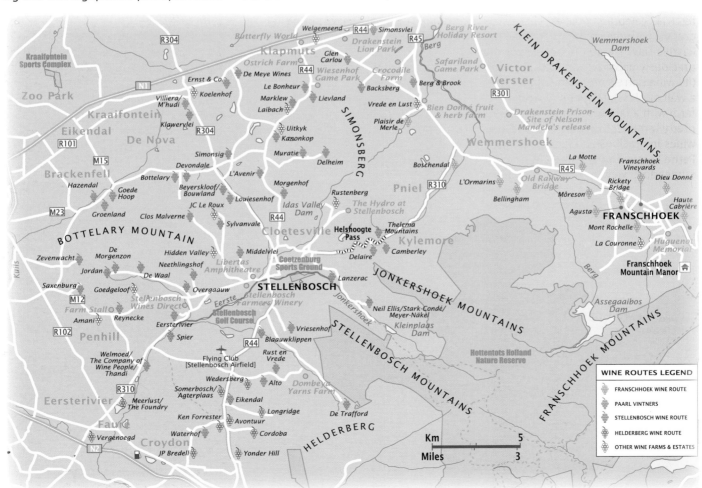

STELLENBOSCH

In streets lined with leafy old oaks, this pretty university town's buildings rub shoulders: historical cottages and Cape Dutch with Cape Georgian, Regency and Victorian houses. Dorp Street is a marvel for its meticulously preserved façades, most of them historical monuments. Stellenbosch buys into café society, and there's a good selection of trendy coffee shops spilling out onto the pavement. The town has some very good art galleries and art museums: Dorp Street Gallery, the gallery at 34 Ryneveld Street, the Rupert Gallery and the Rembrandt van Rijn Art Gallery. You can only expect to successfully visit three or four wine cellars in a day, so plan well. There are around 30 cellars and co-operatives on four major roads within a 12km (7-mile) radius from Cape Town.

A CORNER OF FRANCE

Franschhoek is a den for hedonists; taking its cue from the French, it's a centre for wining and dining, festivals and fun. Year-round, the town stages festivals celebrating olives, cheese, grapes, with the cherry on top being Bastille Day. The top farms include the graciously gabled L'Ormarins, La Motte (its wine barrels are visible through a wall of glass), Môreson (a working farm with a large, airy restaurant and a pretty terrace), Haute Provence (superb wines in gracious surrounds) and La Petite Ferme (lovely lawns and a stupendous view).

THE PEARL OF THE WINELANDS

The Main Street in Paarl, which tails the Berg River, runs an amazing 11km (7 miles) and boasts rows of 18th- and 19th-century Cape Dutch and Georgian houses. About one-fifth of the country's total wine production comes from Paarl, and the most striking symbol of its wine history is La Concorde, a neo-classical building with a sculpted pediment, dating back to 1956. Watch Fairview Wine Estate's Saanen (Swiss) goats nimbly navigate a thin spiral ramp up a tall tower, and then test their milk cheeses. At Zanddrift you can taste wines in a stone chapel that was built in the early 1940s by Italian prisoners of war, while world-famous Nederburg holds an annual wine auction. The swooping white spires on the hill are part of the Taal (language) Monument, a tribute to the Afrikaans *taal*. It has three domes and three small pillars that vary in size and height. Nearby, Paarl Mountain can be climbed with the help of chain handholds. This granite outcrop, the world's second largest after Australia's Uluru, wears its age well – 500 million years and counting.

GREAT WINE REGIONS

· Bordeaux	France
· Stellenbosch	South Africa
· Napa Valley	California, USA
· Alto Douro	Portugal
· Marlborough	New Zealand
· Porto	Portugal
· Sonoma Valley	California, USA
· Chianti	Tuscany, Italy
· Yarra Valley	Melbourne, Australia
· Florence	Tuscany, Italy
· Maipo Valley	Santiago, Chile
· Rhein-Mosel	Germany
· Bilbao-Rioja	Spain

Top to bottom: typical Winelands landscape; wine barrels; grapes of the Carignan variety.

THE GARDEN ROUTE

The official start of the Garden Route, Mossel Bay is famous for its natural gas deposits, but the idiotically brave can enjoy shark cage dives which operate off the coast. The Dias Museum celebrates the 500th anniversary of Dias' historic arrival, while outside by the famous milkwood tree a stone boot acts as a mailbox for visitors' postcards, which are duly marked with a special stamp. The coastline is fed by countless rivers, drenching rains, and mists sweeping in from the sea, keeping it enduringly moist, fertile and green. This is punctuated by wave-lapped beaches, river mouths, lagoons and lakes, making it the natural playground for outdoor types – walkers and hikers, cyclists and mountain bikers, canoeists and windsurfers. The Wilderness Lakes (a loop of sinuous waterways, lakes, a lagoon and estuary) offer bird-watching trails guaranteed to get you close to the tweeters. Knysna's serene 17km-long (10,5-mile) lagoon is guarded at its sea entrance by two sandstone cliffs, the Knysna Heads. The quaint town is one of a number of beach and water-sport havens that are packed during the holiday season.

North of Knysna, Noetzie's stone castles line a stunning curve of beach, which is accessible via steep stairs.

KAYAKING THE GARDEN ROUTE

The more than 200km (125-mile) stretch of scenic coastline between Mossel Bay and the Storms River Mouth is remarkably undeveloped: craggy cliffs, soft beaches, gentle inland waters and endless ocean. Barricaded from the arid interior by the Outeniqua and Tsitsikamma mountains (both offer famed trails through rugged mountains and tangled forest), the Garden Route is a world of cliffs and coves, lakes and lagoons fed by the Indian Ocean, and a playground for the canoeist and kayaker. The wild ocean, placid inlets and lazy lagoons offer many other water sports too: surfing, sailing, waterskiing and angling. The beaches and ocean, blessed with sunny summers and mostly temperate winters, are set against a verdant backdrop. Thousands of hectares of reserves and conservation areas, such as the Garden Route National Park, lie along the beaches, but it is the salty sea air and gentle winds that lure kayakers. Operators are relatively few, but those who do work these shores are knowledgeable and helpful. The best time to take to the waters is at sunset, when dolphins cavort in the waves, seals ply the ocean and gentle 'white horses' ripple across the sea. Remember that the ocean is untamed, and beach-based lifesavers and rescue units are not on duty in the off-season. It is not unheard of for kayaks to be surrounded by relatively harmless hammerhead sharks and even the occasional great white. The weather, although generally faultless, can be temperamental, the waves unpredictable and the sun harsh, but this is a small price to pay for superb kayaking conditions.

THE OTTER AFRICAN TRAIL RUN

Probably the most popular trail run in South Africa, the Otter is one of the best in the world. Participants run a challenging technical route through the Tsitsikamma Section of the Garden Route National Park. First staged in September 2009, the trail consists of 42km of running through fynbos and along beaches, a swim across Bloukrans River, and numerous drops and climbs.

The Otter is not to be taken lightly. It's important to carry the right gear and to be cautious. Sudden changes of weather or flash floods can change the race in an instant. Rescue could take up to an hour because of the inaccessibility of the route. Runners have to carry cellphones, but signal is intermittent.

SURFING AT JEFFREYS BAY

Jeffreys Bay is a surfer's haven, because it has some of the finest surf you're likely to find on earth, according to the locals. Beachcombers, too, will enjoy it. The air is alive with sea spray, the beach sand sprinkled with shells and you can spot pods of dolphins if you're lucky. 'J Bay' is proudly clinging to its laid-back roots despite plenty of local development for the tourist industry.

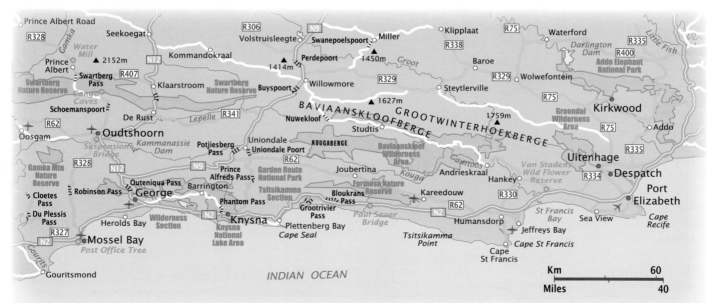

STORMS RIVER

Storms River is a hive of adventure activities, including black-water tubing, abseiling and snorkelling. The big daddy for all the adrenalin junkies out there, however, has to be bungee jumping ... and the Bloukrans bridge has one of the world's highest platforms at a gut-wrenching 216m (708ft). Go on – take the plunge.

ROUTE 62

In much the same way as the famous Route 66 in the USA links the urban and rural communities of Chicago and Los Angeles, Route 62 in South Africa links Cape Town and Port Elizabeth. The route allows travellers to take in the longest wine route in the world, as well as the Breede River Valley and the Little Karoo. The Langeberg Mountains around Ashton have plenty of hiking routes and trails for the adventure seeker, while Soekershof in Robertson is home to one of the world's largest hedge mazes – the Klaas Voogds Maze covers 13,870m^2 (149,241ft^2).

Robertson is famous for its cheese, wine, roses and horses, and is said to be one of the most hospitable towns in the region, but one of Route 62's most famous landmarks has to be Ronnie's Sex Shop, about 25km (15 miles) outside Barrydale. It's certainly worth a visit.

Bonnievale's Tokkelossie Museum describes the culture and history of farm workers as well as the recently outlawed 'dop' system (paying workers with alcohol).

The Breede River Valley is rich in diversity, with an abundance of breath-taking mountain views, sparkling streams, orchards, vineyards (the largest wine producing valley in the Western Cape), indigenous flora, springs and adventure.

Montagu is undoubtedly the B&B capital of Route 62. It is a firm favourite as a 'weekend-away' destination, and its hot springs are a great crowd-puller.

GARDEN ROUTE IN A NUTSHELL
Climate: Conditions are generally good year-round, but winter rains can be bother-some. Summer is the peak holiday period, during which the area is really crowded.
Risk factor: Usually gentle, but the warm ocean can pose a shark risk.
Pack: Some sunscreen and waterproof clothing, but operators should provide the necessary equipment.
Facilities: Facilities offered by operators are generally good to very good, although the nature of the adventure means that participants should be prepared to get at least a little wet, with some discomfort in the cold winter.

Top to bottom: Robberg Nature Reserve; the elusive Knysna Turaco; the Dutch Reformed Church in Swellendam.

THE TWO KAROOS

The Karoo is a vast, dry expanse of desert-like terrain that stretches across sections of the Western Cape and into the Northern Cape. It is divided into the Little and the Great Karoo, according to geological factors as well as topography, vegetation and climate. Its name comes from the indigenous Khoi people's description of it as the 'land of great thirst'.

The Karoo boasts the world's greatest number of succulents (as well as some of the largest specimens), with more than 9000 in the Beaufort West region alone. The scenery is flat, monotonous, and stretches to the horizon, but here and there pancake-layered outcrops reveal the typical Karoo shale and sandstone strata. Dolerite formations do break the monotony – here, the volcanic lava has thrust up through the earth, and over time been weathered into weird and wonderful shapes as the harder rock resisted the moulding and reshaping forces of wind and water. Some of these formations are highly distinctive, with names such as the Three Sisters – three similarly shaped conical hills north of Beaufort West. An enduring image of this slice of South African landscape is, here and there, a lone wind pump, like a sentinel in the crisp, eternally clear Karoo air.

KAROO NATIONAL PARK

Just north of Beaufort West stretch the plains of the Karoo National Park whose sweet grass provides fodder for many antelope species, among them hartebeest and springbok. Other wildlife has been reintroduced to the park, including black rhino, black wildebeest and Cape mountain zebra. The animal best suited to this environment is the gemsbok, with its rapier horns and its ability to endure the tough, dry conditions of the Karoo. The park has a 4x4 trail, and the Fossil (geology) and Bossie (vegetation) walking trails.

BEAUFORT WEST

The N1 is the Great North Road that connects Cape Town and Johannesburg by bisecting the Karoo. Beaufort West, the 'capital' of the Karoo region (or at least its largest town!) is located on the N1. The town has little to commend it, other than its role as a centre of civilisation in the flat, featureless middle of nowhere. Travellers can find a basic, clean place to stay overnight, fill travel-weary tums, refuel their equally travel-weary vehicles, and then stock up with lots of treats to stave off boredom from the many hours spent on the road.

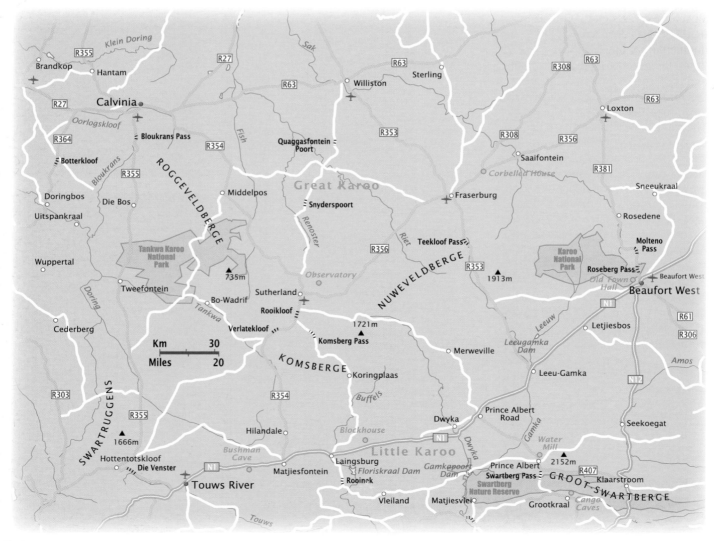

MATJIESFONTEIN

A turn-of-the-century settlement centering on the 1900 Lord Milner Hotel, the entire Matjiesfontein is a heritage site. It was all started by Scotsman James Logan in 1883, when he established a dining place alongside the railway line in an age when trains had no dining coaches. Over time, this expanded to become a hotel, and today, the Lord Milner's decorative iron-lace verandahs and white-painted square turrets are reminiscent of that elegant time.

Despite the lattice-fringed post office nearby, Matjiesfontein is, essentially, a charming hotel complex planted in the middle of the Little Karoo. The iron lace that prettifies South Africa's Victorian homes is locally termed 'broekie' lace – a reminder of the delicate lace edgings of a lady's bloomers!

Matjiesfontein boasts some interesting museums (such as the Transport Museum and the Marie Rawdon Museum), while a trip around town on the local (yet authentic!) London double-decker bus is a must.

OUDTSHOORN

The country's ostrich-farming capital boasts grandiose sandstone mansions (a.k.a. feather palaces). It has earned its reputation and status with dyed feathers, ostrich leather handbags, belts, shoes and painted eggs for sale. Visitors can choose to sit on an ostrich, brave a canter, or rather just sit and watch other people perched atop these giant – albeit flightless – birds.

The Cango Wildlife Ranch has lion and cheetah to spy on (from the safety of an aerial walkway), as well as crocodiles and alligators that snap their ugly teeth at you.

The Cango Caves offer visitors a phantasmagorical display of limestone drip formations as well as hours of fun exploring the age-old caves.

> ### THE FOUR PASSES
> Composed of rough-hewn rock and deep sky, the Four Passes route has an amazing concentration of mountain landscapes, including the Swartberg, Langeberg and Outeniqua mountains. Pass builder Thomas Bain earned his spurs at the base of these rock barriers: Seweweekspoort rises to 2325m (7628ft), Schoemanspoort chisels through a 10km (6-mile) long, narrow chasm, Swartberg winds on for 24km (15 miles) and Meiringspoort bares its cliffs in contorted, burnt-orange folds. According to legend, Seweweekspoort ('seven weeks pass') refers to the time it took the early brandy smugglers to cross this mountain barrier.

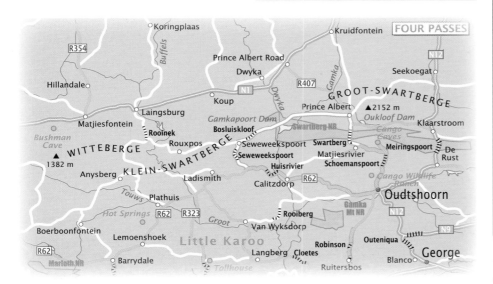

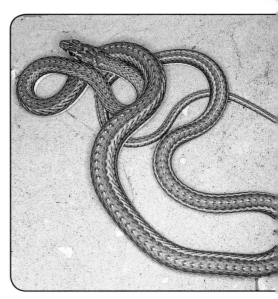

Top to bottom: sand snake; ostriches; a lonely Karoo windmill and dam.

PONY TREKKING IN THE MALUTIS

The landscape of the traditional home of the Basotho people is wild and rugged. Its open veld and golden grassland are skirted by rocky ridges, and much of the land is untamed and inaccessible, even on foot or by 4x4. The largely rural Basotho use horses and the sure-footed Basotho pony to navigate this terrain. These tough and hardy mounts are the most dependable way to traverse Lesotho, and an entire industry (albeit rather basic) has grown around the Basotho pony.

In the summer, the mountains are carpeted with indigenous plants, while winter brings snow to the mountain peaks that still shelter pastoral herdsmen wearing little more than the ornately decorated blankets for which the Basotho are renowned.

Crossing the countryside is not easy: the going is extremely tough in places. Despite this, you do not have to be a practised horse rider to take advantage of the unspoiled wilderness, but do familiarise yourself with some horse-riding basics.

The logistics of most pony trekking tours are carefully planned by operators based in Lesotho and South Africa. It is best to make use of their services rather than rely on your own abilities to interpret local conditions in a landscape that is both challenging and deceptive. Every care needs to be taken to avoid complications on a trip into such an isolated world, making trained guides your most vital 'accessory'.

Amenities on the South African side of the border are far more sophisticated, and the foothills of the Drakensberg are dotted with some fine lodges, private reserves and overnight facilities.

THE MALUTI IN A NUTSHELL
Requirements: Border crossings can be problematic without the correct documentation. Plan carefully.
Climate: Winter temperatures can be icy, with a formidable wind-chill factor contributing to freezing conditions. Summers are moderate to hot.
Facilities: Facilities are virtually non-existent. Be prepared.

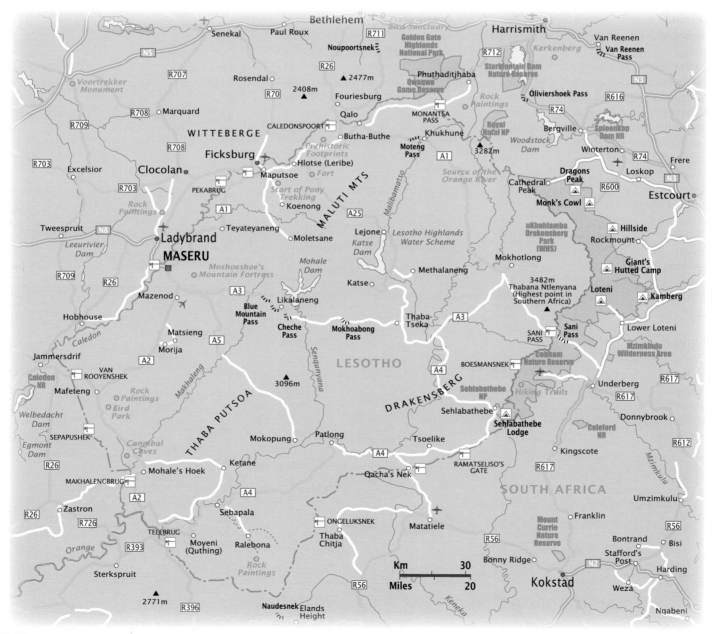

THABANA NTLENYANA

Part of the Drakensberg mountain range, which formed over 150 million years ago, Thabana Ntlenyana, in the northeastern corner of Lesotho, is the highest peak in Southern Africa. Thabana Ntlenyana ironically means 'beautiful little mountain', yet it lies 3482m (11,417ft) above sea level, offering some of Southern Africa's most spectacular views.

In winter, the snow-covered slopes are icy cold, a chilling wind whipping its way through every valley and down rock cliffs. In the balmy summer months, the rains bring with them a green blanket that clothes the rugged terrain. The hike to the top of Thabana Ntlenyana is along 25km (16 miles) of some of Lesotho's roughest terrain, rising to a height of 2000m (6562ft).

SANI PASS

Surrounded by some of the tiny nation's most magnificent scenery stands Sani Mountain Lodge, an eerily windswept haven for hikers and adventurers – the summit offers comfort in the form of the highest pub in Africa! Sani Pass snakes through the Mkhomazana River valley in the Drakensberg from just beyond the tiny village of Himeville up to Sani Top. Sani Pass soars 1000m (3280ft) over a length of only 7km (4.3 miles). The route is demanding at best, perilous at worst. The broader region caters for hikers, trailists and 'pony trekkers', usually led by the blanket-clad local Basotho people.

DRIVING SANI PASS

One of the most jaw-dropping mountain gateways in Southern Africa, Sani Pass is the highest in the region and opens up unsurpassed views over vast tracts of South Africa. The pass is whipped by winds that emit a ghostly wail as they batter the rugged slopes and pummel every nook and crevice. Extremes of weather and vegetation make the countryside all the more picturesque, and the long, winding Sani Pass is the lifeline of this remote expanse of the steep escarpment.

The pass itself is a small but significant chink in the great mountain. Once little more than a rough bridle path crafted by man and beast, and used mostly by blanketed Basotho horsemen and the occasional adventurer, Sani Pass is today the only road link between KwaZulu-Natal and the remote Lesotho highlands. Cut by breathtaking hairpin bends carved into the rocky slopes, even at its least trying the pass is an arduous and difficult climb, twisting and slicing its way along the steep inclines of the valley formed by the meandering Mkhomazana River. This is the simplest way to ascend the 2875m (9500ft) mountain face, and the vistas from even relatively low down on the pass will take your breath away.

DO NOT LOOK DOWN!

This is not a place for sufferers of even mild vertigo. The drops are long and steep, and the 6km (4-mile) route from the South African border post elevates the traveller no less than 1000m (3280ft). Not surprising, then, that no standard sedan vehicle is permitted beyond that point: this is total 4x4 terrain, and every conceivable attribute of an off-road vehicle is put to the test.

A few private individuals operate from the nearby hamlets of Underberg and Himeville. They offer the next best thing to negotiating yourself to the mountainous heights of Lesotho. It is so precipitous that even the Basotho ponies struggle a little – especially when the rocky ground is covered by a soft mantle of snow.

Although local townsfolk know the lie of the land well and are ready for most emergencies, winter snow can play havoc with even the most meticulously planned excursion.

Top to bottom: traditional hut door; shepherd in the Maluti Mountains; Mafika Lisiu Pass.

SANI PASS IN A NUTSHELL
Climate: Snowfalls in the icy winters and heavy downpours in the hot summers make spring (Aug–Nov) the best bet.
Risk factor: Not for the uninitiated or anyone with less than impressive driving skills or no head for heights. Pass is closed in bad weather.
Pack: Warm clothing during the freezing winter. Carry every conceivable necessary spare vehicle part.
Facilities: Comfortable overnight amenities in foothill towns.

RAFTING THE ORANGE RIVER

Slicing through an apparently lifeless landscape is the winding course of the mighty Orange, South Africa's greatest river and 'homeland' of its river-rafting adventures. It is the most revered by water-sport enthusiasts and, with its succession of tortuous bends, raging waters and breathtaking rapids, is justifiably one of South Africa's premier adventure destinations. Time spent on the Orange is unmatched in high-pulse excitement and wonder at the scenic beauty of its banks. The often parched landscape is simply spectacular – and taking it all in from a canoe on the river makes it all the more memorable.

Although more known for its turbulent white waters and adrenalin-pumping rapids, canoe trails and circular routes, including the impress-ive Augrabies Falls National Park, the Orange does have less demanding routes where little experience is required. This is one of the sub-continent's most powerful water-courses, so be sure to keep your wits about you, especially in sections with names like Rollercoaster, Crunch and Crusher. They will call on your strength, knowledge of the river and application of important pointers dispensed by the more experienced water guides and instructors in the introductory lecture offered by operators.

Trips can stretch from one to five days (or longer), and while you aren't expected to have any rafting experience to tackle the Orange, novice canoeists should stick to routes and trips in keep-ing with their ability. It is all too easy for the fun of an exhilarating adventure to end in disaster if you take the river too lightly. Water levels fluctuate ac-cording to the season – the river floods in summer and the rocky riverbed below the cascading waters presents dangers of its own. Sensible handling and the right equipment should ensure a safe and invigorating trip though.

THE ORANGE IN A NUTSHELL

Climate: Best during the summer rains (Nov–Jan) when waters are high.

Risk factor: Moderate to challenging, but professional river guides provide valuable instruction and guidance.

Pack: Protective, waterproof clothing adds to your comfort levels; tour operators will provide most of your requirements. Sunscreen is essential.

Facilities: Facilities offered by operators are generally good to very good, although the nature of the adventure means that participants should be willing to rough it in the wilderness.

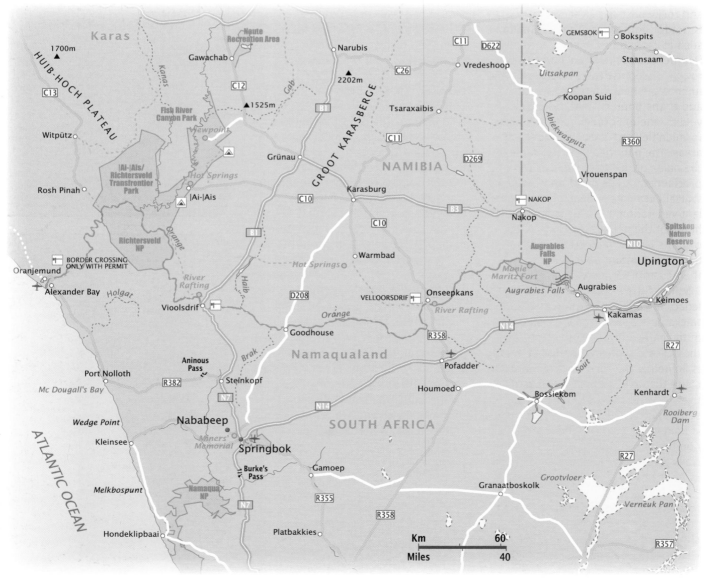

CROSSING THE RICHTERSVELD

Although accessible from a number of points in South Africa and along the Namibian border, many roads leading to the 160,000ha (395,400-acre) Richtersveld National Park may not be numbered, while routes within the park can only accommodate high-clearance and 4x4 vehicles. Situated more than 200km (125 miles) from Springbok, the region is remote, a desert landscape lined with mountains and its plains dotted with granite boulders. Crossing the Richtersveld on foot or by road demands planning and careful navigation. Make good use, too, of the few existing facilities at the camp sites and overnight stopovers.

THE ROADS LESS TRAVELLED

The 4x4 routes and hiking trails that criss-cross the veld, compact sands and rocky passes vary in intensity – it is not for nothing that natural features such as Mount Terror have earned their fearful reputation! Then again, the rough, unsophisticated tracks and often unbearable heat have only served to add to the popularity of the Richtersveld as one of Southern Africa's most formidable (and beautiful) wilderness areas. The national park that shares the name of the broader region was proclaimed in 1991 and, with its geological extremes and variety of succulent vegetation, remains the traditional home of the pastoralist Nama. They still own the land and continue to farm with livestock, keeping alive remnants of their customs and traditions.

Many of the existing 4x4 trails are the legacy of early pioneers who left their tracks here during the prospecting days of the early 20th century. To preserve the delicate ecosystem, off-road driving is limited to these numbered tracks. Because the park's official routes are relatively new, the opportunity to explore some spectacularly unspoiled wilderness is unique and, to keep it that way, the number of vehicles on dedicated 4x4 trails is restricted to three, carrying no more than 12 travellers at a time.

The hiking routes are also limited to specially demarcated zones. There are no organised hikes, due to the shortage of qualified guides, but visitors can arrange their own hikes.

RICHTERSVELD IN A NUTSHELL
Requirements: Permits for hiking, angling and 4x4 trails.
Climate: Winter (May–Aug) is best, as summer heat can be oppressive, with sandstorms and strong winds.
Risk factor: Moderate- to high-risk driving; easy to physically demanding hiking routes.
Pack: Sunscreen is essential, along with a high fluid intake. Strong winds and very basic facilities necessitate a tent that can be sealed.
Facilities: Amenities within the park vary from basic camp sites with no facilities at all to comfortable self-catering, fully equipped accommodation. Official routes and trails are clearly signposted.

Top to bottom: a klipspringer on a rocky path; Augrabies Falls; a weary 'halfmens' tree.

PORT ELIZABETH

Port Elizabeth, or PE (also known as the Friendly City, as well as the Windy City) is known for its beaches, parks and historical architecture and monuments. The city's colonial past is evident, with statues of the likes of Queen Victoria, the Horse Memorial, and the towering Campanile commemorating the arrival of the 1820 Settlers. The Campanile has a spiral staircase leading up the 52m (168ft) tower to a super viewing platform with a great perspective of the city and surrounds. Other sites worth visiting include the 54ha (133-acre) Settlers Park, the Port Elizabeth Museum, the snake park and aquarium. Township tours incorporate some of the surrounding poorer areas into the tourist's itinerary and offer an insight into the daily lives of people living here. Big favourites with locals and tourists are the coastline, with great beaches for hobie sailors and surfers, as well as scores of great diving sites. The 1799 Fort Frederick was the first stone building in the district and was built by the Brits to repel a possible French invasion. The fort never had to fire a shot, either in self-defence or in anger.

SHIPWRECK COAST

A delightfully unspoilt stretch of coastline between Port Alfred and East London offers superb natural vegetation and sandy stretches of beach. This wild, natural haven has seen the unhappy demise of countless ships, and the 64km (39-mile) Shipwreck Hiking Trail takes in some of the sites from the Great Fish River through to the Ncera River. The trail offers a unique hiking and camping experience in South Africa, with greater freedom to camp and make fires where you please. The natural scenery is calming and the views are superb.

ADDO ELEPHANT NATIONAL PARK

Lying just 72km (44 miles) north of PE is the 164,000ha (405,000-acre) refuge for the remainder of the once prolific elephant population that roamed this area. Visitors are sure of seeing elephant here. Also to be seen are spotted hyena, warthog, vervet monkey and numerous smaller mammals, as well as a good variety of antelope.

The park is being expanded into the 686,000ha (1,7-million-acre) 'Greater Addo'. By incorporating part of the coastline into this larger reserve, the natural diversity will be increased to include five of South Africa's seven major vegetation biomes, and visitors will have a chance to see the Big Seven: elephant, rhino, lion, buffalo and leopard, as well as whales and great white sharks.

EAST LONDON

A busy little port city, East London's excellent surfing conditions are a big hit with boarders young and old, notably at the famous Nahoon Beach. Holidays see the main beaches horribly overcrowded, so it's a better idea to surf out of season or slightly further away from the crowds. Besides surfing, the city offers a small aquarium, while the East London Museum has excellent displays of local Xhosa culture as well as two prize 'catches': a coelacanth and the world's only dodo egg.

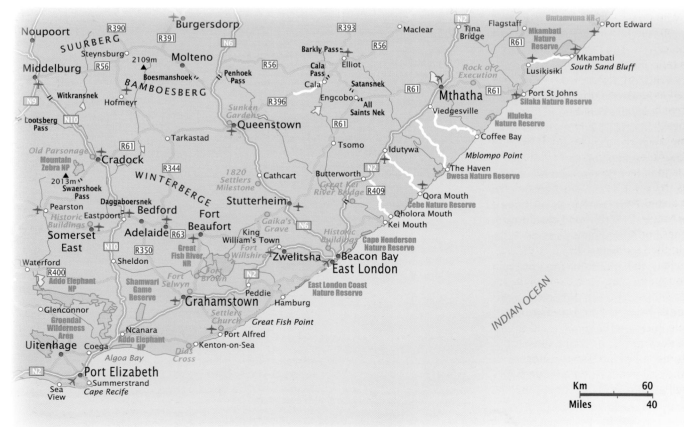

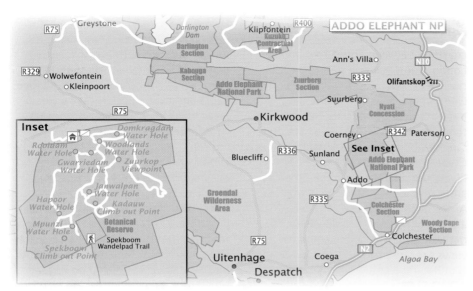

MTHATHA

This town was founded on the Mthatha River in 1871 by European settlers answering a call from the Thembu tribe to offer a barrier to invasions from the rival Pondo warriors. A small museum has interesting displays of beadwork and traditional costumes of the Xhosa.

WILD COAST NATURE RESERVES

Although the Wild Coast Hiking Trail is in a state of disrepair, private operators (e.g. Wild Coast Holiday Reservations, see p. 8) run guided/supported hikes, or you can do it independently by carrying a tent. Mkambati Nature Reserve offers canoe trips up the Msikaba River as well as walking trails. Silaka Nature Reserve boasts Cape clawless otters on the beach, along with White-breasted Cormorants. Hluleka Nature Reserve is a beautifully scenic combination of sea, lagoon and forest from Port St Johns to Coffee Bay (reportedly named after a shipwrecked 'coffee carrier'). Cebe Nature Reserve has great forests, beaches and trails, Cape clawless otters in the lagoon and the impressive Mbanyana Falls. Dwesa Nature Reserve is thought by many to be one of South Africa's most beautiful reserves, with crocodile being reintroduced into the Kobole River and herds of eland that stroll down to the beach at sunset. In the forest areas, attentive visitors may see the shy tree dassie and blue duiker, as well as samango monkeys.

WILD COAST HIKING HOTSPOTS	
· Tsitsikamma Trail	5 days
· Otter Trail	5 days
· Shipwreck Hiking Trail	3 days
· Strandloper Hiking Trail	5 days
· Amatola Trail	6 days
· Evelyn Valley Loop Trail	2 days
· Zingcuka Loop Trail	2 days
· Hogsback area	1–3 days
· Wild Coast Meander	5 days

Top to bottom: Addo Elephant National Park; 'Hole in the Wall', Wild Coast; Hobie Pier, Port Elizabeth.

iSIMANGALISO WETLAND PARK

This World Heritage Site includes a number of game and marine reserves, whose five ecosystems form one of the world's most incredible destinations. The 32,800ha (81,016-acre) area has a coastline that stretches 280km (1730 miles), while the Greater St Lucia Wetland Park on Lake St Lucia has one of Africa's largest estuaries. It acts as a nursery for innumerable species of marine life and teems with crocodile, hippo and numerous bird species, including the African Fish Eagle.

ST LUCIA AND SURROUNDS

Part of the World Heritage Site, St Lucia offers magnificent views from the village, a wide range of arts and crafts and a Crocodile Centre that breeds the endangered dwarf and longsnout crocs.

KOSI BAY AND SURROUNDS

The local Tsonga people build ingenious fish traps close to the mouth of the Kosi Estuary. The primitive but effective system provides vital sustenance.

SODWANA BAY

Sodwana has excellent hotels and lodges as well as self-catering chalets, caravan parks and tent sites located along its coastal forest. Fresh produce and local craftwork are sold at roadside markets. Sodwana is a diving hotspot famous for its marine life.

CAPE VIDAL

Here outdoor enthusiasts can sail, swim, snorkel and fish on a beautiful stretch of beach where record catches of marlin and barracuda have been registered. Saltwater fly-fishermen will enjoy Mission Rocks.

TEMBE ELEPHANT GAME RESERVE

On the South Africa–Mozambique border, Tembe protects the last of the Maputaland elephant population and also offers great viewing for birders. Tongaland's reefs are a great destination for scuba divers.

HLUHLUWE-iMFOLOZI PARK

Among the oldest wildlife sanctuaries in Africa are the two separate parks proclaimed in 1895 – the Hluhluwe and the Umfolozi – that are now united to form one of the continent's most famous reserves. Apart from the Big Five, visitors can observe a variety of other animals and an especially rich bird life.

ITALA GAME RESERVE

Criss-crossed by rivers and hiking trails, this 30,000ha (74,100-acre) reserve has grassland, forested valleys and granite cliffs. Wildlife includes giraffe, antelope, zebra and over 300 bird species. Itala is also a geological wonderland, its rock formations among the oldest in the world. All in all, this reserve offers a choice experience in what is now one of KwaZulu-Natal's premier reserves.

uMKHUZE SECTION OF iSIMANGALISO

One of uMkhuze's unique features is a rare forest of giant fig trees that reach up to 25m (82ft) in height. Nearly 400 bird species enjoy the varied vegetation, and the excellent bird hide at Nsumo Pan takes full advantage of this.

PHINDA RESOURCE RESERVE

Located between the uMkhuze Section and the Sodwana Bay Section, Phinda's seven habitats support the Big Five and 380 bird species. The walking safaris are not to be missed.

THE BATTLEFIELDS ROUTE

The Battlefields Route takes visitors across land that saw grim fighting throughout most of the 1800s, as conflict raged between Boer, Brit and Zulu. Take your time to explore the small towns along the way, and stop at monuments and cemeteries to imagine what it must have been like to face an army of attacking Zulu warriors, sunburnt British soldiers, or charging Boer horsemen.

BLOOD RIVER

A life-size wagon laager provides an awesome monument to this great battle, which saw so much loss of life that the victorious Boers claimed the Ncome River ran red with Zulu blood.

iSANDLWANA

In response to an invasion of their land (an attempt to conquer the mighty Zulu nation), 25,000 Zulu impis defeated the 24th Regiment on 22 January 1879. The loss of life was heavy: over 1000 men died on both sides.

RORKE'S DRIFT

The Rorke's Drift Museum pays homage to a mighty British defence: around 100 soldiers kept 4000 Zulu warriors at bay.

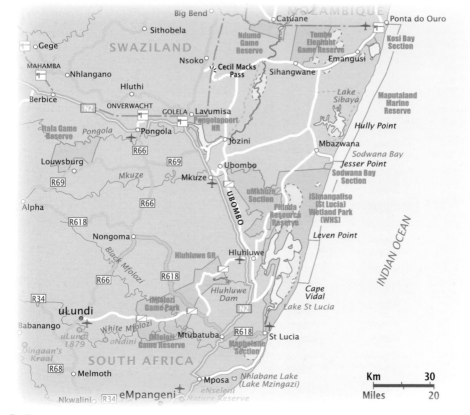

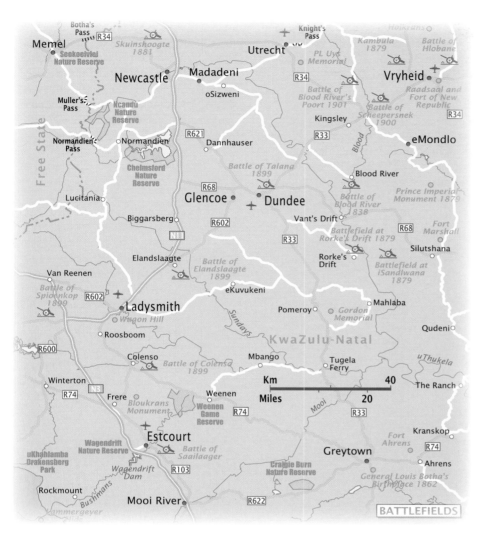

Top to bottom: loggerhead turtle hatchlings; uThukela River.

Their heroism was awarded with 11 Victoria Crosses, the highest number ever for such an engagement.

DUNDEE
Close to many battle sites and the comprehensive Talana Museum, Dundee has historic churches, buildings and a war memorial. Activities around town include horse riding, 4x4ing and hiking.

SPIOENKOP
Spioenkop has a battlefield, a dam and a nature reserve. The nearby Range-worthy Cemetery is the resting place for the fallen of Spioenkop and Bastion Hill.

NEWCASTLE
The mountains around Newcastle are great for hiking. Hilldrop House, now a heritage site, was once the home of Rider Haggard, whose life and work are documented in the museum at Fort Amiel. Fort Terror is one of several

signalling posts in the area, while St Dominic's Pavilion (1916) was originally built as a skating rink.

HIKING THE DRAKENSBERG
The ridge of high peaks that forms the escarpment between South Africa's east coast and the mountainous hinterland is one of Africa's grandest formations. This is hiker's dream of walking trails,

DRAKENSBERG IN A NUTSHELL
Requirements: Permits, where required, are available at the various park entrances.
Climate: Snowfalls in the icy winters and heavy downpours in the hot summer. Spring is best (Aug–Nov).
Pack: Camping equipment, comfortable and firm hiking boots, warm, protective clothing and sleeping bags for the freezing winters; or lightweight clothing and rain gear for the blistering summer days.
Facilities: Accommodation is relatively sophisticated, varying from basic camp sites with ablutions to very comfortable overnight huts and private lodges. Booking is essential. Many routes and trails are well signposted.

as well as arduous climbs that require fitness and commitment.

The scenic beauty is not without danger, however, and even casual hikers are advised to familiarise themselves with this area, known for its precarious drops, steep slopes and the isolation of many routes.

Swaziland

A PROUD KINGDOM

Swaziland is a small landlocked country bordered on three sides by South Africa, with Mozambique lying on its eastern side. The local people are friendly and have a good many traditions and customs, including the traditional dancing that is often on display throughout the countryside. There is also a flourishing handicraft industry. Swaziland offers an extraordinary diversity of scenery, and its excellent national parks have game drives where you can see a wide diversity of game, notably the somewhat elusive rhino. The national bird is the Purple-crested Turaco.

MBABANE

The capital, Mbabane, boasts the Swazi Plaza – a large modern shopping complex, which is a good landmark and houses the Tourist Office – and the interesting Indinglilizi Art Gallery, established in 1982 in order to show- case the work of many talented local artists. The Siteki Inyanga Sangoma School trains traditional healers and diviners, while the Muti-Muti Nature Reserve is used by the school's trainers and students as a rich source of vital herbs which grow abundantly throughout the reserve.

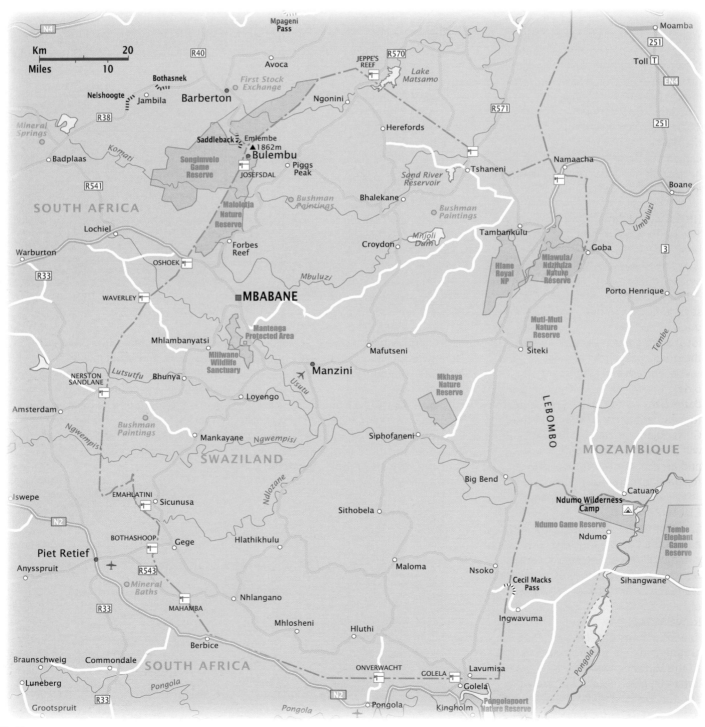

PIGGS PEAK

Located in the far north of Swaziland, Piggs Peak was once a gold mining centre named after an early prospector, William Pigg. Modern-day prospectors swarm to the new gambling centre in the hope of striking it rich, or simply just to enjoy a few hours of entertainment at a casino.

Inside the Malolotja Reserve, just 40km (24 miles) south of Piggs Peak, is the old Forbes Reef Gold Mine. Visitors can safely explore the abandoned horizontal mine shafts with the visual aid of a torch.

HIGHS AND LOWS

The smallest country in the southern hemisphere, Swaziland's highest point is at Emlembe, which is a popular climb at 1862m (6107ft) above sea level.

The Sibebe Rock is the world's second-largest granite rock and is a good picnic spot near to Mbabane. The local Sibebe beer is named in honour of the great rock.

The Ngwenya Mine is one of the oldest known mines in the world and dates back to 41,000BC. You can get to it by car. A visit to the Ngwenya Glass Factory (just west of Mbabane) will showcase some of the glasswork and art that the locals are famous for producing.

CULTURE VULTURE

Ezulwini Valley (also close to Mbabane) has all the cultural attractions you could wish for and is, in addition, a relaxing place to unwind in – understandably, since locals call it 'the place of heaven'. Not to be missed is the Incwala ceremony and the Umhlanga dances. Ezulwini is the nation's entertainment centre and the valley is home to the Mlilwane Wildlife Sanctuary. Lobamba is the royal family residence, and the Royal Kraal, Somhlolo National Stadium and the National Museum are all interesting cultural hotspots. The National Museum offers displays on Swazi origin, tradition, dress and lifestyle. Next to the museum are the parliament buildings as well as the King Sobhuze II Memorial.

NOT VERY RESERVED

Mkhaya Nature Reserve is the kingdom's VIP destination and is a refuge for endangered species – this 6200-hectare (15,314-acre) bird-watchers' paradise is particularly memorable if you are interested in raptors.

Mlilwane is a private reserve dominated by the striking Nyonyane (little bird) Peak and boasting a good collection of wildlife, including hippo and Black Eagles. The name of the reserve means 'little fire', after the many fires started by lightning strikes in the region.

Hlane Royal National Park has very good accommodation and offers visitors some of the best game viewing in Swaziland, with up to 10,000 animals gathering here during the dry season.

Mantenga is a small protected area of 725ha (1790 acres) in a corner of the Ezulwini Valley and is bordered by the little Usutu River in the south and Mlilwane to the north and west. Possibly the reserve's most famous attraction is the Mantenga Falls, the largest (in terms of volume) in Swaziland. Bird life here is abundant and includes the endangered Bald Ibis.

Top to bottom: a woman weaving baskets; Phophonyane Falls; horseback safari in the Mlilwane Wildlife Sanctuary.

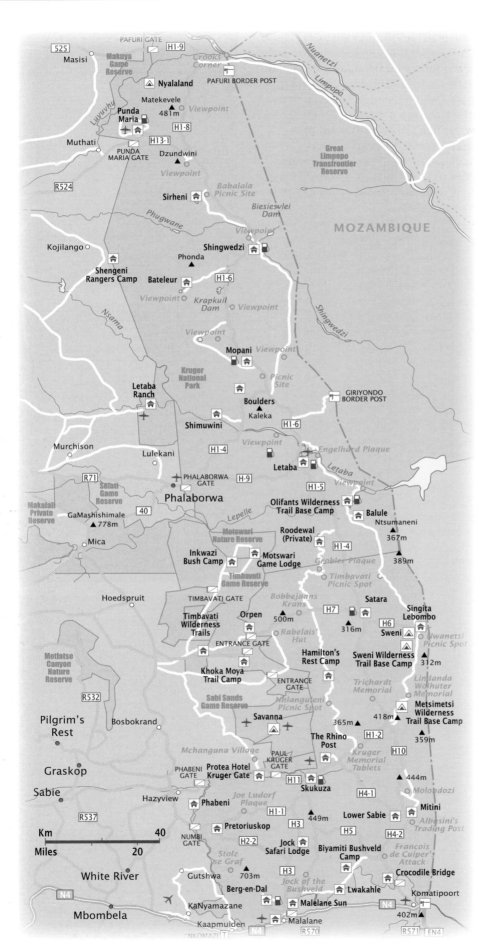

BEST GAME VIEWING IN AFRICA
· Mombo Camp,
   Moremi National Park, Botswana
· Il Moran Camp – Governor's Camp,
   Masai Mara National Park, Kenya
· Ngorongoro Crater Lodge,
   Ngorongoro Crater National Park, Tanzania
· Migration Camp,
   Serengeti National Park, Tanzania
· Singita,
   Sabi Sands Game Reserve, South Africa

AS OLD AS THE HILLS
In Kruger's northern region you can take a drive to Baobab Hill to see the majestic solitary baobab tree that has been there for centuries. This northern area may be remote, but it's definitely worth visiting – besides baobabs, numerous other tree species can be seen across the plains. Trees are an important food source for several animals, notably elephants.

THE LION THING
King of the animal world, the lion tops the wish list of most visitors when it comes to Things To See In Kruger. Many animals will make a noise if a lion is nearby, but you should also watch the skyline for giraffes: they often stare fixedly in the direction of any danger (i.e. lions).

A BIG SIX
There is such an abundance of birds compared with mammals, it's understandable that the compilers of the 'must-see' bird list couldn't agree on just five, hence the Birding Big Six: Ground Hornbill, Kori Bustard, Lappet-faced Vulture, Martial Eagle, Pel's Fishing Owl and the Saddle-billed Stork. Kruger has many superb bird hides, which offer plenty of excellent 'twitching' opportunities.

ONE, TWO, TREE

Of course trees had to get in on the act as well. The five tree species experts advise you to seek out for your check list are: Baobab, Fever Tree, Knob Thorn, Marula and Mopane. Baobabs are the great-great-grandpapa of the floral world, mopane are among the most abundant in Kruger, while the marula is surely the tastiest (when transformed into the delectable liqueur, that is).

A LOT OF LOGS IN ONE RIVER

It's something of an irony that Kruger has an uMgwenya (Crocodile) River and a Lepelle River (previously known as the Olifants), and yet the Lepelle, not the uMgwenya, is the one that boasts one of the highest densities of crocodile in all of Africa.

JOCK OF THE BUSHVELD

Dogs provide game rangers with companionship and protection, during which time strong bonds develop; hence the dog's graveyard where 'fallen friends' are buried. The most famous dog to have trodden Kruger's soil was Jock, immortalised in Percy Fitzpatrick's book, *Jock of the Bushveld*. Jock Safari Lodge was named in honour of that brave staffie, a statue commemorates his duel with a sable antelope, and other tributes to him can be seen in the park.

DRIVING TRIPS FURTHER AFIELD

You can't go wrong spending three days driving around the central region of Kruger, between the Sabie and Lepelle rivers. The Satara/Timbavati River Route is particularly enjoyable and should offer sightings of elephant and giraffe, but the Nwanetsi River to Lindanda Route is not to be missed, with magnificent scenery and many animals to be seen. The Sabie River drive will excite kids of all ages, as it covers the famous 'lion route' through lush riverside vegetation packed with wildlife. Keep the binoculars handy for your experience of the Kanniedood Dam drive – apart from marvellous scenery, monkeys, elephants and crocodiles, the birding is superb. Night drives afford some of the best wildlife spotting opportunities as many animals are livelier in the cooler evenings, which in turn attracts the predators.

THE SOUTHERN KRUGER LOOP TRIP

This part of the park is a big favourite with tourists for the abundant wildlife, varied landscapes and diverse vegetation. Driving around the southern parts of Kruger leads visitors to numerous water holes, as well as great picnic spots, viewpoints and memorials. Using Skukuza as your base, you have several choices and options, depending on the time available and your interests. The routes also link up with two exit gates, making the trips ideal as a final excursion on your way out of the park.

Top to bottom: baobabs at sunrise; a giraffe grazing on the treetops; Tawny Eagle.

PILGRIM'S REST

The town of Pilgrim's Rest sprang up as a result of the 1873 gold rush, with almost 1500 prospectors massing to the area within the year to seek their fortune. The gold held out for more than a hundred years. The restored town is now a heritage site and visitors can explore the Old Print House, Miner's House, St Mary's Anglican Church, Joubert Bridge, the cemetery (with its infamous Robber's Grave) and Dredzen & Co's general dealer store. To get a taste of life as a Pilgrim's Rest prospector, try panning for gold at the Diggings Site on the banks of Pilgrim's Creek. There are gold-panning demonstrations to watch first if you don't want to risk throwing your name (or a 'valuable' nugget) away. If you take to panning like a duck to water, then stick around till November for the annual National Gold Panning Championships, a fun festival spread over five days. Each competitor receives a bucket of sand and a regulation gold pan. Only the officials know how many nuggets are in the buckets – contestants are penalised for any nuggets they miss. The 'prospector' who pans out the most nuggets in the shortest time is declared the winner.

THE TROUT TRIANGLE

The legendary Trout Triangle lies between the sleepy country towns of eMakhazeni (Belfast), eNtokozweni (Machadodorp), Dullstroom, Emgwenya (Waterval-Boven), and Mashishing (Lydenburg). This area is a magnet for fly-fishermen and there are well-developed facilities to cater for locals and tourists alike. Sabie and Pilgrim's Rest are two other prime fishing sites. Trout are not indigenous to the area, however. Popular legend has it that the fish were introduced into the dams and rivers around Dullstroom some 80 years ago by two local enthusiasts: Mr Gurr, the postmaster, and a watchmaker by the name of Brown.

Hatcheries in Mpumalanga produce 60 percent of South Africa's trout for the retail market. These hatcheries also ensure that dams and rivers remain well stocked. They provide stock for the European export market, too. Rainbow and Brown Trout are found happily gliding through the water in most dams and rivers.

Apart from fishing guides and trips, you can arrange for one-on-one lessons or even group and corporate fishing lessons, as well as advice sessions.

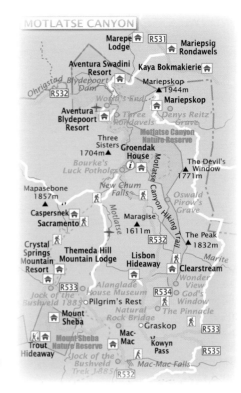

MOTLATSE (BLYDE) CANYON NATURE RESERVE

The majestic 20km (12.4-mile) long Motlatse Canyon reaches depths of 700m (2296ft) in places, its dramatic cliffs and slopes covered by dense bush and tangled forest. Antelope, small mammals, the full range of Southern Africa's primate family and a large variety of birds live in the nature reserve, along with an abundance of flowering plants, orchids, lichens, mosses and montane forest. The much-photographed Three Rondavels is a trio of rocky outcrops that has eroded into a shape reminiscent of the traditional round Zulu or Xhosa tribal huts. Two other favourite visual feasts for visitors to indulge in from the road running above the canyon are World's End and Lowveld View.

Popular activities in this area include the circular drive, short hikes and overnight trails, kloofing, microlighting and leisurely boat trips that take in the wide array of wildlife within the canyon, as well as some of the best whitewater rafting to be found in South Africa.

BOURKE'S LUCK

Looking down from the bridge across the potholes, you will stare in awe at the amazing cylindrical holes scooped out of the yellow dolomite rock floor. Over millions of years, swirling pebbles and gushing water from the Motlatse and Sefogane rivers created these dramatic natural 'rock carvings'.

ECHO CAVES

The Echo Caves are a sprawling mass of dolomite cut out by an underground river. Legend has it that the Sotho hid here from Swazi warriors and used the cave's stalactites to make spears, which is why so many of them are broken.

SUDWALA CAVES

The Sudwala Caves are the world's oldest dolomite caves, with a floor surface of 14,000m² (45,920 sq. miles). The caves feature weird and wonderful dripstone formations – stalagmites, stalactites, and the fossilised remains of 'collenia' (a form of algae believed to be the very origins of life on earth). Many of the rock formations in the caves have biblical names, such as Devil's Workshop, Samson's Pillar and the Weeping Madonna.

A five-hour tour of the Crystal Chambers can be organised. Outside the caves is a timeline of humankind as well as a 'dinosaur' park: life-size models of prehistoric wildlife that lived here 100 million years ago are set amid cycad and palm species.

SUDWALA CAVES

Top to bottom: fly-fishing in comfort; the Three Rondavels; hiking in the Motlatse Canyon.

39

Namibia

QUICK FACTS

Capital: Windhoek
Area: 824,290km² / 318,260mi²
Population: 2,1 million
Main ethnic groups:
· Ovambo (50%)
· Kavango (9%)
· Herero (7%)
· Damara (7%)
· White (6%)

Main languages:
· English
· Afrikaans
· Ovambo
· Kavango
· German
Main religions:
· Christian and Lutheran (90%)
Currency: Namibian dollar (100 cents)

IN THIS CHAPTER

Top to bottom: Giant's Playground; walking a red dune in Sossusvlei.

Namibia

10 TOP ADVENTURES

1. Hiking
2. Rock climbing
3. Stargazing
4. Quad biking
5. Sandboarding
6. 4x4ing
7. Fishing
8. Rafting
9. Ballooning
10. Skydiving

Hiking in the Fish River Canyon.

One-stop shop
Abenteuer Afrika Safari
www.abenteuerafrika.com
+264 64 404 030
Namibia Tourism
www.namibiatourism.com.na
+264 61 290 6000 or
+27 21 422 3298

ON LAND

Hiking
 MILD
The tough, multi-day Fish River Canyon and Namib-Naukluft hiking trails are world renowned, but there are numerous spectacular shorter hikes. One of the best is the guided trail at Twyfelfontein (/Ui-//aes), a World Heritage Site thanks to its vast and outstanding collection of rock petroglyphs.

Namibia Wildlife Resorts
www.nwr.com.na
+264 61 285 7101
Tok Tokkie Trails
www.toktokkietrails.com
+264 61 264 521

Twyfelfontein Country Lodge
www.twyfelfonteinlodge.com
+27 21 855 0395
Wilderness Safaris
www.wilderness-safaris.com
+27 11 883 0747

Rock climbing
WILD
Sticking abruptly out of the Namib Desert, the sharp 1730m (5676ft) Spitzkoppe is known as the Matterhorn of Southern Africa. The standard route on the spectacular granite peak is the country's most famous rock climb, but there are masses of sport and traditional climbing routes on Spitzkop itself and on the surrounding Pontoks. Aussenkehr, overlooking the Orange River in southern Namibia, offers fantastic climbing on the hard dolerite crags of the spectacular King's Throne Canyon.

Peak High Mountaineering
www.peakhigh.co.za
+27 33 343 3168
Blue Mountain Adventures

www.samountain.co.za/bluemountain
+27 21 461 6077
Norotshama Resort
www.norotshamaresort.com
+264 63 297 215

Stargazing
TO DO
No light pollution means a starry, starry sky. Stop anywhere in the wilderness and gaze up at the night sky for a mind-blowing display, or treat yourself to a stay at Sossusvlei Mountain Lodge and let the resident astronomer give you a guided tour of the heavens.

&Beyond
www.andbeyondafrica.com
+27 11 809 4300

Quad biking
MILD
Roar up dunes near Swakopmund, take a leisurely ride to Sandwich Harbour and the other historic sites near Walvis Bay, or enjoy an eco-sensitive tour of the Kulula Wilderness Reserve, learning all about the unique desert fauna and flora.

Dare Devil Adventures
www.daredeviladventures.com
+264 81 149 1261
Wilderness Adventures
www.wilderness-adventures.com
+27 11 257 5111

Sandboarding
WILD
The dunes around Swakopmund, some of the highest in the world, are a perfect playground for sandboarders. Choose to stand up on your board and learn to carve tracks in the sand, or simply lie down on a piece of plywood and whizz down at speed. Experienced operators provide tuition and gear – and take the schlepp out of the adventure by ferrying you back to the top of the dune on a quad bike!

Dune 7 Sandboarding
www.duneseven.com
+264 81 127 7636

Dare Devil Adventures
www.daredevil adventures.com
+264 81 149 1261

4x4ing
MILD
The wide open spaces of Namibia beg to be explored in a 4x4. You can head out for a day's off-road driving from Walvis Bay or Swakopmund, but if you've got a week to spare, test your driving skills and nerves on the dunes between Lüderitz and Walvis Bay. Listen to jackal calls at night, do some stargazing, lose yourself running up dunes and explore the fascinating history of this coastline.

Coastway Tours
www.coastways.com.na
+264 63 202 002
Uri Adventures
www.uriadventures.com

+264 64 220 571
Mola Mola Safaris
www.mola-namibia.com
+264 64 205 511

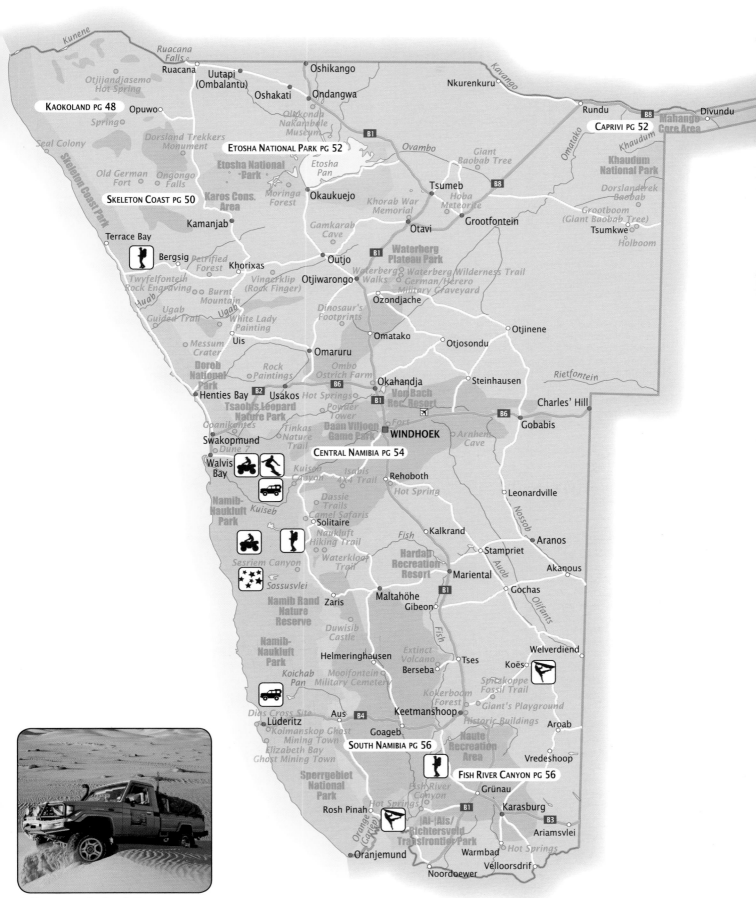

KAOKOLAND PG 48

Kunene

Ruacana Falls

Ruacana

Uutapi (Ombalantu)

Oshikango

Nkurenkuru

Kavango

Rundu

B8

Divundu

Mahango Core Area

Otjijandjasemo Hot Spring

Opuwo

Oshakati

Ondangwa

Spring

B1

Ovambo

CAPRIVI PG 52

Omatako

Khaudum

Seal Colony

Dorsland Trekkers Monument

Olukonda Nakambale Museum

ETOSHA NATIONAL PARK PG 52

Giant Baobab Tree

Khaudum National Park

Skeleton Coast Park

Old German Fort

Ongongo Falls

Etosha National Park

Etosha Pan

Tsumeb

B8

Dorslandtrek Baobab

SKELETON COAST PG 50

Karos Cons. Area

Moringa Forest

Okaukuejo

Khorab War Memorial

Hoba Meteorite

Grootfontein

Grootboom (Giant Baobab Tree)

Tsumkwe

Kamanjab

Otavi

Holboom

Terrace Bay

Gamkarab Cave

Bergsig

Petrified Forest

Khorixas

Outjo

B1

Waterberg Plateau Park

Twyfelfontein Rock Engraving

Vingerklip (Rock Finger)

Otjiwarongo

Waterberg Walks

Waterberg Wilderness Trail

German/Herero Military Graveyard

Huab

Ugab Guided Trail

Ugab

White Lady Painting

Uis

Dinosaur's Footprints

Ozondjache

Messum Crater

Omaruru

Omatako

Otjosondu

Otjinene

Doreb National Park

Rock Paintings

Ombo Ostrich Farm

Okahandja

Steinhausen

Rietfontein

Henties Bay

B2

Usakos

Hot Springs

B6

B1

Von Bach Rec. Resort

Charles' Hill

B6

Tsaobis Leopard Nature Park

Powder Tower

Daan Viljoen Game Park

Fort

Gobabis

Goanikontes

Tinkas Nature Trail

WINDHOEK

Arnhem Cave

Swakopmund

Dune 7

CENTRAL NAMIBIA PG 54

Walvis Bay

Kuiseb Canyon

Isabis 4x4 Trail

Rehoboth

Leonardville

Namib-Naukluft Park

Kuiseb

Dassie Trails

Hot Spring

Nossob

Camel Safaris

Solitaire

Kalkrand

Aranos

Naukluft Hiking Trail

Fish

Stampriet

Waterkloof Trail

Hardap Recreation Resort

Mariental

Akanous

Sesriem Canyon

Auob

Sossusvlei

B1

Gochas

Olifants

Namib Rand Nature Reserve

Zaris

Maltahöhe

Gibeon

Namib-Naukluft Park

Duwisib Castle

Extinct Volcano

Welverdiend

Helmeringhausen

Tses

Koës

Spitzkoppe Fossil Trail

Berseba

Koichab Pan

Mooifontein Military Cemetery

Kokerboom Forest

Giant's Playground

Dias Cross Site

Aus

B4

Keetmanshoop

Historic Buildings

Aroab

Lüderitz

Goageb

Kolmanskop Ghost Mining Town

Haute Recreation Area

Elizabeth Bay Ghost Mining Town

SOUTH NAMIBIA PG 56

Vredeshoop

Sperrgebiet National Park

Fish River Canyon

FISH RIVER CANYON PG 56

Grünau

Rosh Pinah

Hot Springs

|Ai-|Ais/ Richtersveld Transfrontier Park

B1

Karasburg

B3

Orange (Gariep)

Oranjemund

Warmbad

Hot Springs

Ariamsvlei

Noordoewer

Velloorsdrif

4x4ing across the Namib Desert.

43

Each activity is rated as 'To do', Mild or Wild based on intensity

TO DO **MILD** **WILD**

1 **2** **1**

 ## ON WATER

MILD

Fishing

The stretch of coast between Walvis and Henties Bay is one of the best spots in Southern Africa to hook a shark, but remember the law states that once you've reeled in your prize it has to be returned to the sea alive. The inland lakes and rivers of the Caprivi are known for their superb tiger and bream fishing.

Ocean Adventures & Angling Tours
www.fishingtoursnamibia.com
+264 64 404 281
Sunrise Fishing
www.sunrisetours.com.na
+264 64 404 561
Mola Mola Safaris
www.mola-namibia.com
+264 64 205 511

Levo Tours
www.levotours.com
+264 64 207 555
Ichobezi River Lodges
www.ichobezi.co.za
+27 79 871 7603
Kalizo Lodge
www.kalizolodge.com
+264 66 686 802

Orange River.

MILD

Rafting

Paddling down the Orange River is one of those quintessential African adventures that everyone should do at least once. Chill out, watching the birds and taking in the dramatic rocky desert scenery of southwestern Namibia as you meander down the river, stopping to picnic and overnight on sandy riverbanks. Intrepid whitewater hounds should head for thrills and spills on the remote, crocodile-infested Kunene River on the border with Angola.

Felix Unite
www.felixunite.com
+27 87 354 0578
Wildthing Adventures
www.wildthing.co.za
+27 87 354 0578
Gravity Adventure Group
www.gravity.co.za
+27 21 683 3698
Amanzi Trails
www.amanzitrails.co.za
+27 21 559 1573 or +264 63 297 255
Epupa Camp
www.epupa.com.na
+264 61 232 740
Kunene River Lodge
www.kuneneriverlodge.com
+264 65 274 300

Majestic red sand dunes.

 ## IN THE AIR

TO DO

Ballooning

If you're after romance, take a sunrise balloon ride over the Namib Desert, one of the oldest, and most beautiful, deserts on earth. Red dunes rise majestically before you, while beyond the white clay pan studded with dead trees are rugged, ancient volcanic mountains.

Namib Sky Balloon Safaris
www.balloon-safaris.com
+264 63 683 188
Wilderness Safaris
www.wilderness-safaris.com
+27 11 883 0747

WILD

Skydiving

There is nothing like the rush of skydiving, and nowhere like the empty plains of Namibia to really make it feel extreme. Take a tandem jump, or if you're feeling brave you can sign up for a static-line course and jump solo.

Skydive Swakopmund
www.skydiveswakop.com.na
+264 64 402 841
Alter-Action
www.alter-action.info/web/
+264 64 402 737

Kunene

Ruacana Falls

Otjijandjasemo Hot Spring

Ruacana

Uutapi (Ombalantu)

Oshikango

Nkurenkuru

Kavango

KAOKOLAND PG 48   Opuwo

Spring

Oshakati

Ondangwa

Dorsland Trekkers Monument

Olukonda Nakambale Museum

ETOSHA NATIONAL PARK PG 52

B1

Ovambo

Rundu

B8   Mahango Core Area   Divundu

CAPRIVI PG 52

Khaudum

Old German Fort

Ongongo Falls

Etosha National Park

Etosha Pan

Giant Baobab Tree

Omatako

Khaudum National Park

SKELETON COAST PG 50

Karos Cons. Area

Moringa Forest

Okaukuejo

Tsumeb

B8

Hoba Meteorite

Dorslandtrek Baobab

Grootboom (Giant Baobab Tree)

Skeleton Coast Park

Kamanjab

Gamkarab Cave

Khorab War Memorial

Otavi

Grootfontein

Tsumkwe

Holboom

Terrace Bay

Bergsig

Petrified Forest

Khorixas

Outjo

B1

Waterberg Plateau Park

Waterberg Wilderness Trail

Twyfelfontein Rock Engraving

Huab

Vingerklip (Rock Finger)

Otjiwarongo

Waterberg Walks

German/Herero Military Graveyard

Burnt Mountain

Ugab Guided Trail

White Lady Painting

Dinosaur's Footprints

Ozondjache

Otjinene

Messum Crater

Uis

Omatako

Otjosondu

Rietfontein

Doroб National Park

Rock Paintings

Omaruru

Ombo Ostrich Farm

Okahandja

Steinhausen

Henties Bay   B2   Usakos

Hot Springs

B6

Von Bach Rec Resort

Charles' Hill

Tsaobis Leopard Nature Park

Goдikontes

Powder Tower

B1

B6

Gobabis

Tinkas Nature Trail

Daan Viljoen Game Park

Fort

WINDHOEK

Arnhem Cave

Swakopmund

Dune 7

CENTRAL NAMIBIA PG 54

Walvis Bay

Kuiseb Canyon

Isabis 4x4 Trail

Rehoboth

Hot Spring

Leonardville

Namib Naukluft Park

Dassie Trails

Camel Safaris

Kuiseb

Solitaire

Nossob

Kalkrand

Aranos

Naukluft Hiking Trail

Fish

Hardap Recreation Resort

Stampriet

Akanous

Sesriem Canyon

Waterkloof Trail

Auob

Mariental

Sossusvlei

Namib Rand Nature Reserve

Zaris

Maltahöhe

B1

Gibeon

Gochas

Olifants

Welverdiend

Namib-Naukluft Park

Duwisib Castle

Helmeringhausen

Extinct Volcano

Tses

Koës

Koichab Pan

Mooifontein Military Cemetery

Berseba

Kokerboom Forest

Spitzkoppe Fossil Trail

Giant's Playground

Dias Cross Site

Aus   B4

Keetmanshoop

Historic Buildings

Aroab

Lüderitz

Kolmanskop Ghost Mining Town

Goageb

SOUTH NAMIBIA PG 56

Naute Recreation Area

Vredeshoop

Elizabeth Bay Ghost Mining Town

Sperrgebiet National Park

FISH RIVER CANYON PG 56

Grünau

Karasburg

Rosh Pinah

Hot Springs

Fish River Canyon

Ai-/Ais/ Richtersveld Transfrontier Park

B1

B3

Ariamsvlei

Orange (Gariep)

Oranjemund

Warmbad

Hot Springs

Velloorsdrif

Noordoewer

45

Namibia

ON LAND

Game viewing
The vast pan of Etosha NP is the country's premier game viewing destination, finest in the dry season – particularly July to October – when huge herds of animals can be seen around the water holes. Less visited is the Caprivi Strip, also Big Five country and famous for its outstanding bird life, and Damaraland, where sightings include desert-adapted elephant, Hartmann's mountain zebra, spotted hyena, gemsbok and other buck.

Namibia Wildlife Resorts
www.nwr.com.na
+264 61 285 7101
Wilderness Safaris
www.wilderness-safaris.com
+27 11 883 0747
&Beyond
www.andbeyond.com

+27 11 809 4300
Chameleon Safaris
www.chameleonsafaris.com
+264 61 247 668
Harnas Wildlife Foundation
www.harnas.org
+264 62 568 828/38

Birding
Walvis Bay Lagoon, a RAMSAR site and the most important coastal wetland in Southern Africa, is famous for its vast flocks of flamingos and pelicans and is also visited by African and Palaearctic migrants. The flood plains and lush savanna of the Caprivi Strip and the Kunene region are also prime destinations for twitchers.

Levo Tours
www.levotours.com
+264 64 207 555
Ichobezi River Lodges
www.ichobezi.co.za
+27 79 871 7603

Epupa Camp
www.epupa.com.na
+264 61 232 740

Mountain biking
Cycling is hard work in this dry, harsh landscape, but is unbelievably rewarding. Take your own bike, organise maps and other useful info from Namibia Tourism or Namibia Wildlife Resorts, then head off on the dirt roads. Alternatively, sign up for a guided mountain biking safari and explore little visited sections of the Namib Desert. This is serious outback territory: desolate, beautiful and far away from it all. There are no fences, no farming, mining, industry, villages or towns, just abundant wildlife in a pristine natural environment. Competitive mountain bikers will enjoy the annual Klein-Aus Vista MTB Challenge and the five-day Desert Knights Mountain Biking Tour from the Fish River Canyon viewpoint to the Richtersveld NP in South Africa.

Mountain Bike Namibia
www.mountainbikenamibia.com
+264 64 402 078 or
+264 81 128 4900
Klein Aus Vista
www.klein-aus-vista.com
+264 63 258 021

Namibia Wildlife Resorts
www.nwr.com.na
+264 61 285 7101
Bike & Saddle
www.bikeandsaddle.com
+27 21 813 6433

Horse riding
A horseback safari allows you to really appreciate the incredible emptiness and extraordinary scenery of Namibia. Rides range from a couple of hours to the 10-day traverse of the Namib Desert – billed as one of the toughest horse rides in the world!

Namibia Horse Safari Company

www.namibiahorsesafari.com
+264 63 258 021

ON WATER

Sea kayaking
Playful seals and dolphins are your companions on Eco Marine's stunning half-day sea kayak adventure from Pelican Point near Walvis Bay. The trip starts with a 4x4 journey to the tip of the long spit on the far side of the lagoon, spotting flamingos, terns and gulls before launching near the seal colony.

Eco Marine Kayak Tours
www.emkayak.iway.na
+264 64 203 144

Kitesurfing
Walvis Bay and Lüderitz have ideal wind conditions for expert kitesurfers to practise their skills, while the sheltered lagoon is ideal for beginners. And if you're really hooked, check out Walvis Bay's annual Speed Week.

Walvis Bay Kite Center
www.namibiakite.com
+264 81 373 9402

Free Air Guesthouse
www.namibia-walvisbay-guesthouse.com/index2.html
+264 64 202 247

Marine safaris
Cruise around Walvis Bay harbour and Pelican Point, checking out the pelicans and other sea birds as seals and dolphins play around the boat.

Laramon Tours
www.laramontours.com
+264 81 124 0635
Mola Mola Safaris
www.mola-namibia.com
+264 64 205 511
Levo Tours
www.levotours.com
+264 64 207 555

Cruising along the river.

OTHER ADVENTURES

1. Game viewing
2. Birding
3. Mountain biking
4. Horse riding
5. Sea kayaking
6. Kitesurfing
7. Marine safaris
8. Flying safaris

Giraffes in Etosha.

IN THE AIR

Flying safaris

If jumping out of a plane sounds too extreme, stay on board and enjoy a scenic flight!

Pleasure Flights and Safaris
www.pleasureflights.com.na
+264 64 404 500

KAOKOLAND PG 48

Flying safaris

SKELETON COAST PG 50

ETOSHA NATIONAL PARK PG 52

Game viewing

CAPRIVI PG 52

Birding

Flying safaris

Birding

Walvis Bay
Sea kayaking;
Kitesurfing;
Marine safaris

CENTRAL NAMIBIA PG 54

Mountain biking;
Horse riding

Flying safaris

Kitesurfing

SOUTH NAMIBIA PG 56

Flying safaris Mountain biking

FISH RIVER CANYON PG 56

KAOKOLAND

Kaokoland refers to the vast, rocky, mountainous terrain bordered in the north by the Kunene River and by the Hoanib in the south, and immediately inland of the northern Skeleton Coast. It is a wild and unpredictable wilderness populated largely by the Himba and Herero-speaking people (who gave the area its name). Kaokoland's rivers are home to crocodiles, while small herds of Kaokoland elephant roam the desolate landscape, which fell victim to devastating drought in the 1970s. Much of its wildlife was decimated, but the land is slowly recovering and Kaokoland, especially its lumbering great elephants, remains a popular tourist drawcard.

DRIVING THROUGH KAOKOLAND

The nearly 50,000km² (19,500 sq. miles) of rough roads and mountain terrain are not immediately inviting to the traveller. The tracks are unpredictable and difficult to navigate, and the landscape is wild and, to a large degree, empty of inhabitants other than the local Himba. Still isolated from Western influence, the Himba are simple subsistence farmers who remain true to custom, so problems with your vehicle here are not going to be solved by the locals. Indeed, the locals are friendly, approachable and hospitable, but

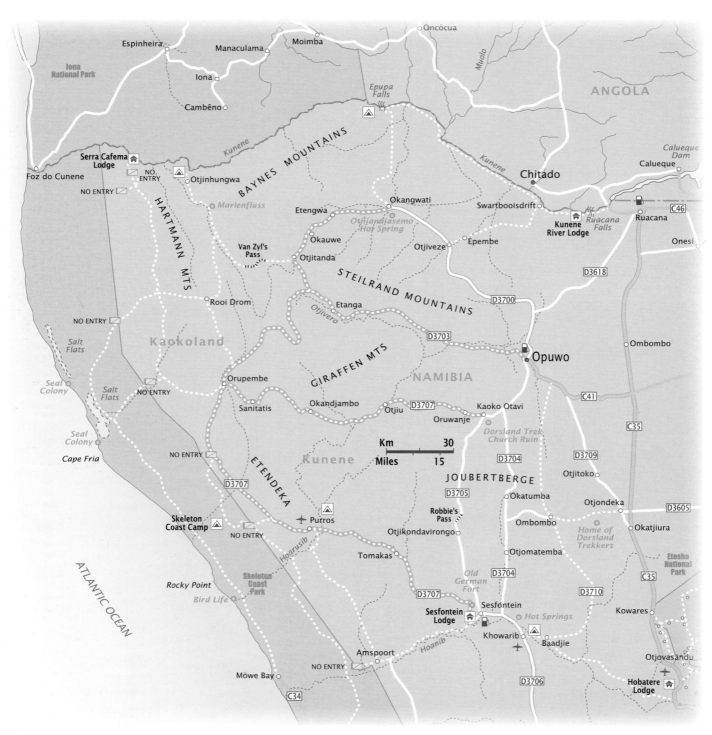

it is best not to rely on them for anything more than a welcome drink and a cheery smile. At the same time, though, they know their homeland best and if you find yourself lost – and can decipher the elaborate hand gestures (few people here speak English) – you may decide to ask for directions. Remember, however, that the locals use different names to those on maps.

THE FAMOUS DESERT ELEPHANTS

Apart from the perils of the desert landscape, the natural splendour remains the attraction. Namibia's desert-dwelling elephants, although mistakenly considered an entirely separate species from the African elephant, have simply adapted to the harsh Kaokoland. The most notable deviations from other elephants is, of course, their diet. Here they browse on the indigenous ana trees. The elephants may spend days in search of water, trudging in excess of 60km (37 miles) for a drink. Other wild animals, too, will make their way from one water supply to another as the available supply dwindles away in the dry season.

Travellers should be aware that there are no reliable open water sources in this region and that it is essential to take along your own water rations.

GREAT AFRICAN RAFTING SPOTS

Burundi	Luvironza River
Zambia	Zambezi River
Uganda	Nile River
Namibia	Kunene River
South Africa	Orange River
South Africa	uThukela River

RIVER RAFTING ON THE KUNENE

The mighty Kunene in the north of Namibia forms part of its border with Angola for about 325km (200 miles). Winding and twisting through a rough, primeval landscape, the great river is characterised by fearsome crocodiles, thundering waterfalls, tranquil streams and the raging whitewater rapids that have made it one of the continent's premier rafting destinations. The untamed waters (almost entirely white in parts from the turbulence that roars beneath the surface) cascade over long-time popular adventure thrills like the renowned Epupa and Ruacana falls. Nail-biting rapids such as those at Enyandi and Ondorusu test you out before you arrive at the more treacherous rapids like The Crusher, Dead Man's Grave and Smash.

KAOKOLAND IN A NUTSHELL

Best times: Moderate to hot all year, best times are May–Aug.
Climate: Winters are moderate but cool; heavy summer rains (Jan-Mar).
Risk factor: Isolated and inhospitable to the ill-prepared traveller. Party of at least two 4x4s essential on roads that are essentially dust tracks. Professional assistance in planning is advised.
Health: Malaria is endemic to the northern area. There is a risk of AIDS and bilharzia in this region.
Pack: Sunscreen and comfortable lightweight clothing, first-aid supplies, water rations and vehicle parts.
Facilities: Although locals are generally accommodating, guesthouses are few and far between – visitors need to be entirely self-sufficient. Some reliable tour operators service this area.

Top to bottom: Kaokoland desert elephant; Himba woman; the endangered white rhino.

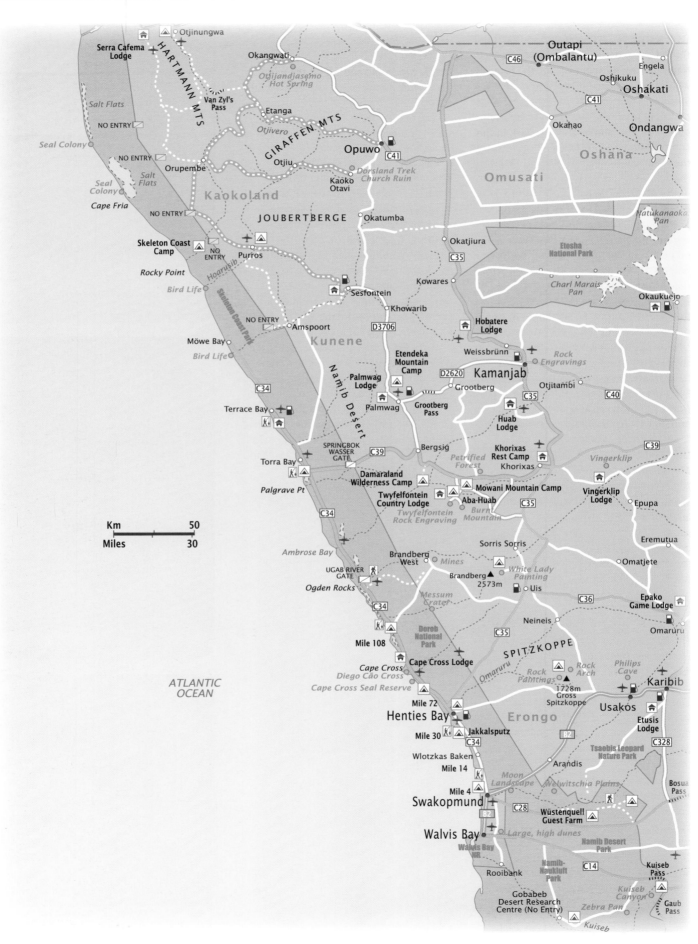

Serra Cafema Lodge
Otjinungwa
HARTMANN MTS
Salt Flats
NO ENTRY
Seal Colony
NO ENTRY
Salt Flats
Seal Colony
Cape Fria
NO ENTRY
Skeleton Coast Camp
NO ENTRY
Rocky Point
Bird Life
NO ENTRY
Möwe Bay
Bird Life
C34
Terrace Bay
Torra Bay
Palgrave Pt
Ambrose Bay
UGAB RIVER GATE
Ogden Rocks
C34
Mile 108
ATLANTIC OCEAN
Cape Cross
Diego Cão Cross
Cape Cross Seal Reserve
Mile 72
Mile 30
Wlotzkas Baken
Mile 14
Mile 4
Swakopmund
Walvis Bay

Van Zyl's Pass
Otjijandjasemo Hot Spring
Okangwati
Etanga
Otjivero
GIRAFFEN MTS
Opuwo
C41
Otjiu
Kaoko Otavi
Dorsland Trek Church Ruin
Orupembe
Kaokoland
JOUBERTBERGE
Okatumba
Purros
Hoarusib
Skeleton Coast Park
Sesfontein
Khowarib
Amspoort
Kunene
D3706
Namib Desert
Etendeka Mountain Camp
Palmwag Lodge
Palmwag
Grootberg Pass
SPRINGBOK WASSER GATE
C39
Bergsig
Damaraland Wilderness Camp
Twyfelfontein Country Lodge
Twyfelfontein Rock Engraving
Mowani Mountain Camp
Aba-Huab
C35
Burnt Mountain
C34
Brandberg West
Mines
Sorris Sorris
White Lady Painting
Brandberg ▲ 2573m
Uis
Messum Crater
Neineis
C35
Dorob National Park
Cape Cross Lodge
Omaruru
SPITZKOPPE
Rock Paintings
Rock Arch
1728m Gross Spitzkoppe
Henties Bay
Erongo
Jakkalsputz
C34
Moon Landscape
Arandis
Tsaobis Leopard Nature Park
Welwitschia Plains
Large, high dunes
B2
C28
Wüstenquell Guest Farm
Namib Desert Park
Walvis Bay NR
Rooibank
Namib-Naukluft Park
C14
Gobabeb Desert Research Centre (No Entry)
Zebra Pan
Kuiseb
Kuiseb Canyon
Gaub Pass
Kuiseb Pass

Outapi (Ombalantu)
C46
Engela
Oshikuku
C41
Oshakati
Okahao
Ondangwa
Oshana
Omusati
Natukanaoka Pan
Etosha National Park
Charl Marais Pan
Okaukuejo
Kowares
Hobatere Lodge
Weissbrünn
Rock Engravings
Kamanjab
D2620
Grootberg
Okatjiura
C35
Otjitambi
C35
C40
Huab Lodge
Khorixas Rest Camp
Khorixas
Petrified Forest
Vingerklip
C39
Vingerklip Lodge
Epupa
Eremutua
Omatjete
Philips Cave
Karibib
Epako Game Lodge
Omaruru
C36
Usakos
C328
Etusis Lodge
B2
Bosua Pass

Km   50
Miles   30

SKELETON COAST

One of the most extraordinary of Namibia's many spectacles is the bone-white sands that comprise the great Skeleton Coast, an eerie expanse of beach that extends from the country's northern border to the Namib-Naukluft Park in the south. Hemmed in by the cold Atlantic in the west and the dry interior to the east, the 1.6 million hectares (4 million acres) of the Skeleton Coast Park is an untamed wilderness divided into two main regions. The baking sand of the Namib covers the northern stretch, while the south is made up of dry gravel plains scattered with boulders and laced, in part, with seasonal rivers. Although there are few mammal species, the Skeleton Coast is renowned for its abundant bird life. The volatility of the elements and the relentless battering of wave and wind lend to this landscape an almost surreal beauty. The coast can be shrouded in mist for days, which helped to earn it the reputation as the world's largest shipping graveyard – over 100 vessels have run aground here.

DRIVING THE SKELETON COAST

The Skeleton Coast is an extensive wilderness and a traveller's paradise. Although sparsely vegetated, it boasts a unique array of life forms that have made unusual adaptations to live on this sandy, dry and wind-blown shore stretching from the country's northernmost border with Angola down to the dry and dusty plains of the Namib-Naukluft Park.

FUN ON FOUR WHEELS

The rocky coast is battered by winds and pummelled by the ocean, and much of it is traversed over bumpy dirt roads or tarred roads in a sad state of disrepair. The southern reaches are covered by the sandy dunes of the Namib, and the gravel plains of the north are liberally sprinkled with boulders, rocks and rivers. Visitors travelling through the region in a 4x4 are advised to drive carefully, particularly in areas that have had rain after having had none for a long time. The scenic beauty of the coastline might seem idyllic to romantic adventurers, yet these lengthy stretches of beach are considerably less hospitable when you are stranded and helpless under the blazing sun. Despite the aridity of the region, the Namibian coast is a haven for adventurers, but the golden rule is: do your homework first.

WALVIS BAY

Positioned between the searing sands of the Namib in the south and the wind-swept shore of the Skeleton Coast in the north, Walvis Bay is the unofficial capital of Namibia's coastal stretch. Much of the social and economic activity of this little city centres on its vital natural harbour, the deepest in southwestern Africa. For centuries, small indigenous settlements remained undisturbed in this forgotten corner of the country until Dutch, German and British colonial powers stumbled upon the harbour. Walvis Bay is a vital instrument in the national economy (servicing the freight and fishing industries) and is a convenient base for some adventure activities that are on offer at certain times of the year, including 4x4 and desert exploration, as well as bird-watching. Take the popular lagoon drive to enjoy the flamingos, pelicans, storks and cormorants; if you're there at the right time the lagoon will be pink with flamingos.

SKELETON COAST PARK IN A NUTSHELL
Best times: May–Aug.
Climate: Generally moderate, often misty. Heavy summer rains (Jan–Mar) often bring flash floods and high temperatures.
Risk factor: Private trips should be well planned, taking into account the volatility of both desert and ocean.
Pack: Warm clothing for the fogbound coast; sunscreen is essential; comfortable light-weight clothing for hot days.
Facilities: Some plush private operations, but generally simple to rustic camping and overnight facilities.

Top to bottom: Skeleton Coast stretching into the horizon; driving the dunes; one of the many wrecks along the coast.

51

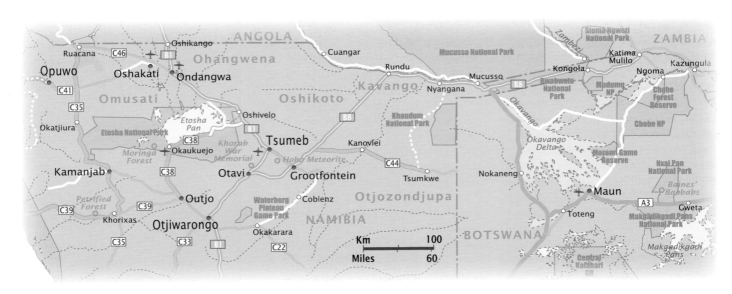

ETOSHA NATIONAL PARK

Etosha ('great white place' in Herero, due to the bright sun) is one of the finest game reserves to be found in Southern Africa and is a vital sanctuary for the entire region. The park is home to 114 species of mammal, 340 bird species, 110 different reptiles, 16 species of amphibian and yet just one fish species. All this wildlife is found in the 22,000km^2 (13,670 sq. miles) that make up the park, which is named after the massive dry pan that covers a vast 5000km^2 (3107 sq. miles), stretching roughly 120km (74.5 miles) from east to west and some 70km (43.5 miles) across at its widest point. The pan seldom has much (if any) water as it is fed by the rains rather than reliable rivers, and even when the rains fall hard, few areas fill up or flood due to the incredibly high rate of evaporation. Etosha is best explored in your own car

without a guide. The roads are good and the open landscape allows for excellent wildlife spotting, although there are also sections that are thick, bushy and wooded. Oryx (or gemsbok) tend to congregate around Etosha's water holes. The rainy season signals the arrival of summer migrants in the form of mammals and birds. In good years the pan is alive with thousands of flamingos. The western reaches of Etosha feature some unique areas, including the fascinating Moringa Forest or Haunted Forest, dubbed 'Sprokieswoud' in Afrikaans. The Haunted Forest is littered with weirdly contorted moringa trees which were, quite possibly, shaped by browsing herds of elephant and giraffe. Etosha's three main rest camps (Namutoni, Halali and Okaukuejo) have perimeter fencing and superb floodlit water holes that can be visited 24 hours a day. The park was the world's

largest game reserve until the 1960s, when its surface area was (over time) reduced by nearly 80%. Nonetheless, Etosha remains one of Africa's largest and greatest parks.

AN IDEAL BASE CAMP
Katima Mulilo boasts really good facilities for travellers. It is an excellent base from which to explore and embark on adventure activities, as it's located on the banks of the mighty Zambezi River, and it is an easy hop into Zambia, Zimbabwe or Botswana.

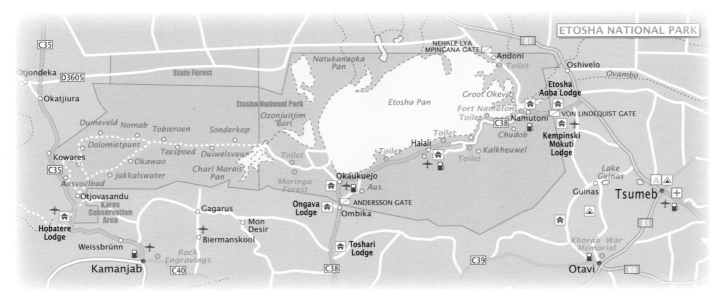

KHAUDUM NATIONAL PARK

Khaudum is wild 4x4 country and, while its remoteness might add to its charm, it also demands travelling in a group with adequate supplies. The lack of fencing around Khaudum (with the exception of the boundary with Botswana) allows animals to leave the park in search of fresh grazing and water during the rainy season, thus ensuring a proliferation of wildlife to watch, particularly wild dogs and roan antelope. Artificial water holes provide some of the best wildlife spotting. Winter is best for game viewing, but you'll need patience: free-roaming animals don't tolerate noise, particularly from humans and loud vehicles. The heavier summer rain thickens the dry woodland savanna (located on settled parts of the Kalahari's sand dunes), thus encouraging a vibrant bird life.

THE WATERBERG PLATEAU

The Waterberg Plateau Game Park dominates the surrounding landscape. Steep cliffs rise hundreds of metres above the surrounding plains, making the plateau something of a refuge for wildlife. Many of Namibia's endangered species have been rehomed here to safeguard them from poachers and predators. Due to its conservation success, it supplies rare species of game and wildlife to many of Namibia's other parks. Its amazing biodiversity also allows this small park to support a wide array of animals. You can drive around the park on one of the organised game drives but NOT on your own. Walking in the park offers incredible scenery and game viewing, with 200 bird species (Verreaux's Eagles and Cape Vultures), age-old dinosaur tracks and San rock art.

TSUMEB

Tsumeb's name can be translated as 'to dig a hole in loose ground' – appropriate for one of Namibia's key mining towns that has attained a worldwide reputation in the mining community. The Tsumeb Museum offers visitors a window into the past, while the Tsumeb Cultural Village is an open-air museum that allows a first-hand look at the traditional way of life of the area.

GROOTFONTEIN

Grootfontein (it means 'large fountain') was named for its natural springs. The fascinating Old Fort Museum has interesting historic photographs, gems, rocks and a display on the old art of wagon and cart manufacture. The 60-ton Hoba Meteorite (the largest recorded on earth) can be found 50km (31miles) outside town. Almost 3m^2 (9.8ft^2) in area and 75–122cm (30–48in) thick, it may be 200 to 400 million years old. Hoba slammed down here around 80,000 years ago.

> **TOP TRIPS**
> · An hour outside Otjiwarongo are fossilised footprints that date back around 200 million years! You will stare in awe at the massive set of prints made by a very large two-legged dinosaur.
> · A 2km (1.2-mile) drive out of Otavi will bring you to the Khorab War Memorial. Erected in 1920, it marks the spot where the German forces capitulated to General Louis Botha's South African forces in 1915.

Top to bottom: a pensive zebra; the enduring welwitschia plant; a pair of oryx.

WINDHOEK

Albeit relatively small and underdeveloped, the Namibian capital is the great tourist centre and economic hub of the nation, a vibrant, colourful and relatively modern city catering for international travellers. The nightlife is lively, the facilities adequate and the infrastructure impressive, while the colours, cultures and panoramic vistas are a photographer's dream. In recent years there has been a healthy resurgence in the tourism market. Windhoek has become every inch the modern city and remains the gateway to the adventures promised by the coast, desert and wild expanse beyond waiting to be explored. The nearby Daan Viljoen Game Park is equipped for travellers and sedan cars are able to negotiate its roads. The park

has three main trails: Wag-'n-Bietjie (buffalo-thorn) Trail, Rooibos (bushwillow) Trail and Sweet-thorn Trail. The game spotting is good and the bird life prolific (including the Damara Rockjumper and the Rosy-faced Lovebird).

NAMIB-NAUKLUFT PARK

Larger than Switzerland, the 50,000km^2 (31,070 sq. miles) of fantastically scenic desert landscape occupied by the Namib-Naukluft Park ranks it among the biggest in all of Africa. The park represents a vital effort to conserve the pristine nature of the Namib Desert, which vies with the Atacama Desert in South America for the title of oldest on earth. You'll need plenty of time to enjoy all that the park has to offer. The Namib has an amazing array of wildlife, despite the aridity, and the hardy

plant life in its mountainous region is surprisingly prolific. This is an area enjoyed by the rare Hartmann's mountain zebra as well as leopards and other shy animals who appreciate the vegetation and the sanctuary offered by the caves, gorges and rocky terrain. Numerous small nocturnal creatures (insects and reptiles) can be found in the area. Bird-watchers will delight in the bustling air traffic around the deep kloofs that have water year-round. Horse riding and hiking are popular on guest farms. Hikes range from a few hours to the more advanced eight-day, 120km (74-mile) Naukluft Hiking Trail.

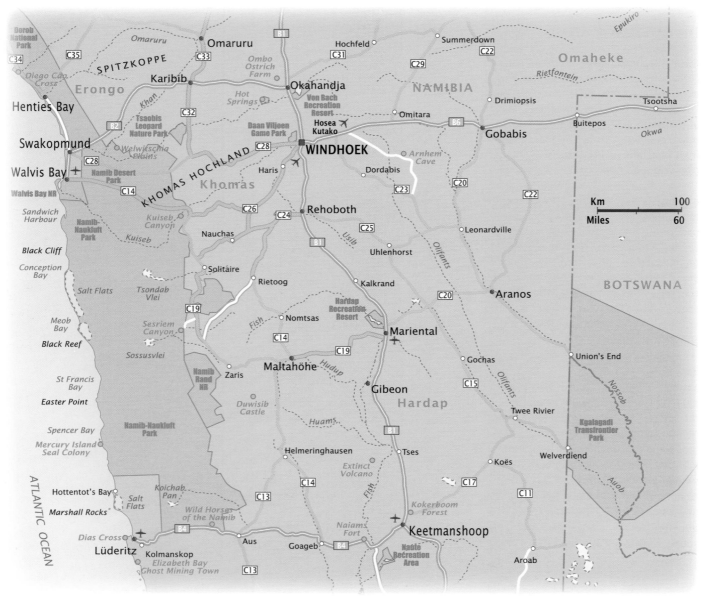

OKAHANDJA

Okahandja's open-air markets specialise in souvenirs such as wood-carvings (notably enormous hippos, huge giraffe and up to 2m/6.5ft tall human busts) as well as art from all around Southern and Central Africa. The Herero's administrative 'capital', Okahandja, hosts a large and colourful annual festival in August to honour the Herero forefathers. There are numerous historic sights in and around town, including Moordkoppie (Murder Hill, the scene of the 1850 Herero massacre) and many graves of local leaders from the last 100 years (including that of the Oorlam leader, Jan Jonker Afrikaner).

MARIENTAL

Forget peace and tranquillity: Mariental suffers from an unhappy climate. Atrocious summer heat, biting winter cold, and the changes in season bring strong winds that blow dust everywhere. Local industry focuses on cultivating animal fodder, fruit and vegetables, as well as ostrich meat and karakul pelts. Nearby is the Hardap Dam (Namibia's largest reservoir), enjoyed by anglers, hikers, birders and boating enthusiasts. Herman Brandt, the first colonial settler in the area, made his wife happy by naming it Marie's Valley ('Mariental' in German).

GOBABIS

Gobabis has a special charm for passing tourists on this vital route through to Botswana. There are pretty old church buildings in town and a golf course. A statue of a bull at the town's western entrance bears testament to the importance of cattle to the Omaheke region.

HENTIES BAY

Hentie van der Merwe first started fishing here in 1929, and little did he know that a town would grow here and adopt his name. A sleepy hollow, Henties wakes up for the summer season to welcome the 10,000-plus visitors who flock to this fisherman's paradise, many with an eye on casting a line into the ocean or swinging their clubs at the nine-hole golf course that runs through a valley down towards the beach. The town has plenty of petrol stations to cater for the lack of supply further north.

NAMIBIA'S NATURAL WONDERS
- Namibia's massive parkland covers approximately 11.22 million hectares (27.7 million acres)
- Etosha Pan's amazing wildlife hangs out at the huge salt depression
- The dramatic dunes of Sossusvlei
- Age-old rock engravings
- The Fish River Canyon
- The vast Namib Desert
- The unforgiving Kaokoland
- The ancient Petrified Forest
- The Spitzkoppe hills

Top to bottom: dry, cracked desert floor; animal tracks on the face of a dune; climbing in the Namib-Naukluft National Park.

FISH RIVER CANYON

FISH RIVER CANYON FACTS
Estimated age: 2,000,000 years
Length: 160km (100 miles) long
Widest point: 27km (17 miles)
Deepest point: 600m (2000ft)
Smaller than: Only the Grand Canyon in North America is bigger than the Fish River Canyon.

FISH RIVER CANYON

The Fish River Canyon comprises wind-carved depressions, inclines and rock formations moulded from the inland plateau. The canyon is dramatic, with valleys and gullies slicing through its ancient geological foundations. Its grandeur lies more in the spectacle than in the geological records and data that make up this natural phenomenon. The Fish River Canyon's steep inclines and roughly hewn rock faces, eroded over time by the forces of nature and its ravaging elements, are second in size only to the Grand Canyon.

HIKING THE FISH RIVER CANYON

The Fish River rises in the Khomas Hochland Mountains southwest of Windhoek and flows some 800km (500 miles) before it meets the Orange River far to the south. The remarkable rock erosion has carved a network of paths and trails into the rock and sand. The last 160km (100 miles) of the river's fierce and often turbulent course winds through a deep canyon that forms the backdrop to Namibia's most challenging hiking trail. Although this trail is popular with ardent walkers and climbers, it is not standard tourist fare and remains entirely un-spoiled – unlike the mass-oriented tourist drawcards of the big cities. For the first 65km (40 miles) of its course, the gorge of the Fish River Canyon is, in effect, a canyon within a canyon, making for some remarkable walking. Almost in retaliation against the forces that shifted the rocks and sediment millennia ago, the Fish River be-gan to cut a deep channel in the bed of the original trough – only much deeper, narrower and far more spectacular. In places, the canyon floor is more than 500m (1640ft) below the level of the pla-teau. Fortunately, it is a relatively gentle world of placid pools and mighty boulders strewn across beds of sand, with little evidence of life. Naturally, this sort of isola-tion (in a spot that is relatively inhospitable) presents dangers of its own. As long as wary travel-lers use their common sense and

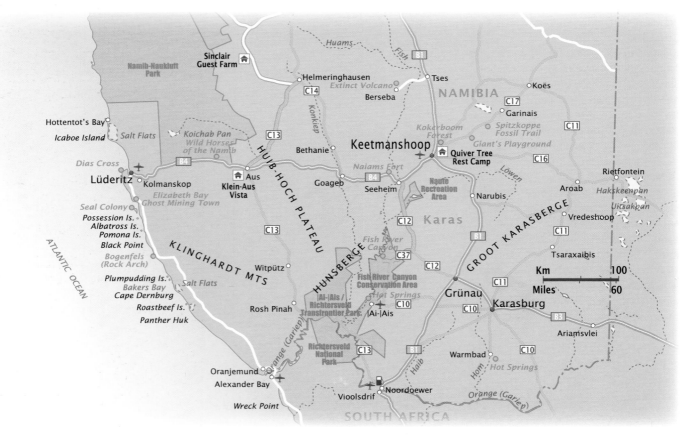

take no chances, there should be little to worry about – just the endless stretch of undulating path that lies ahead (albeit not always particularly well signposted, but the river is an able guide).

KEETMANSHOOP

Keetmanshoop (shortened to 'Keet' by the locals) is a small, sunny town with a few examples of attractive German colonial architecture, pretty gardens and a rustic museum. 'Keet' lies almost 500km (310 miles) south of Windhoek and is roughly 1000m (3281ft) above sea level. The original church was built in 1866 but, sadly, 24 years later a freak flood washed the entire building away. Its replacement (the current town museum) was put up five years later … this time on somewhat higher ground!

KOLMANSKOP GHOST TOWN

The desert ghost town of Kolmanskop lies just 10km (6 miles) from Lüderitz. The diamond rush saw this town spring up in 1908 and become the centre of the region's diamond industry. During its boom years the streets and businesses bustled with determined and starry-eyed prospectors, readily diving into the desert sands in search of their personal fortunes. It is today a tourist stop to explore the sand-ravaged houses and buildings that have been deserted for over 40 years. Naturally, you won't be able to enjoy the town's former facilities of an ice factory and casino, but the theatre and skittle alley have been restored to working order.

LÜDERITZ PENINSULA

A trip around the peninsula (in calm weather) will present some fabulous views and swimming possibilities at one of the many bays along the coast (Dias Point and Griffith Bay offer stunning views), while the rusted remnants of Sturmvogel Bucht's 'deceased' Norwegian Whaling Station are worth a look. A friendly, small town with slow-paced hospitality, rich in German tradition and history, Lüderitz is worth the effort to visit for a day. Sitting more than 360km (223 miles) from Keetmanshoop, Lüderitz is literally and figuratively isolated from the rest of the world, but it's not cut off completely. Part of Lüderitz's charm is that its isolation for so many years has left the town with much original architecture and character-ful buildings from the 1900s. The town has an element of fun in the garishly bright colours of the houses and the mid-day siren that doubles as a fire alarm! Kolmanskop and Elizabeth Bay ghost towns are a comfortable drive from Lüderitz and are both worth visiting.

Top to bottom: Fish River Canyon; Sossusvlei's dramatic dunescape; quiver trees (kokerbome).

Botswana

QUICK FACTS

Capital: Gaborone
Area: 600,372km² / 231,805mi²
Population: 2 million
Main ethnic groups:
 · Tswana (75%)
 · Shona (12%)
 · San (3%)
 · White (1%)
Main languages:
 · English
 · Tswana
 · Shona
 · San
 · Ndebele
Main religions:
 · Traditional beliefs (50%)
 · Christian (mostly Anglican) (50%)
Currency: Pula (100 thebe)

IN THIS CHAPTER

Lake
Liambezi
Kasane
Linyanti
Swamp
Chobe
Chobe Forest
Reserve
King's Pool
Pandamatenga
Savuti
Marsh
Chobe
NP
kavango
Delta
Moremi
GR
Nxai Pan
NP
Tsuli
Shorobe
Nxai Pan
un
Matlapaneng
Kudiakama
Pan
Nata
Bridge
Matopi
Gweta
Nata
Makgadikgadi
Pans GR
Makgadikgadi
Pans
Sowa
Pan
Sebina
Dzibui
Pan
Ntwetwe
Pan
Rakops
Orapa
Francistown
Madzilobge
Lake Xau
Mopipi
Letlhakane
Shashe Dam
Shashe
Shashe
Deception
Pans
A1
Selebi-
Serule
Phikwe
Bobonong
Central Kalahari
Game Reserve
Serowe
Sefophe
Lotsane
Palapye
Chief's Grave and
Mission Site
Shoshong
Sherwood
Mahalapye
Khutse
GR
Lephepe
Makwate
Salajwe
Dutlwe
Letlhakeng
A1
Sekoma
Molepolole
Mochudi
A2
Rock Paintings
Engravings
Gaborone GR
Khakhea
Jwaneng
Thamaga
Mokoledi GR
GABORONE
Manyelanong
Ramotswa
Vulture Colony
Lobatse
Ramatlabama

Clockwise top to bottom:
Elephant viewing;
mokoro as transport;
wetlands sunrise.

59

Botswana

10 TOP ADVENTURES

1. Game viewing
2. Horse riding
3. Quad biking
4. 4x4ing
5. Kalahari Bushmen Safari
6. Mountain biking
7. Walking with elephants
8. Birding
9. Mokoro trips
10. Tiger fishing

Horse riding.

ON LAND

Game viewing

TO DO

The diversity of Botswana means that there are endless possibilities, whether you're into big game or tiny creepy-crawlies. Walking safaris are popular, and mobile tented safaris allow you to explore various different environments. One of the beauties of the country is that you can plan really exciting self-drives, either camping or staying at up-market lodges.

&Beyond
www.andbeyond.com
+27 11 809 4300
Moremi Safaris and Tours
www.moremi-safaris.com
+27 11 463 3999
Bush Ways Safaris
www.bushways.com
+267 686 3685
Wilderness Safaris
www.wilderness-safaris.com
+27 11 883 0747

Letaka Safaris
www.letakasafaris.com
+267 680 0363
Flame of Africa
www.flameofafrica.com
+27 31 762 2424
Roger Dugmore Safaris
www.rogerdugmoresafaris.com
+267 686 2427

Horse riding

MILD

There's nowhere like Botswana when it comes to horseback safaris. If you want big game, saddle up and explore the incredible wetland, woods, meadows and papyrus-lined waterways of the Okavango Delta or the mopane forests of the Tuli. Or ride out through the lunar landscapes of Makgadikgadi Pans or the starkly beautiful Kalahari.

Okavango Horse Safaris
www.okavangohorse.com
+267 686 1671
African Horseback Safaris
www.africanhorseback.com
+267 686 3154
Limpopo Valley Horse Safaris
www.lvhsafaris.co.za
+267 7232 0024

David Foot Safaris
www.ridebotswana.com
+267 7248 4354
Uncharted Africa
www.unchartedafrica.com
+27 11 447 1605

Quad biking

MILD

Take a quad bike safari and sleep out under the stars in the middle of the vast Makgadikgadi Pans.

Uncharted Africa
www.unchartedafrica.com
+27 11 447 1605

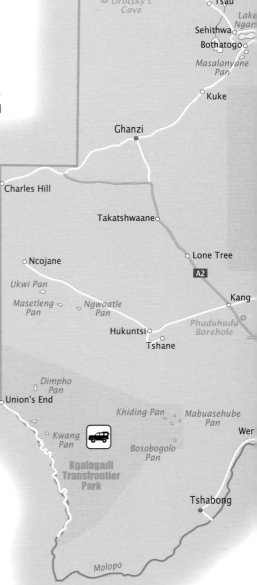

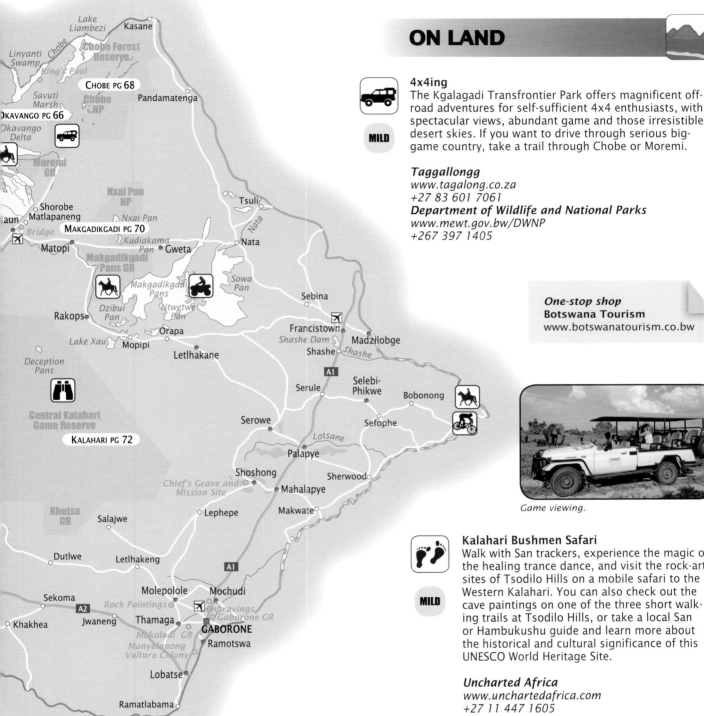

ON LAND

4x4ing

MILD

The Kgalagadi Transfrontier Park offers magnificent off-road adventures for self-sufficient 4x4 enthusiasts, with spectacular views, abundant game and those irresistible desert skies. If you want to drive through serious big-game country, take a trail through Chobe or Moremi.

Taggallongg
www.tagalong.co.za
+27 83 601 7061
Department of Wildlife and National Parks
www.mewt.gov.bw/DWNP
+267 397 1405

One-stop shop
Botswana Tourism
www.botswanatourism.co.bw

Game viewing.

Kalahari Bushmen Safari

MILD

Walk with San trackers, experience the magic of the healing trance dance, and visit the rock-art sites of Tsodilo Hills on a mobile safari to the Western Kalahari. You can also check out the cave paintings on one of the three short walking trails at Tsodilo Hills, or take a local San or Hambukushu guide and learn more about the historical and cultural significance of this UNESCO World Heritage Site.

Uncharted Africa
www.unchartedafrica.com
+27 11 447 1605

Mountain biking

WILD

Mashatu, in the Tuli Block, just over the border from South Africa, is one of the few Big Five parks to offer mountain biking. Cycle Mashatu run regular, multi-day guided trips, and once a year you can ride through the reserve on the Tour de Tuli.

Cycle Mashatu
www.cyclemashatu.com
+27 82 446 6810
Tour de Tuli
www.tourdewilderness.com *(online bookings only)*

Mountain bikers get close to a herd of elephants.

61

Botswana

ON LAND

Walking with elephants
Walk next to the gentle giants, holding their trunks and learning about their habits and habitats.

MILD

Stanley's Camp
www.sanctuaryretreats.com
+44 20 7190 7728
Living With Elephants
www.livingwithelephants.org
+267 686 3198
Adventure Safaris
www.adventure-safaris.com
+267 370 0166

Birding
Birding opportunities abound throughout Botswana, and an interesting project is the community-initiated Nata Bird Sanctuary, at the mouth of the Nata River on the Sowa Pan – it's an important flamingo and pelican breeding ground.

TO DO

Bush Ways Safaris
www.bushways.com
+267 686 3685
Letaka Safaris
www.letakasafaris.com/
+267 680 0363
Moremi Safaris and Tours
www.moremi-safaris.com
+27 11 463 3999

Uncharted Africa
www.unchartedafrica.com
+27 11 447 1605
Wilderness Safaris
www.wilderness-safaris.com
+27 11 883 0747

Top: Elephant safari.
Right: What a catch!

ON WATER

Mokoro trips

Sit back in a mokoro, a traditional Botswanan dugout canoe, as a poler expertly guides you through the crystal-clear waters and reed-lined channels of the delta. The bird life is fantastic and you'll often see hippo, croc and buck, but the trip is just as much about chilling out and enjoying the incredible sounds and smells of the wilderness. If you want a rustic, community-run experience, hook up with the Poler's Trust at Mbiroba Camp.

TO DO

Desert & Delta Safaris
www.desertdelta.co.za
+267 686 1559

Moremi Safaris and Tours
www.moremi-safaris.com
+27 11 463 3999

Adventure Safaris
www.adventure-safaris.com
+267 370 0166

Wilderness Safaris
www.wilderness-safaris.com
+27 11 883 0747

Uncharted Africa
www.unchartedafrica.com
+27 11 447 1605

&Beyond
www.andbeyond.com
+27 11 809 4300

Mbiroba Camp
www.okavangodelta.co.bw
+267 687 6861

Flame of Africa
www.flameofafrica.com
+27 31 762 2424

Roger Dugmore Safaris
www.rogerdugmoresafaris.com
+267 686 2427

David Foot Safaris
www.ridebotswana.com
+267 7248 4354

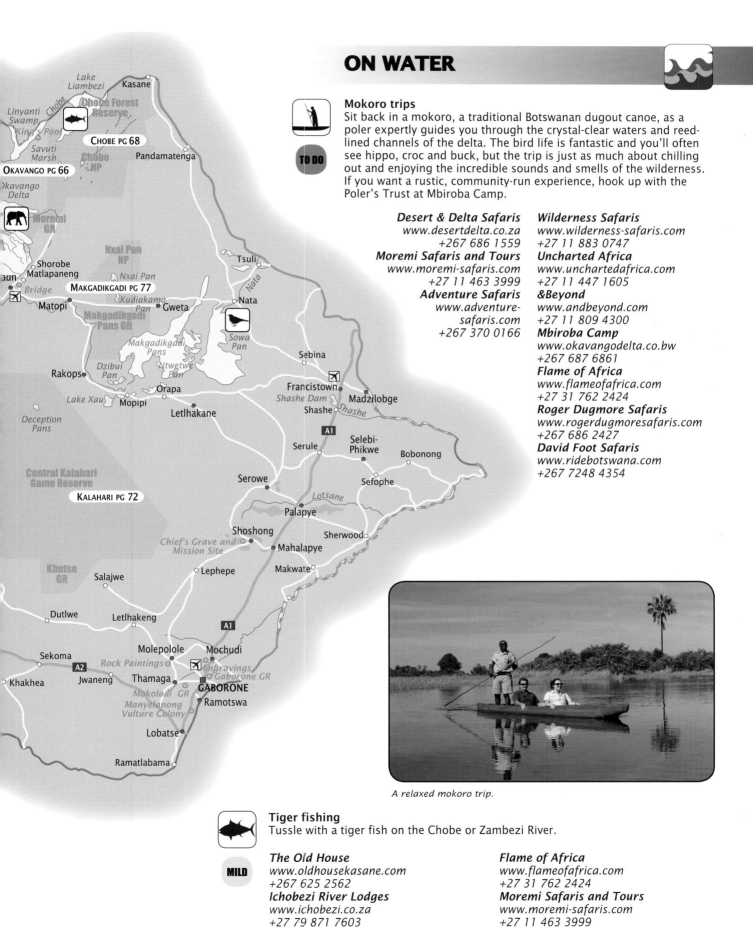

A relaxed mokoro trip.

Tiger fishing

Tussle with a tiger fish on the Chobe or Zambezi River.

MILD

The Old House
www.oldhousekasane.com
+267 625 2562

Ichobezi River Lodges
www.ichobezi.co.za
+27 79 871 7603

Flame of Africa
www.flameofafrica.com
+27 31 762 2424

Moremi Safaris and Tours
www.moremi-safaris.com
+27 11 463 3999

63

Botswana

OTHER ADVENTURES

1. No. 1 Ladies' Detective Agency Tours
2. Stargazing
3. Meerkat encounters
4. Canoe safaris
5. Houseboating
6. Flying safaris

 ON LAND

No. 1 Ladies' Detective Agency Tours
You've read Alexander McCall Smith's books, now visit Mma Ramotswe's haunts.

African Insight
www.africainsight.com
+267 316 0180

Stargazing
There's little light pollution outside the cities, so the night sky twinkles. A top spot for stargazing is the Makgadikgadi Pans – a true astronomers' paradise.

Uncharted Africa
www.unchartedafrica.com
+27 11 447 1605

Meerkat encounters
Mingle with meerkats on an overnight safari from Planet Baobab.

Uncharted Africa
www.unchartedafrica.com
+27 11 447 1605

Springbok grazing.

ON WATER

Canoe safaris
Between April and October, paddling the Selinda Spillway in the remote north of Botswana is a great four-day adventure. Or if you're really strong, you could embark on a Trans Okavango Safari of 300–500km! If you fancy a lazy day on the river, the half-day trip downstream of Kasane, which takes you past Impalila Island, is a gem. The scenery is fantastic, the birding is great and there's a little rapid to add to the excitement.

David Foot Safaris
www.ridebotswana.com
+267 7248 4354
Kayaktive Adventure Safaris
www.kayakbotswana.com
+267 7280 8561

The Old House
www.oldhousekasane.com
+267 625 2562

Houseboating
Cruise the Chobe River in a floating palace, enjoying the birds, the wildlife coming down to drink, and a spot of fishing. And the best bit is that you get to stay in the park once all the day-trippers have left.

Ichobezi River Lodges
www.ichobezi.co.za
+27 79 871 7603
Zambezi Queen
www.zambeziqueenrivercruise.com
+27 31 762 2424

The Zambezi Queen.

IN THE AIR

Flying safaris
Take a flight into the Okavango Delta in a light aircraft, at times almost skimming the water. Flying over this natural wonder, with its Ilala palms and blue water, offers game viewing opportunities second to none.

Moremi Air
www.moremiair.com
+267 686 3632

Map labels:
Kasane
Lake Liambezi
Canoe safari
Linyanti Swamp
Chobe Forest Reserve
Houseboating
Chobe
CHOBE PG 68
Savuti Marsh
Chobe NP
Pandamatenga
KAVANGO PG 66
Okavango Delta
Moremi GR
...ng safari
Shorobe
Matlapaneng
Nxai Pan NP
Nxai Pan
Tsuli
...aun
Bridge
MAKGADIKGADI PG 77
Matopi
Kudiakama Pan
Gweta
Nata
Nata
Makgadikgadi Pans GR
Meerkat encounters
Makgadikgadi Pans
Sowa Pan
Sebina
Rakops
Dzibui Pan
Stargazing
Orapa
Francistown
Madzilobge
Lake Xau
Mopipi
Shashe Dam
Shashe
Shashe
Deception Pans
Letlhakane
A1
Serule
Selebi-Phikwe
Bobonong
Central Kalahari Game Reserve
Serowe
Sefophe
KALAHARI PG 72
Lotsane
Palapye
Shoshong
Sherwood
Chief's Grave and Mission Site
Mahalapye
Khutse GR
Salajwe
Lephepe
Makwate
Dutlwe
Letlhakeng
No. 1 Ladies' Detective Agency Tours
A1
Mochudi
Sekoma
A2
Molepolole
Gaborone GR
Khakhea
Jwaneng
Thamaga
GABORONE
Mokolodi GR
Ramotswa
Manyelanong Vulture Colony
Lobatse
Ramatlabama

OKAVANGO DELTA

The Okavango flood plain is the world's largest inland delta, over 15,000km² (5790 sq. miles) in dry years, while higher rainfall can fan it out over a monstrous 22,000km² (8500 sq. miles). It is a vast green oasis in the middle of otherwise inhospitable terrain, but unfortunately much of the water is lost to evaporation, while irrigation and domestic consumption further reduce the water level. Conservationists are fighting to have the delta declared a World Heritage Site to secure its protection.

HIGHS AND LOWS

Ironically, the river's highest levels are achieved during Botswana's dry season, reaching their peak in June and July.

In Botswana's rainy season (October to March) the Okavango's pans and the many rivers and streams are dry and the formerly lush water channels become inaccessible by boat. This is a result of the delta's dependence on the Angolan section of the river: rain falling in Angola's rainy season provides the watery lifeblood to the Okavango's main tourist sections.

THE AHA HILLS

These remote hills straddle the border with Namibia and form a plateau stretching for 245km² (151 sq. miles), the bulk of it made up of limestone, dolomite and marble. The rocks date back some 700 million years.

FAMOUS RIVER DELTAS

Nile Delta	Egypt
Ganges Delta	India
Mississippi Delta	USA
Rhone Delta	Germany
Okavango Delta	Botswana
Amazon Delta	Brazil
Orinoco Delta	Venezuela
Rhine Delta	Germany

TSODILO HILLS

Located in the remote northwestern corner of Botswana, these hills have been revered by the locals for centuries. Richly adorned with rock art by the early inhabitants, the hills are said to represent a male, female and child.

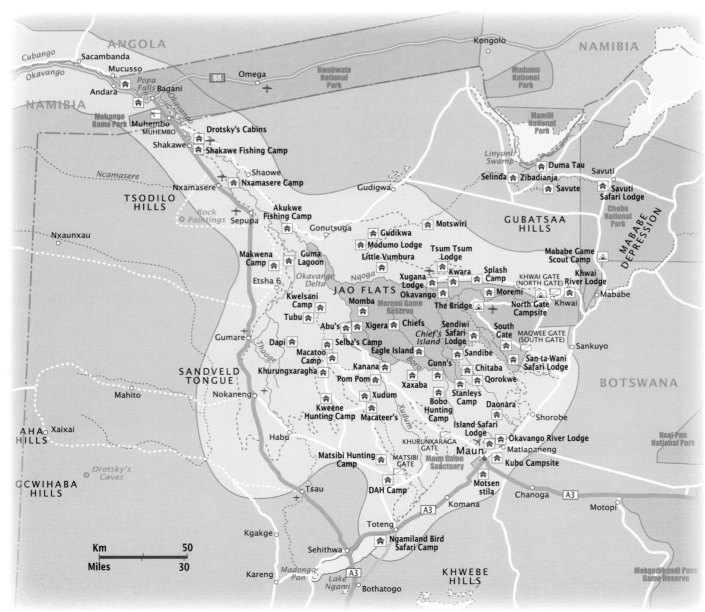

DROTSKY'S CAVES AND GCWIHABA HILLS

The interesting circular route from Nokaneng to Tsau, which also takes in the Aha Hills, is a journey of around 320km (198 miles), so prepare for an overnight stay and ensure the tank is full of petrol and the spare tyre in good nick. Drotsky's Cave is officially known as Gcwihaba (hyena's lair) Cave. This two-million-year-old site has dramatic stalactites, stalagmites and flow-stones, particularly in the large chamber.

GABORONE

Compact Gaborone has enjoyed phenomenal growth since it became Botswana's capital in the 1960s. Largely because of its considerable mineral wealth, it is one of the fastest-growing urban settlements on the African continent, with good restaurants, hotels, casinos and other entertainment centres.

AROUND GABORONE

The modern city has retained some of its distinct African flavour, and few other urban centres of similar status can boast the same number of small reserves and conservation land on their doorstep. Mount Kgale overlooks Gaborone, with a relatively easy walk along the Lobatse Road being all that separates you from great views of the capital. Just 12km (7.5 miles) south of Gaborone, Mokolodi Nature Reserve offers wildlife education for children and guided wildlife walks.

LOBATSE AND MOCHUDI

The town of Lobatse, 68km (42 miles) south of Gaborone, enjoys a lovely setting, yet the town itself is dull, except for St Mark's Anglican Church with its unusual thatched roof. Mochudi, on the other hand, is one of southeastern Botswana's more interesting villages. The Kwena first settled here in the 1500s, followed some 350 years later by the Kgatla who were avoiding migrating Voortrekkers. The Phuthadikobo Museum proudly displays Kgatla history, as well as that of Mochudi itself.

MAUN AND ITS MINI GAME RESERVE

Maun is a banking and administrative hub whose frontier image is fading fast as development westernises it to cash in on the tourist market, but the women of its big Herero population (former Namibian refugees) remain popular photographic subjects in their traditional dress. Just be sure to negotiate permission first. Nhabe Museum is worth a visit, as is the Craft Centre and the Shorobe Basket Co-operative. Maun's tiny game reserve occupies just 3km² (1,8 sq. miles) on the Thamalakane River but supports a variety of antelope. Nearby Matlapaneng bridge leads to the village of the same name that is popular with budget tourists.

Top to bottom: Mabokushu tribe members fishing; the Okavango Delta; African Fish Eagle.

CHOBE AND MOREMI RESERVES

Whereas the Okavango region is predominantly wetland, the Moremi Game Reserve is a vast 2000km² (770-sq.-mile) expanse of contrasts: flood plain and lagoon, dry bushveld and mopane woodland. The Moremi is roamed by big-game species such as lion, leopard, cheetah, elephant, buffalo, wild dog, kudu, tsessebe and Botswana's ubiquitous lechwe. Like Moremi, Chobe National Park's habitat is varied, alternating between swamp and grassland, flood plain and bushveld. The northern border of its 10,000km² (3800 sq. miles) of wilderness is carved by the Linyanti-Chobe river system. The Chobe is Botswana's only perennial river and, although more than 30km (19 miles) of its banks have been commandeered by responsible tourism, it continues to act as the life force for much wildlife.

Most notable are the more than 35,000 elephants, but there are also over 450 bird species.

One of the most remarkable attempts to accommodate local communities has found fruition in the arid Kgalagadi Transfrontier Park between South Africa and Botswana (see map, page 73). In an effort to preserve the natural habitat and its characteristic game species, government and conservation officials established this cross-border park, which is home to an amazing range of plant, mammal and bird life. Covering an area of more than 2 million hectares (5 million acres), Kgalagadi effectively unites South Africa's former Kalahari Gemsbok National Park and Botswana's old Gemsbok National Park – Africa's first formally gazetted transboundary reserve.

CHOBE IN A NUTSHELL
Climate: Riverside conditions are good year-round (best in May–Oct), while further inland conditions are best from Nov–May.
Health: Chobe is in a malaria area.
Risk factor: Drive with caution in any densely wooded areas: you may stumble across the path of an elephant!
Pack: Fuel is only available at Maun and Kasane.

MOREMI DELTA IN A NUTSHELL
Climate: Game viewing, good all year, is best in the dry season (May–Nov). Birders will delight at the influx of migrant species during the summer months. There's an added bonus in the scores of foaling antelope.
Risk factor: After any heavy rains many of the tracks can become totally impassable. Drive with care, carry along provisions and spares, and take your time – do not try to rush your way out of a bad position.
Health: Moremi is in a malaria area.
Pack: Fuel is only available at Maun and Kasane. Remember that your fuel consumption is higher in sandy areas.

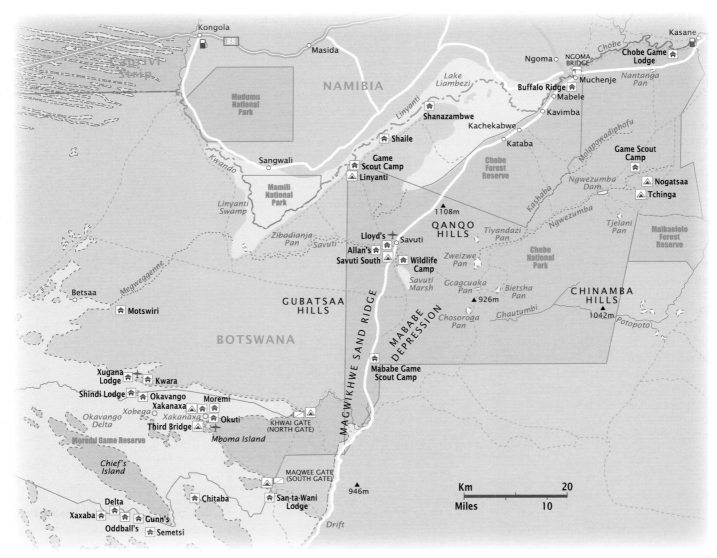

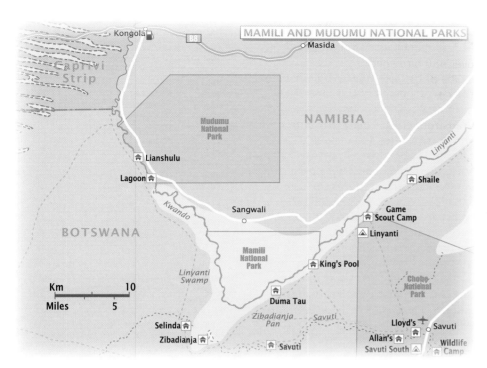

NAMIBIA'S MAMILI NATIONAL PARK

The 32,000ha (79,000-acre) Mamili National Park was opened at the same time as Mudumu (1990) – these are the eastern Caprivi's only protected areas. The Linyanti Swamp is a major draw-card when the Kwando River is running full (often flooding around June), opening up lazy mokoro (dugout) forays to the forested islands, wetlands and reeded channels. Naturally, the bird life is abundant (more than 430 species). Other wildlife ranges from elephant and lion to giraffe and hippo, along with numerous buck species. Mokoro and 4x4 are the only way to get around Mamili, and this is not the place to take personal risks, as help can be a long time coming. Rangers are on patrol throughout the park, but they may not cross your path in time if you find yourself in a spot of bother. Game viewing is best before the rainy season, which can start as early as October. The best birding opportunities are between December and March when the migrants move in, but then the 'black cotton' clay (road) tracks could become totally inaccessible.

NAMIBIA'S MUDUMU NATIONAL PARK

Spread across 100,000ha (247,000 acres), Mudumu is hugged to the west by the Kwando River, which is alive with crocodile, hippo and numerous water-loving buck such as sitatunga, red lechwe and reedbuck. Covered in mopane woodlands, the reserve is well-populated with elephant, giraffe and zebra, in addition to impala, kudu, red lechwe and the somewhat uncommon roan antelope species. These animals enjoy the shelter and foliage offered by the abundant mopane. Bird-watchers will fall in love with Mudumu, especially if they get to spot the African Fish Eagle, the Narina Trogon, Pel's Fishing Owl, or any of the many species found nowhere else in Namibia. It's best to explore Mudumu by 4x4, but Lianshulu Lodge and Lianshulu Bush Lodge offer guided walks. For a cultural diversion, visit the Lizauli Traditional Village just outside Mudumu to learn about traditional Caprivi lifestyles (from food to farming methods, medicine to crafts and tool-making). Lizauli is one of many local upliftment programmes and is worth supporting.

Top to bottom: male lion; tented camp at Linyanti; sunset over the Zibadianja Pan.

MAKGADIKGADI PANS

The world's largest natural salt pans, Makgadikgadi once formed part of a massive inland lake, but all that exists today on the remaining plains is an endless sea of empty, cracked, salt-encrusted pans, the most notable among them being Makgadikgadi's Sowa, Ntwetwe and Nxai pans. Following climatic changes and immense seismic shifts, the waters that once covered this landscape receded to leave the 12,000km² (4600-sq.-mile) seasonal salt pans. Summer rains fill the depressions, which become the lifeblood of the wildlife that is drawn here during the rainless winter. The plains of the Makgadikgadi and Nxai Pan parks cover 7500km² (2850 sq. miles). Established operators know the region and are quick to warn of the dangers of the dry pans and the havoc they wreak.

QUAD BIKING IN MAKGADIKGADI

The general mode of transport here is the quad bike, a small, sturdy but reliable four-wheel vehicle with limited impact on the sands – almost all other vehicles tend to cause irreparable damage to the ecosystems. Because of the unforgiving terrain, travellers (usually in pairs) are given impromptu lessons on how to handle quad bikes – but be warned that it is not as simple as pushing the pedal and steering. Beyond Kibu Island, mirages appear and disappear under the harsh sun as the 'quad-bike caravans' negotiate shallow but bone-rattling gullies and crests on the hard salty clay – a deceiving 'lid' over water lying below the surface. This is clearly no ride in the park, and there are pitifully few, if any, landmarks by which to navigate. Don't drive on, hoping to

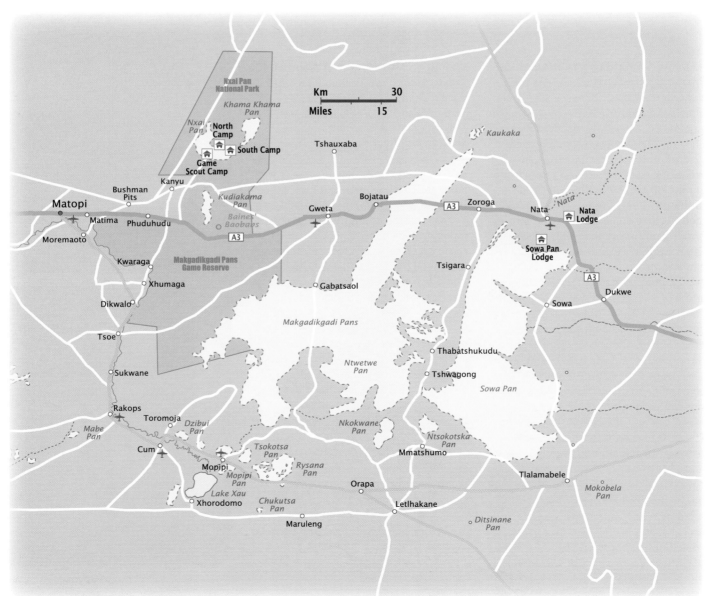

is not encouraged, but there are also adventure operators offering diversions into the wilds.

NO NEED TO ROUGH IT
While some established concerns pride themselves in providing every luxury, the smaller ones offer the most tactile and memorable experiences, stretching from three to 10 days. Night drives are not permitted in Botswana, and the Tuli Trail is reserved for days only. Most family cars are able to negotiate the well-signposted roads, but game viewing is rather limited from there: horseback safaris increase your chances of encountering wild animals! No inexperienced horse riders are permitted on the trails, and even those who are fairly well versed in horsemanship should heed the warning of guides. In most cases, even the horses are carefully screened for their controlled temperament and ability to withstand the perils of the veld. Groups are advised to stick to the tracks already etched into the dry riverbeds.

BAINES' BAOBABS
The stands of baobabs that dot pockets of the otherwise empty interior symbolise the grandeur of this sparse country. From the outskirts of settlements to the featureless pans, the horizon is broken by the silhouette of these indigenous residents who have lived here for centuries. The most prominent are the Seven Sisters referred to as Baines' Baobabs. This cluster of 'upside-down' trees is named after Thomas Baines, the artist and explorer who captured them on canvas in 1862. Baines' Baobabs stand on the rim of Kudiakama Pan.

stumble onto the correct course: every inch further into the pans could mean another inch further away from help. Travellers making their way across the pans need to be well prepared and supremely self-sufficient. Even if you have the foresight to bring a winch, there's nothing in the pans to which you can attach the rope. It's therefore essential to travel in a group. Tour operators have learned the hard way, and should know all the tricks; paying for their services and expert advice is in your long-term interests.

ON HORSEBACK THROUGH TULI
The Tuli Block comprises reserves, concession areas and agricultural land covering 12,000ha (30,000 acres). This is indeed big-game country, and the primitive landscape has contributed much to making Botswana one of Africa's top wildlife safari destinations. Riding horseback through Tuli is one of those once-in-a-lifetime experiences. The open veld, wide blue skies and plethora of wildlife in an untamed wilderness call to you: lion, leopard, cheetah, Burchell's zebra, wildebeest, hippo and the Tuli elephant all have a home here. The horizon is punctuated with clusters of boulders and baobabs, while impala, klipspringer, honey badgers and bat-eared foxes dart in and out of sight. Much of the land here is private, so venturing off gravel roads

Top to bottom: Ilala palms on the Makgadikgadi Pans; brown hyena; Baines' Baobabs.

71

KALAHARI DESERT

The Kalahari is the largest continuous stretch of sand in the world. Flat, dry and empty, it covers more than 80 per cent of Botswana, stretching from the Orange River towards the equatorial regions. This wide, open expanse – whipped by clouds of dust, lashed by the summer rains and baked by the sun – was formed 200 million years ago when the supercontinent Gondwana began to break up to form the landmasses of the southern hemisphere.

A KALAHARI SAFARI

The tourism industry is currently one of Botswana's most lucrative sectors, and a vital element of this burgeoning business is ecotourism, an increasingly popular trend throughout Africa.

Ecotourism has rapidly usurped the position of Botswana's hunting industry as one of the country's top foreign-exchange earners. Botswana is now one of Africa's leading destinations. The sandy tracks first cut through this countryside by early explorers have given way, in parts, to a more developed infrastructure, but gravel and dust roads are still the paths most travelled in Botswana's wild areas. This adds to the rustic mood of untrammelled wilderness so sought after by travellers to Africa.

A SENSITIVE ECOLOGY

Much of Botswana comprises arid and sparsely vegetated terrain, and the ecological balance is a sensitive one, easily destabilised. Yet this parched land is unusually rich in game and bird species. Game viewing is at its finest in the dry winter from May to August, when wildlife congregates at the remaining water sources. Wet summers provide the animals with an abundance of water, at which time they are far more reclusive. Summers also introduce a greater risk of malaria.

THE WORLD'S GREATEST DESERTS
- Sahara Desert, North Africa 9,065,000km² (3,500,000mi²)
- Gobi Desert, Mongolia-China 1,295,000km² (500,000mi²)
- Kalahari Desert, Southern Africa 582,000km² (225,000mi²)
- Great Victoria Desert, Australia 338,500km² (150,000mi²)
- Great Sandy Desert, Australia 338,500km² (150,000mi²)

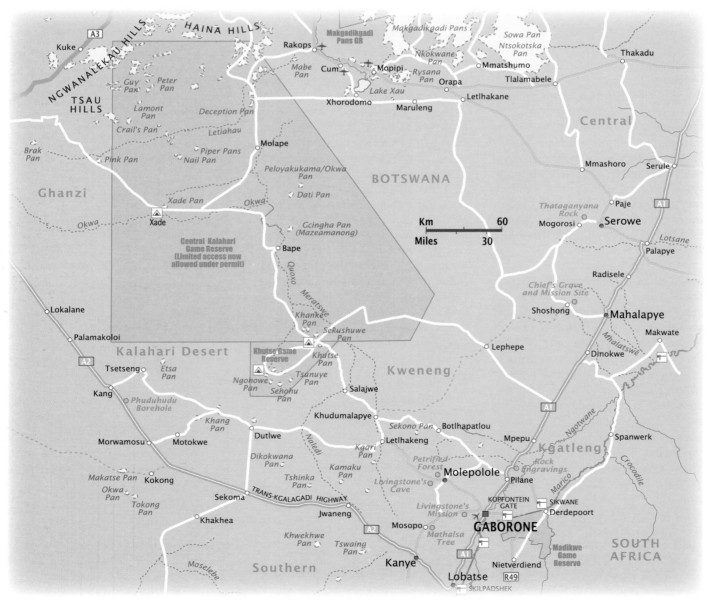

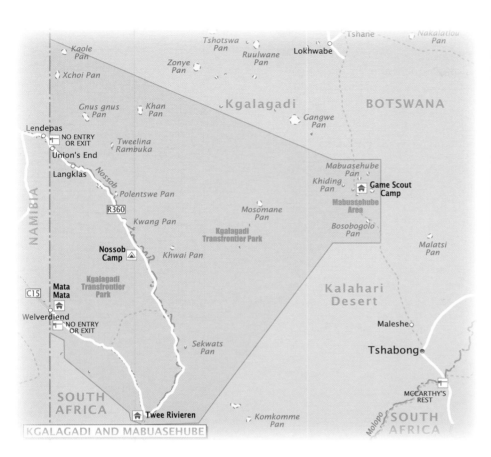

KHUTSE AND MABUASEHUBE

Hugging the southernmost border of the Central Kalahari Game Reserve, Khutse Game Reserve is a small sanctuary located fairly close to Gaborone. Made up largely of undulating savanna within typical pan countryside, Khutse is 4x4 territory and its numerous pans yield good wildlife sightings. The bird life, too, is rich. Mabuasehube Game Reserve (now part of the Kgalagadi Transfrontier Park) is located in a remote region that is time-consuming and costly to reach ... yet it yields rich rewards for those who invest the time and money to enjoy what it has to offer: the simple beauty of the stark pans, the natural burnt ochres and browns of the desert, and reliably abundant game. The rare brown hyena is frequently spotted in the area, while wildebeest, hartebeest, eland, springbok and gemsbok are seen around the many pans, particularly during the rainy season (October to April). During the drier months game (and, as a result, most of the tourists) is concentrated largely around three of the major watering points: Lesholoago Pan, Mpaathutlwa Pan and Mabuasehube Pan.

Top to bottom: meerkats on the lookout; Nossob dry riverbed; gemsbok.

Zimbabwe

QUICK FACTS

Capital: Harare
Area: 390,580km² / 150,800mi²
Population: 12,5 million
Main ethnic groups:
· Shona (71%)
· Ndebele (16%)
· White (11.5%)
· Asian (0.5%)
Main languages:
· English
· Shona
· Ndebele
Main religions:
· Syncretic (combination Christian/traditional beliefs (50%)
· Christian (26%)
· Traditional beliefs (24%)
Currency: US Dollar, Euro, South African Rand

IN THIS CHAPTER

Zambezi

Sapi Safari Area
Kanyemba

Mana Pools NP
Dande Safari Area
urungwe afari Area

Chewore Safari Area
Hunyani

Makuti

Doma Safari Area

Muzarabani

Mukumbura

Charara Safari Area
A1

Centenary

Mavuradonha Wilderness Area (Community Chalets)

Mt Darwin

Ruya

Karoi

Mhangura

Mvurwi

Unfurudzi Safari Area

Portuguese Forts

Mazowe

Nyamapanda

Magunje

Chinhoyi Caves National Park

Howard Institute

Katiyo

Bindura

Mutoko

Chinhoyi

Mazowe

Paradise Pools

Ruenya

A1

Murombedzi

Murewa

Umfuli Recreational Park

A2

Lake Manyame Rec. Park

HARARE

Norton

Regina Coeli

Hartley Safari Area

Chitungwiza

Ruins

Chegutu

Lake Chivero Rec. Park

Macheke

Ruins

Nyanga NP

Kadoma

Marondera

Ruins

A3

Juliasdale

Ngezi Dam Rec. Park

A4

Caves

Rusape

Hande Viewpoint

A5

Sebakwe Dam Rec. Park

Fort Charter

Odzani Falls

Watsomba

Kwekwe

MUTARE

Fort Ingwenya

Chivhu

Bunga Forest Botanical Reserve

Vungu

A17

Mvuma

Ruins

Save

Gweru

Ruins

Muchuchu Ruins

A5

Shurugwi

Odzi Gorge

A9

Nalatale Ruins

Muzhwi Dam

A4

Nyika

Ruins

Chimanimani

Ruins

Dhlo Dhlo Ruins
Fort Rixon

Masvingo

A9

Chibvumani Ruins

Thomas Moodie's Grave

Chimanimani NP

Memorial

Mushandike Sanctuary

Mutirikwi Rec. Park

Chipinge

Lake Cunningham Rec. Park

Zvishavane

Great Zimbabwe National Monument

Chipinge Safari Area

alabala

A9

Manjirenji Rec. Park

Mt Selinda

Insiza

Ngundu

Bangala Dam Rec. Park

Save

Ichelo Cave

Bubiana

Manyuchi Dam

Chiredzi

A6

Mzingwane

Runde

Chilojo Cliffs

Mwenezi

A4

Bengi Spring

Giraffe Petroglyph

Hot Spring

Gonarezhou NP

Tuli Safari Area

Malapati Safari Area

Pioneer Memorial

Chipise Hot Spring

Beitbridge

Limpopo

Top to bottom: aerial view of Lake Kariba; a cruise to Victoria Falls; local curios on sale.

Zimbabwe

10 TOP ADVENTURES

1. Hiking
2. Game viewing
3. 4x4ing
4. Horse riding
5. Elephant safaris
6. Canoeing
7. Whitewater rafting
8. Houseboating
9. Bungee jumping
10. Scenic flights

Game viewing.

ON LAND

Hiking

MILD

The Chimanimani Mountains are criss-crossed with long-distance hiking trails that lead through meadows of wild flowers to hidden caves and pools. Peak baggers should aim for the highest summit, Monte Binga (2436m), on the border with Mozambique. Matobo NP, the burial place of Cecil John Rhodes, offers a fine combination of scenery, wildlife and history, including numerous cave paintings.

Chimanani NP
www.zimparks.org
+263 026 555
Matobo NP
www.zimparks.org

+263 083 8257
Wild Frontiers
www.wildfrontiers.com
+27 72 927 7529

Game viewing

MILD

Hwange NP is the jewel in the crown of Zimbabwe's national parks. You can combine an elephant-back safari with black rhino tracking and a Big Five game drive in the Victoria Falls Private Game Reserve, and there are plenty of up-market lodges in Malilangwe and other reserves for those looking for a spoil.

Wild Frontiers
www.wildfrontiers.com
+27 72 927 7529
Singita
www.singita.com
+27 21 683 3424
Natureways
www.natureways.com
+263 772 335 038

Wilderness Safaris
www.wilderness-safaris.com
+27 11 883 0747
Hwange NP
www.zimparks.org
+263 18 371
Stanley & Livingstone
www.stanleyandlivingstone.com
+27 11 658 0633 or
+258 21 301 618

4x4ing

MILD

Zimbabwe has plenty of dirt roads for self-sufficient adventurers to explore. There are lodges and camp sites for wild camping in Big Five territory at Mana Pools and Matusadona national parks, and guided trips through game-rich Kariba and Hwange national parks.

Parks & Wildlife Management Authority
www.zimparks.org
+263 4 706 077/8

Taggallongg
www.tagalong.co.za
+27 11 975 3293

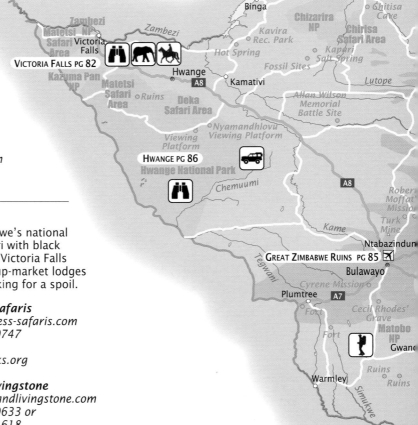

Horse riding

Ride out on short trails or multi-day safaris along the game paths around Victoria Falls.

MILD

Flame of Africa
www.flameofafrica.com
+27 31 762 2424
Safari Par Excellence
www.safpar.com
+260 213 320 606
Matobo NP
www.zimparks.org
+263 083 8257

Elephant safaris

The high vantage of an elephant's back offers a different perspective on Victoria Falls National Park.

MILD

Wild Horizons
www.wildhorizons.co.za
+263 134 4571

One-stop shop
Flame of Africa
www.flameofafrica.com
+27 31 762 2424
Wild Horizons
www.wildhorizons.co.za
+263 134 4571
Wild Frontiers
www.wildfrontiers.com
+27 72 927 7529
Zimbabwe Tourist Office
www.zimbabwe.net
+263 478 0651/4
NB: Many activities listed around Vic Falls/ Livingstone can be organised from both the Zimbabwean and Zambian side.

Elephant safari.

ON WATER

Canoeing

MILD

Canoe safaris on the Zambezi River cater for all sorts. Choose between a leisurely wine route on the upper section, or a multi-day safari on which you experience some small but exciting rapids, sleep out on remote sandbanks and get a water-side view of game on the lower Zambezi.

Natureways
www.natureways.com
+263 772 335 038
Cansaf Adventures and Canoeing Safaris
www.cansaf.com
+263 4293 3687
Safari Par Excellence
www.safpar.com
+27 11 781 3851 or +260 213 320 606
Wild Horizons
www.wildhorizons.co.za
+263 134 4571
Wild Frontiers
www.wildfrontiers.com
+27 72 927 7529

Whitewater rafting.

Canoeing on the Zambezi.

Whitewater rafting

Shooting the rapids of the mighty Zambezi is not for sissies. But it carries serious bragging rights!

WILD

Shearwater Adventures
www.shearwatervictoriafalls.com
+263 134 4471/2/3
Frontiers Rafting
http://africanadrenalin.co.za/frontiers/index.htm
+263 134 1092
Safari Par Excellence
www.safpar.com
+260 213 320 606
Wild Horizons
www.wildhorizons.co.za
+263 134 4571

Houseboating

TO DO

Cruising around Lake Kariba in a houseboat with the family or a few mates – chilling, enjoying the sunsets and trying a spot of tiger fishing – is one of the quintessential African adventures.

Flame of Africa
www.flameofafrica.com
+27 317 622 424

KARIBA PG 84

VICTORIA FALLS PG 82

HWANGE PG 86

GREAT ZIMBABWE RUINS PG 85

Chiru

Karib

Lake Kari
Rec Par

Matusadon
NP

Lake
Kariba

Chete
Safari Area

Lake Kariba
Rec. Park

Binga

Chizarira
NP

Chitisa
Cave

Chirisa
Safari Area

Zambezi

Kavira
Rec. Park

Kapari
Salt Spring

Hot Spring

Fossil Sites

Lutope

Victoria
Falls

Zambezi
Matetsi
NP
Safari
Area

Kamativi

Kazuma Pan
NP

Matetsi
Safari
Area

Hwange

A8

Ruins

Deka
Safari Area

Allan Wilson
Memorial
Battle Site

Viewing
Platform

Nyamandhlovu
Viewing Platform

Hwange National Park

Chemuumi

A8

Rober
Moffo
Missio

Kame

Turk
Mine

Ntabazindu

Bulawayo

Tegwani

Cyrene Mission

Plumtree A7

Fort

Cecil Rhodes'
Grave

Fort

Matobo
NP

Gwan

Warmley

Simukwe

Ruins

Ruins

Bungee jumping

WILD

You can access the iconic 111m bungee of the Victoria Falls Bridge from either the Zimbabwean or the Zambian side of the falls. So you've no excuse not to do it!

Shearwater Adventures
www.shearwateradventures.com
+263 134 4471/2/3

Bungee over the falls.

Scenic flights

TO DO

No matter what you've heard about it, the Flight of Angels will surpass all expectations. If you want to really feel the power of the falling water, take a microlight flight – or keep your distance in a helicopter.

Shearwater Adventures
www.shearwatervictoriafalls.com/
+263 134 4471/2/3
Batoka Sky
www.livingstonesadventure.com
+260 213 323 589

Zimbabwe

OTHER ADVENTURES

1. Walk with lions
2. Victoria Falls Marathon/Zambezi Man
3. Viewing the falls
4. Walking safaris
5. Mountain biking
6. Abseiling
7. Sunset cruising
8. River boarding
9. Bridge swinging

The spectacular Victoria Falls.

 ON LAND

Walk with lions
Come face to face with the king of Africa. The walk, through riverine vegetation, is educational and a stunning opportunity to get close-up images of the playful lion cubs.

Wild Horizons
www.wildhorizons.co.za
+263 134 4571

Wild Frontiers
www.wildfrontiers.com
+27 72 927 7529

Victoria Falls Marathon/Zambezi Man
One of the most scenic marathons in the world, the route takes runners on a magnificent tour of Africa's premier adventure centre, a highlight of which is crossing the roaring Zambezi on the Vic Falls Bridge for a brief visit to the Zambian side of the falls. And if you really want bragging rights, how about the multi-disciplinary Zambezi Man Challenge?

Wild Frontiers
www.wildfrontiers.com
+27 72 927 7529
www.zam-man.com

Viewing the falls
There are various viewpoints from which to ogle at the falls, the most dramatic of which is Cataract View. Danger Point is also superb, but the trek to it can be extremely slippery.

Walking safaris
Guided walks and wilderness trails can be booked in most of the national parks, but the three-day full-moon walks at Mana Pools NP are a must for fit adventurous sorts. If you've got bush skills you can also take off on unguided walks – just watch out for the big game!

Parks & Wildlife Management Authority
www.zimparks.org
+263 470 6077/8

Mountain biking
Experience the rolling thunder of Victoria Falls, Hwange and the Matobo on two wheels, or explore the ancient ruins of Great Zimbabwe.

Bike and saddle
www.bikeandsaddle.com
+27 21 422 3302

Abseiling
Scramble up then abseil down the magnificent granite rock faces of the Matobo Hills near Bulawayo.

Camp Amalinda
www.campamalinda.com
+263 964 868/9

Sunset cruise.

Sunset cruising

Exclusive dining doesn't come better than this. A luxury boat takes you on a sunset cruise, then, once you're upriver, the engines are cut, the lanterns lit and you drift back to the mooring, listen to the sounds of the bush and feast on superb cuisine washed down with fine wines. The big bonus is that all the other boats have to be off the water at sunset – so you have the Zambezi River all to yourself. Just a wee bit special.

Flame of Africa
www.flameofafrica.com
+27 31 762 2424
Wild Horizons
www.wildhorizons.co.za
+263 134 4571

River boarding

An exciting combo for adrenalin junkies is a day of rafting and river boarding, where you hop off the raft at key action spots to play in the waves.

Safari Par Excellence
www.safpar.com
+260 213 320 606

Cable slide.

Bridge swinging

Not content with throwing you off the Victoria Falls Bridge with a bungee cord strapped to your ankles, Shearwater Adventures have added a new bridge swing to their portfolio. And if you think that's for sissies, think again – it's guaranteed to make even grown men scream. Wusses can, of course, opt for the less terrifying cable slide from the edge of the gorge, or the highly educational, and scenic, bridge tour.

Shearwater Adventures
www.shearwatervictoriafalls.com
+263 134 4471/2/3

THE SMOKE THAT THUNDERS

The mighty Victoria Falls (a.k.a. Mosi-oa-Tunya, 'The Smoke that Thunders') is one of Africa's greatest natural wonders, a vast and remarkably rugged vista of rainforest and riverine landscape. As the focal point of adventure in both Zambia and Zimbabwe, tour operators abound in and around Victoria Falls and the Zambezi Gorge, which is rated one of the world's wildest whitewater rafting destinations. The section between Lake Kariba and Victoria Falls is considered among the least tamed of the river's course (as well as one of the most spectacular) and is also the home territory of crocodiles and hippos, with even the occasional elephant spotted along the rugged banks.

VICTORIA FALLS ADVENTURES

Everything is bigger and better, deeper and steeper at the much-publicised junction of Zimbabwe and Zambia. Whitewater rafting can be breathtaking, bungee jumping terrifying, elephant-back safaris out of this world and the scenic flights by plane or helicopter are the stuff of lifetime memories. There are also walking routes,

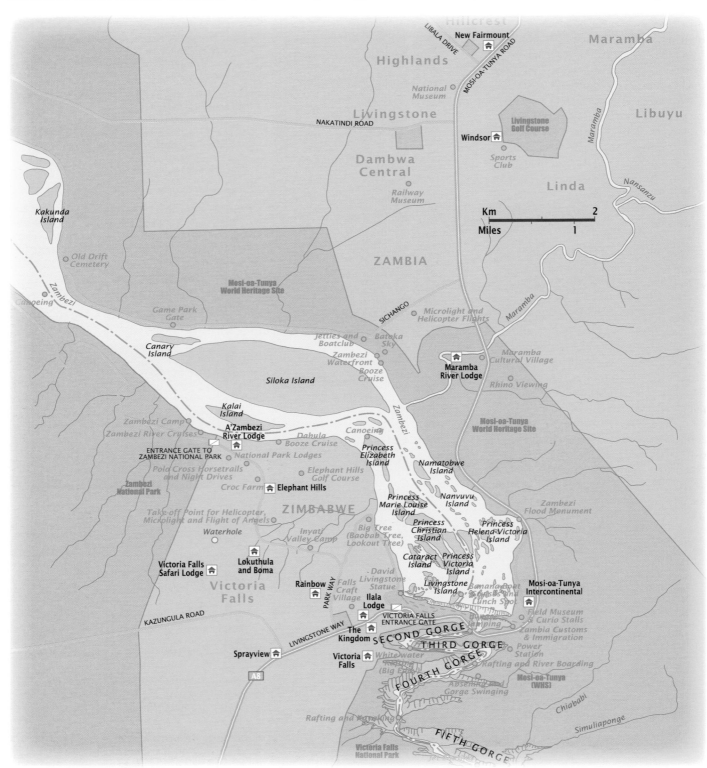

hiking trails, 4x4 excursions, sundowner cruises and game-viewing safaris. The Zimbabwean side is particularly well serviced by the hospitality industry and is, therefore, not cheap. The Zambian side is less 'developed' and not as spectacular, but it does offer a different, less glitzy view, with a better opportunity to get close to the waters of the falls.

HIGHLIGHTS OF THE FALLS

Highlights are undoubtedly the awesome 110m (360ft) bungee jump, hailed as the highest commercial bridge leap in Africa. Queues may be long, the wait frustrating and the cost expensive, but the experience is unbeatable. Another unforgettable experience is the much vaunted Flight of Angels over the falls in a seaplane, helicopter, microlight or a twin-engined aircraft. Prices depend on the agent, aircraft and how long you stay airborne, but the experience is exhilarating, although frowned upon by conservationists.

The main attraction is, however, the whitewater rafting, and the Zambezi Gorge is known to be one of the wildest whitewater spots in the world. High-water trips are available from either the Zimbabwean or the Zambian side, but, depending on the rains, are restricted to July and early August. Low-water runs are tackled between mid-August and the end of December. While the waters above the falls are shallow, more than 20 rapids punctuate the waters below. When the waters are low, the dangers are greater, and August to December are graded 5 – extremely demanding (Grade 6 is given to rapids that are unrideable!). The three-day, 65km (40-mile) whitewater trail from Kazungula ends at Big Tree at the falls.

THE WORLD'S HIGHEST FALLS

Angel Falls, Venezuela	979m	3212ft
uThukela, South Africa	850m	2800ft
Utigord, Norway	800m	2625ft
Monge, Norway	774m	2540ft
Mutarazi, Zimbabwe	762m	2499ft
Yosemite, United States	739m	2425ft
Espelands, Norway	703m	2307ft
Lower Mar Valley, Norway	655m	2151ft
Tyssestrengene, Norway	647m	2123ft
Cuquenan, Venezuela	610m	2000ft

RAPID FIRE

Victoria Falls provides a daunting yet breathtaking backdrop for the site's highly challenging but massively rewarding rapids. It's natural that great whitewater rafting is centred around impressive waterfalls. Africa has a good number to speak of.

· Blue Nile Falls	Ethiopia
· Murchison Falls	Uganda
· Augrabies Falls	South Africa
· The Great Usutu	Swaziland
· Oribi Gorge Falls	South Africa
· Bragança Falls	Angola
· Epupa Falls	Namibia
· Ruacana Falls	Namibia
· Kagera Falls	Burundi

VICTORIA FALLS NATIONAL PARK

The dramatic falls and surrounding rainforest lie at the heart of the Victoria Falls National Park, a small but green and thriving 2300ha (5680 acres) of walking trails, woodland and riverine habitat. The forest that borders the falls is a thick jungle with dense undergrowth and a high canopy filled with ferns and orchids. Stands of wild fig and sausage trees are alive with bird calls. Small primates also inhabit these wooded slopes.

VICTORIA FALLS VILLAGE

Within relatively easy walking distance of the thundering waters is Victoria Falls village, which is still rather rustic in appearance. Expeditions into the forest, elephant safaris, bungee jumps and cycling excursions can be arranged here; visitors' amenities crowd the 'village'. Considerably more tame is the quaint little Zambezi Nature Sanctuary, a small but rewarding haven for some of the region's indigenous wildlife, notably some 5000 Nile crocodiles.

Top to bottom: microlighting over Victoria Falls; a section of the main falls; bungee plunge off the Zambezi River bridge.

83

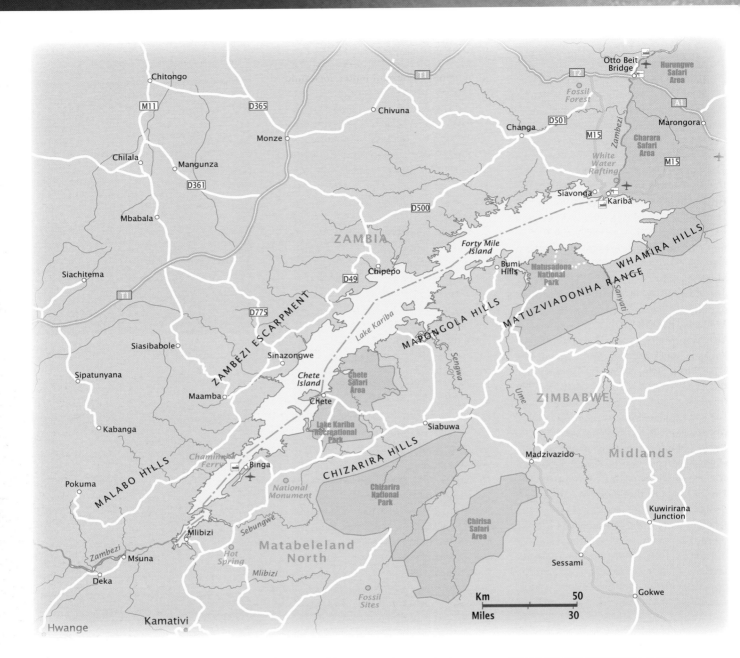

LAKE KARIBA

Lake Kariba is Zimbabwe's principal source of hydroelectricity and the third-largest artificial body of water in Africa, covering a total of 5000km² (1930 sq. miles). Some of Zimbabwe's finest parks, reserves and wilderness areas are found on its shores.

SAILING LAKE KARIBA

The heart of the lake's leisure industry is Matusadona National Park. There are walking trails, boat cruises, sailing and sport fishing as well as plenty of marinas and anchorage. The game lodges on the water's edge boast excellent facilities. Game viewing and bird-watching from the water is rewarding, with crocodile, Fish Eagles, cormorants, kingfishers, darters and herons, and even elephant and buffalo. Given the lake's location and popularity, certain parts of the shore are very expensive. Prices vary from outrageous to very reasonable. Most affordable are the budget picnic cruises, many of which depart regularly from the lake's marinas.

A FERRY GOOD TIME

The Kariba Ferry leaves Kariba town once a week and takes two to three days to reach Binga. Amenities are basic and you should bring your own supplies. Some operators offer special day packages for small groups, usually including a day on the water. Accommodation, including tents, is not hard to find, but you may want to book in advance.

MANA POOLS NATIONAL PARK

This World Heritage Site is wild and remote. It is a great spot for fishing, but even better for wildlife viewing, with hippo, croc, zebra, antelope and elephant all sure to be seen. Day visitors are welcome, but you'd definitely want to spend a few nights in one of the rustic camp sites or in a more up-market lodge!

LAKE KARIBA IN A NUTSHELL
Climate: Temperatures are the highest in the country; nights can, however, be cold, especially mid-year.
Risk factor: Crocodiles.
Health: Malaria, bilharzia and AIDS are prevalent. Drinking water is fairly safe.
Pack: Malarial prophylactics, sunscreen and personal supplies.
Facilities: Good to excellent.

GREAT ZIMBABWE

The ruins of Great Zimbabwe comprise the most impressive medieval site in Africa south of the Sahara. About 30km (19 miles) from Masvingo, it was established more than 1000 years ago by the Karonga, ancestors of the local Shona. The walled city harboured around 10,000 citizens, but it was abandoned in the 1450s. There are guided tours.

EXPLORING CHIMANIMANI

Chimanimani National Park is popular with backpackers. The region has a rich flora and fauna, and within easy reach are two of the area's top attractions: Chimanimani Eland Sanctuary and Bridal Veil Falls. Chimanimani mountain range lures hikers: the granite massif is crowned by the 2436m (7995ft) Mount Binga (Kweza), which lies on the other side of the Mozambique border. Paths and trails take hikers through mountain wilderness dotted with caves, gorges, streams and grassy slopes dotted with msasa trees.

MANY WAYS TO SCALE A PEAK

There are various options to reach the lofty heights of Mount Binga, including a one-day walk to the Southern Lakes by way of the Banana Grove Trail, and the relatively gentle walk up Skeleton Pass, which should take less than an hour. About 20km (12 miles) from Chimanimani village is Mutekeswane Base Camp, the starting point for three routes. Camp sites are basic; the most popular accommodation options are offered at caves such as Digby's Falls, North Cave and Peterhouse Cave. All provide easy access to some of the most spectacular hikes in the area.

MATOBO HILLS

These granite hills are the final resting place of mining magnate and statesman, Cecil John Rhodes, who played a significant role in the troubled history of Southern Africa. The spot at Malindidzimu is known as 'View of the World' and provides one of the finest panoramas in southwestern Zimbabwe. Matobo National Park – 50km (31 miles) south of Bulawayo – has a small assortment of wild and rare animals. Giant granite outcrops and precariously balanced rock formations characterise the area. It also boasts one of the world's most astounding collections of indigenous rock art.

Top to bottom: Kariba Dam wall and Nyaminyami statue; crocodiles at the Kariba crocodile farm; aloes and western ridge stone wall.

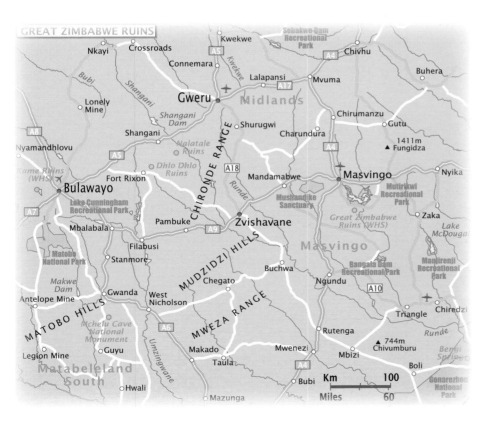

HWANGE NATIONAL PARK

A former hunting reserve for Ndebele kings, Hwange was one of Africa's best-stocked parks until the 1970s, thanks partly to the creation of dozens of artificial water holes. Located alongside the Kalahari Desert, it was created as a means of enticing people into viewing animals en route to the more famed Vic Falls nearby. The easy little two-hour Ten Mile Drive that loops through the best wildlife areas of the park is the staple attraction for most visitors, with the highlight being the Nyamandhlovu Viewing Platform above the popular (among the animals) Nyamandhlovu Pan. More adventurous visitors will take their choice of the Ngwethla Loop, an overnight stay at Sinamatella Camp (with its amazing views and chilling night-time animal 'talk'), or ranger-escorted walks.

ZAMBEZI NATIONAL PARK

The Victoria Falls and Zambezi national parks preserve an incredible natural heritage that includes spectacular waterfalls, thousands of hectares of protected land and some of Africa's most impressive wildlife populations. Much of Zimbabwe is still untamed. The Zambezi NP extends to over 56,000ha (138,350 acres) and is considerably larger than Victoria Falls NP. Zambezi is home to elephant, buffalo, rhino, zebra, lion, leopard and cheetah, in addition to countless other species that have made their home in the Zambezi Basin. Less developed than the rather tourist-oriented falls, Zambezi National Park offers a taste of Zimbabwe at its finest.

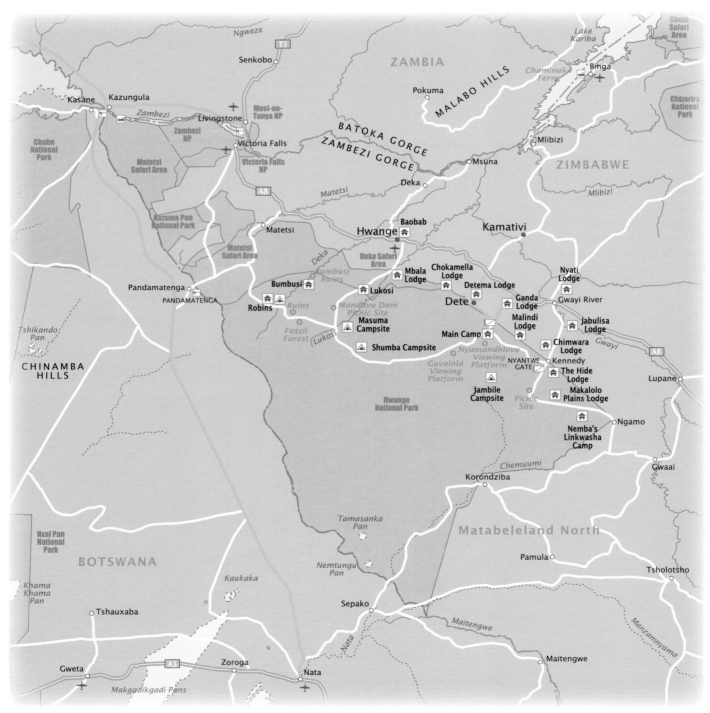

TACKLING THE ZAMBEZI

Depending largely on the season and the rains, the high-water expeditions on the Zambezi are limited to late winter (July and August), while low-water runs are best between mid-August and December. The waters are not always easy to navigate – especially beyond the favoured tourist stopovers – and when the waters are low the existing risks are even greater. This is particularly true from August to December when Grade 5 rapids are fraught with danger, to be tackled only by the exceptionally fit and equally skilled.

Trip durations vary on the Zambezi, but the most popular are the 24-hour, 22km (14-mile) excursion with seven other 'sailors' on an inflatable rubber craft, and the less demanding three-day, 65km (40-mile) whitewater trail from Kazungula to Victoria Falls' Big Tree – a very different experience to the rather menacing whirlpools at Mupata Gorge, which require a lot more skill to negotiate and are potentially hazardous for the uninitiated.

HARARE

Founded just over 100 years ago, Zimbabwe's capital was once hailed as the most African of the continent's principal cities. Harare (formerly known as Salisbury) was pronounced the official capital of Southern Rhodesia in 1923 and was declared a city in 1935. It has seen better days and is plagued intermittently with fuel shortages and barren supermarket shelves. Despite problems such as growing urban crime, the capital remains a beautiful city that has retained at least some of its charm. It also serves as an important centre for the country's arts and crafts industry, notably the soapstone sculptures, the best of which are found about 8km (5 miles) from town at Chapungu Kraal, a model Shona village that offers a glimpse of tribal life. Harare is set against an inspiring backdrop of bushveld savanna dotted with a series of rock formations (the most famous being the Epworth Balancing Rocks) and an impressive number of rock-art sites.

Top to bottom: a pride of female lions resting; 4x4 vehicle in a flooded plain; Ilala palms at sunset.

Mozambique

QUICK FACTS

Capital: Maputo
Area: 799,380km² / 308,642mi²
Population: 22,8 million
Main ethnic groups:
· Makua-Lomwe (47%)
· Tsonga (23%)
· Malawi (12%)

Main language:
· Portuguese
Main religions:
· Traditional beliefs (60%)
· Christian (30%)
· Muslim (10%)
Currency: Metical (100 centavos)

IN THIS CHAPTER

Top to bottom: 4x4 trip near Barra Lagoon; pristine beach.

Namuiranga

Mocímboa da Praia

Negomane
Mueda

Niassa
National Reserve

Rovuma

Manda
Wilderness

Mecula

Cóbuè

Sanga Community
Wildlife Project

Lake Malawi

Quinta Capricórnio
Permaculture Farm

Lichinga

Lugenda

Marrupa

Sunate

Pemba

Messalo

Montepuez

Lúrio

Baia de Memba

Fernão Veloso

Mandimba

Lagoa
Amaramba

Rock
Climbing

Namialo

Mualádzi
Cassacatiza

Lisula

Cuamba

Ribáue

Rock Paintings

Mozambique

Nampula

Fingoè

Mountain
Trails

Miruro

Cahora
Bassa Dam

Zóbuè

Alto Molócuè

Panhame

Magoè

Boroma
Mission

103

Milange

Angoche

Mucumbura

Tete

Gili
Reserve

Ruins of Massangano
Citadel (1730–1870)

103

Changara

Chiramba

Mocuba

Canxixe

102

Zambezi

Hot Springs
Mont
Morrumbala

Pebane

Nicuadala

Quelimane

Grove of Mary
Moffat Livingstone

Inhamitanga

Gorongosa
NP

Marromeu
GR

Gorongosa

Chimoio

EN6

Dondo

Rotanda

EN6

Monta
Binga

Beira

EN1

Ruins of
Fortress (1501)

Espungabera

Ancient Dhow
Anchorage
Save

INDIAN OCEAN

Zinave
NP

Bazaruto
Island

Mabote

Pambarra

Chicualacuala

Banhine
NP

Mapai

Limpopo
National
Park

Massingir
Dam

Inhambane

Macarretane

Inharrime

Lagoa Dongane

Jantiguè

Viewing
Point

Lagoa Poelela

Limpopo Flats

Lagoa Quissico

Ressano
Garcia

EN1

Lagoa Nhanzume

EN4

Baia de Maputo

MAPUTO

Namaacha

Migrating
Elephants

Maputo
Game Reserve

Ponta do Ouro

Mozambique

10 TOP ADVENTURES

1. 4x4ing
2. Horse riding
3. Game viewing
4. Ocean safaris
5. Scuba diving
6. Kitesurfing and stand-up paddle boarding
7. Sailing
8. Game fishing
9. Sea kayaking
10. Dolphin safaris

4x4 vehicles crossing a river.

ON LAND

4x4ing

A 4x4 is a must if you're planning to explore the sandy back roads of Mozambique. If you prefer some support, take the guided self-drive Shingwedzi 4x4 Trail through Mozambique's Limpopo National Park, or, if you want to see the Big Five, the Luvuvhu Trail through Letaba Ranch and Makuya Park.

MILD

Transfrontier Parks Destinations (TFPD)
www.dolimpopo.com
+27 21 701 7860

Horse riding

Head out into the glorious golden dunes of Bazaruto Island, on the beaches or through the plantations and farmlands around Barra Lodge.

MILD

Indigo Bay Resort
www.indigobayresort.com
+27 11 658 0633 or +258 21 301 618
Barra Lodge
www.barralodge.co.za
+258 29 320 561

Game viewing

Don't go to Mozambique expecting to quickly tick off the Big Five – the game is scarcer and more skittish than in the Kruger National Park or the famous East African reserves. But safaris in the Limpopo NP, Gorongosa NP, and the Niassa National Reserve are rewarding for those seeking a true wilderness experience. Day and overnight safaris are also offered in the Manda Wilderness, home to sable, elephant, reedbuck, leopard and over 300 species of birds.

WILD

Manda Wilderness Reserve
www.mandawilderness.org
+44 20 3239 6253
Explore Gorongosa
www.exploregorongosa.com
+27 21 813 9534
Lugenda Wilderness Camp
www.lugenda.com
+27 11 658 0633 or +258 21 301 618
Hartleys Safaris
www.hartleys.co.za
+27 11 467 4704

ON WATER

Ocean safaris

Sightings of whale sharks are almost guaranteed in Whale Shark Alley near Tofo, and when one's spotted you can slip into the water and snorkel with the biggest fish in the sea. Whales, manta rays, dolphins and turtles are among the other species often spotted on these spectacular marine safaris.

TO DO

Liquid Adventures
www.liquidadventures.co.za
+258 845 060 9218
Barra Dive Centre
www.barradiveresorts.com
+27 11 023 9901

Kitesurfing and stand-up paddle boarding

Warm waters and rolling waves make Tofo the ideal place to learn to surf, kitesurf or stand-up paddle board (SUP).

WILD

Tony Cook Adventures
www.kitesurfingafrica.co.za
+27 82 783 8392
Liquid Adventures
www.liquidadventures.co.za
+258 845 060 9218

Whale shark.

Each activity is rated as 'To do', Mild or Wild based on intensity

TO DO **1** MILD **3** WILD **1**

ON WATER

MILD

Scuba diving

For sheer variety of dive experiences, southern Mozambique is hard to beat. Ponto do Ouro, just over the border from Kosi Bay, is a popular self-drive destination for budget travellers, and there are resorts to suit all budgets around Inhambane and Vilanculos. The little-known Nacala Bay area offers stunning diving with plenty of new sites for adventurous divers to discover. If you have the bucks, you should head to the Bazaruto or Quirimbas archipelagos for pristine diving from luxury lodges.

Devocean Diving
www.devoceandiving.com
+27 82 332 9029
Simply Scuba
www.simplyscuba.co.za
+27 11 678 0972
Hartley's Oceans and Islands
www.hartleys.co.za
+27 11 467 4704
Adventure Diving Safaris
www.adventuredivingsafaris.com
+27 12 991 3134
Peri-peri Divers
www.peri-peridivers.com
+258 825 505 661
Tofo Scuba
www.tofoscuba.com
+258 828 260 140 or +258 29 329 030
Moz Divers
www.mozdivers.com

+258 827 030 750 or +27 83 514 6846
Barra Dive Centre
www.barradiveresorts.com
+27 11 023 9901
Guinjata Bay
www.guinjata.com
+27 13 741 2795
Jeffs Pro Dive Centre
+258 842 391 100
Liquid Adventures
www.divingtofo.com
+258 845 060 9218
Blue Footprints
bluefootprints.com
+258 848 900 507
Rani Resorts
www.raniresorts.com
+27 11 658 0633 or +258 21 301 618
Azura Retreats
www.azura-retreats.com

+27 11 258 0180
Marlin Lodge
www.marlinlodge.co.za
reservations@marlinlodge.co.za
+27 12 460 9410
Odyssea Dive
www.odysseadive.com
+258 827 817 130
Coral Lodge 15.41
www.corallodge1541.com
+258 26 240 239
Pelago Adventure Centre
www.kwalala-lodges.com
+258 26 520 214
C.I. Divers (Pemba)
www.cidivers.com
+258 826 822 700 or +258 27 220 102
Vamizi Island
www.vamizi.com
+44 12 8576 2218

TO DO

Sailing

Board a yacht in Vilanculos and sail out over the turquoise ocean to the Bazaruto Archipelago, looking out for whales, turtles and manta rays. The numerous combined sailing, diving and fishing adventures include Robinson Crusoe-style overnight stays on picturesque islands and time to stroll the deserted beaches in search of pansy shells.

Sailaway Dhow Safaris
www.sailaway.co.za
+258 29 382 385
Island Quest Sailing and Diving
www.islandquest.co.za
+27 12 329 2917
Marlin Lodge
www.marlinlodge.co.za
+27 12 543 2134
Hartleys Safaris
www.hartleys.co.za
+27 11 467 4704

Pestana Bazaruto Lodge
www.pestana.com
+258 21 305 000
Pestana Inhaca Lodge
www.pestana.com
+258 21 305 000
Wildlife Adventures
www.wildlifeadventures.co.za
+27 21 422 2017
Mozambique Dhow Safaris
www.mozambiquedhowsafaris.com
+27 21 702 0285

Pemba Beach Resort
www.pembabeachresort.com
+27 11 658 0633 or
+258 21 301 618
Indigo Bay Resort
www.indigobayresort.com
+27 11 658 0633 or
+258 21 301 618

WILD

Game fishing

The waters off Mozambique offer some of the best game in the world with hard-fighting species like wahoo, kingfish, billfish and tuna.

Jeff's Palm Resort
www.jeffsmoz.com
+27 13 932 1263
Charles Norman Safaris
www.sportfishafrica.co.za
+27 11 888 3591
Marlin Lodge
www.marlinlodge.co.za
+27 12 543 2134
Rani Resorts
www.raniresorts.com

+27 11 658 0633 or
+258 21 301 618
Pestana Bazaruto Lodge
www.pestana.com
+258 21 305 000
Marlin Lodge
www.marlinlodge.co.za
+27 12 543 2134
Azura Retreats
www.azura-retreats.com
+27 76 705 0599

Diving.

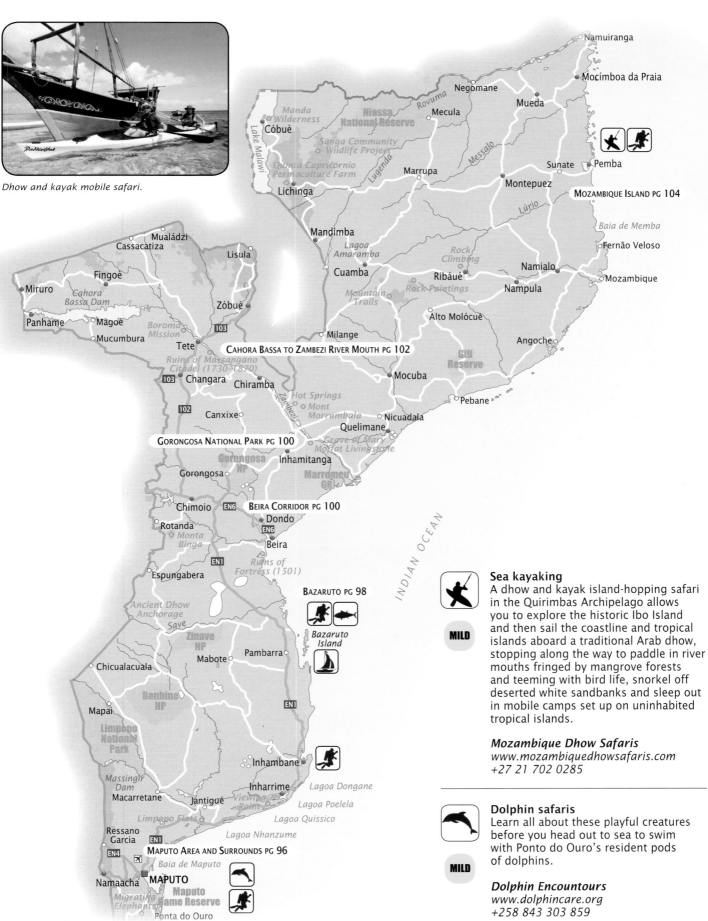

Dhow and kayak mobile safari.

Namuiranga

Mocímboa da Praia

Negomane

Mueda

Mecula

Manda Wilderness

Niassa National Reserve

Cóbuè

Lake Malawi

Sanga Community Wildlife Project

Quinta Capricórnio Permaculture Farm

Lichinga

Lugenda

Rovuma

Marrupa

Messalo

Sunate

Pemba

MOZAMBIQUE ISLAND PG 104

Montepuez

Lúrio

Baia de Memba

Mandimba

Lagoa Amaramba

Cuamba

Rock Climbing

Ribáue

Rock Paintings

Namialo

Fernão Veloso

Mozambique

Nampula

Mualádzi

Cassacatiza

Lisula

Mountain Trails

Alto Molócuè

Fingoè

Miruro

Cahora Bassa Dam

Zóbuè

Milange

Angoche

Panhame

Màgoé

Boroma Mission

Mucumbura

Tete

Ruins of Massangano Citadel (1730-1870)

CAHORA BASSA TO ZAMBEZI RIVER MOUTH PG 102

Mocuba

Gili Reserve

103

103 Changara

Chiramba

Canxixe

102

Hot Springs

Mont Morrumbala

Nicuadala

Pebane

Quelimane

GORONGOSA NATIONAL PARK PG 100

Grave of Mary Moffat Livingstone

Gorongosa NP

Inhamitanga

Marromeu GR

Gorongosa

Chimoio

EN6

BEIRA CORRIDOR PG 100

Dondo

Rotanda

Monta Binga

EN6

Beira

Espungabera

EN1

Ruins of Fortress (1501)

INDIAN OCEAN

Ancient Dhow Anchorage

Save

BAZARUTO PG 98

Bazaruto Island

Zinave NP

Mabote

Pambarra

Chicualacuala

Mapai

Banhine NP

EN1

Limpopo National Park

Massingir Dam

Macarretane

Inhambane

Inharrime

Lagoa Dongane

Jantigué

Viewing Point

Lagoa Poelela

Lagoa Quissico

Limpopo Flats

Ressano Garcia

Lagoa Nhanzume

EN1

MAPUTO AREA AND SURROUNDS PG 96

Baia de Maputo

EN4

Namaacha

MAPUTO

Migrating Elephants

Maputo Game Reserve

Ponta do Ouro

Sea kayaking

A dhow and kayak island-hopping safari in the Quirimbas Archipelago allows you to explore the historic Ibo Island and then sail the coastline and tropical islands aboard a traditional Arab dhow, stopping along the way to paddle in river mouths fringed by mangrove forests and teeming with bird life, snorkel off deserted white sandbanks and sleep out in mobile camps set up on uninhabited tropical islands.

MILD

Mozambique Dhow Safaris
www.mozambiquedhowsafaris.com
+27 21 702 0285

Dolphin safaris

Learn all about these playful creatures before you head out to sea to swim with Ponto do Ouro's resident pods of dolphins.

MILD

Dolphin Encountours
www.dolphincare.org
+258 843 303 859

OTHER ADVENTURES

1. Quad biking
2. Birding
3. Mountain biking
4. Hiking
5. Snorkelling
6. Canoeing

Mozambique offers plenty of walking and hiking opportunities.

ON LAND

Quad biking

Guided quad bike tours through the coconut plantations and cashew nut farms around Barra Lodge near Inhambane give you superb coastal views as well as an insight into village life.

Barra Lodge
www.barralodge.co.za
+258 29 320 561

Birding

Lake Malawi, on Mozambique's western border, attracts a vast range of bird species including large numbers of migratory birds. Birding guides will take you out from Nkwichi Lodge, or you can head out with a map and check list and explore the local area on your own.

Nkwichi Lodge
www.mandawilderness.org
+44 20 3239 6253

Mountain biking

Take off and explore on your own wheels or sign up for a cycle holiday from Maputo to Vilanculos.

Bike & Saddle
www.bikeandsaddle.com
+27 21 813 6433

Hiking

Hike through Big Five territory on the multi-day, guided and porteraged Lebombo Trail, or explore the area around the Palarangala and Machampane rivers on the four-day Palarangala Wilderness Trail.

Mount Binga (2436m/7993ft), the highest mountain in Mozambique, is one for peak baggers (though it's much easier to climb from Chimanimani across the border in Zimbabwe). You can climb the escarpment behind Manda Lodge for spectacular views over Lake Malawi in the Rift Valley, or take short guided or self-guided hikes on Inhaca, Bazaruto and Ibo islands.

Transfrontier Parks Destinations (TFPD)
www.dolimpopo.com
+27 21 701 7860
Manda Wilderness Reserve
www.mandawilderness.org
Pestana Bazaruto and Inhaca Lodges
www.pestana.com
+258 21 305 000
Ibo Island Lodge
www.iboisland.com
+27 21 702 0285

ON WATER

Snorkelling

You don't need to be a scuba diver to appreciate the diversity of Mozambique's marine life. The natural aquariums found in the shallow reefs off Bazaruto, Tofo and Nuarro are perfect for snorkelling. You can also don a mask and snorkel to check out Lake Malawi's colourful cichlids.

Nkwichi Lodge
www.mandawilderness.org
+44 20 3239 6253
Azura Retreats
www.azura-retreats.com
+27 11 258 0180
Nuarro
www.nuarro.com
+258 823 044 049

Canoeing

Explore the mangroves from Ibo or Quilalea islands in the Quirimbas Archipelago, or sign up for a multi-day canoe trip down the Rio Elefantes, overnighting in bush camps on the riverbank.

You can head out in a canoe to explore the eastern shores of Lake Malawi/Niassa or catch the action in the annual Manda Wilderness Canoe Race.

Ibo Island Lodge
www.iboisland.com
+27 21 702 0285
Quilalea Private Island
www.azura-retreats.com
+27 76 705 0599
Ibo Island Lodge
www.iboisland.com
+27 21 702 0285

Transfrontier Parks Destinations (TFPD)
www.dolimpopo.com
+27 21 701 7860
Manda Wilderness
www.mandawilderness.org
+44 20 3239 6253

Namuiranga

Mocímboa da Praia

Negomane

Mecula

Mueda

Rovuma

Niassa National Reserve

Snorkelling; Canoeing

Cóbuè

Birding; Hiking

Lake Malawi

Sanga Community Wildlife Project

Quinta Capricórnio Permaculture Farm

Lichinga

Lugenda

Marrupa

Messalo

Montepuez

Sunate

Canoeing

Pemba

MOZAMBIQUE ISLAND PG 104

Lúrio

Baia de Memba

Fernão Veloso

Mandimba

Lagoa Amaramba

Cuamba

Rock Climbing

Ribáue

Rock Paintings

Namialo

Nampula

Mozambique

Muáladzi

Cassacatiza

Lisula

Fingoè

Mountain Trails

Alto Molócuè

Angoche

Miruro

Cahora Bassa Dam

Zóbuè

103

Milange

CAHORA BASSA TO ZAMBEZI RIVER MOUTH PG 102

Gilé Reserve

Panhame

Mágoè

Boroma Mission

Mucumbura

Tete

Ruins of Massangano Citadel (1730-1870)

103

Changara

Chiramba

Mocuba

Pebane

102

Canxixe

Hot Springs

Mont Morrumbala

Nicuadala

Zambezi

Quelimane

Grave of Mary Moffat Livingstone

GORONGOSA NATIONAL PARK PG 100

Gorongosa NP

Inhamitanga

Gorongosa

Marromeu GR

INDIAN OCEAN

Chimoio

EN6

BEIRA CORRIDOR PG 100

Dondo

Rotanda

Monta Binga

EN6

Beira

EN1

Ruins of Fortress (1501)

Espungabera

BAZARUTO PG 98

Snorkelling

Ancient Dhow Anchorage

Save

Bazaruto Island

Zinave NP

Mabote

Pambarra

Chicualacuala

Banhine NP

Mapai

EN1

Quad biking

Limpopo National Park

Inhambane

Massingir Dam

Inharrime

Lagoa Dongane

Macarretane

Jantigué

Viewing Point

Lagoa Poelela

Limpopo Flats

Lagoa Quissico

Ressano Garcia

EN1

Lagoa Nhanzume

MAPUTO AREA AND SURROUNDS PG 96

EN4

Baia de Maputo

Namaacha

MAPUTO

Mountain biking

Migrating Elephants

Maputo Game Reserve

Ponta do Ouro

Canoeing.

95

MAPUTO

No more than a small, haphazard collection of temporary shelters in the 16th century, Maputo (known in fairly recent times as Lourenço Marques) is a lively port city criss-crossed by palm-fringed avenues lined with jacaranda and flame trees. Following a period of civil strife and political uncertainty that ended only in 1992, many of Maputo's grand palaces, synagogues, markets, museums, and even humble Creole-style homes (particularly in the larger urban centres) still bear the physical scars of civil war. However, Maputo is emerging from the ashes to slowly regain some of the glory of its heyday. It is home to a thriving population of bohemian artists and receives a steady trickle of travellers. It has a vigorous nightlife which centres on the late-night bars of Rua do Bagamoio, the revelry spilling over into the evening markets and brightly lit seafront. Rather dilapidated in parts, the city is dotted with historic Portuguese forts. A highlight is its must-see Museum of the Revolution.

MAPUTO GAME RESERVE

Also known as Maputo Elephant Reserve, this protected area lies across Maputo Bay – an area of shimmering lakes, stretches of grassland and mile upon mile of unspoiled white sand beaches. There are no large herds of game, but elephants are relatively plentiful in the reserve (thanks to excellent conservation efforts). The bird-watching is rewarding and the scenery spectacular. The coastline is rich in colourful tropical fish, coral and a host of marine life. It is also an important breeding ground for the amazing leatherback turtles that weigh in at around 646kg (1421 pounds). These maritime giants lay up to 1000 eggs per season.

THE LAND

Mozambique covers 799,380km² (308,561 sq. miles), which makes up a greater landmass than France and Great Britain combined. A relatively flat land, its average altitude is just over 350m (1148ft), and it enjoys a spectacular coastline that runs for more than 2500km (1554 miles), which provides much of the country's tourist activity.

The multitude of rivers and mountains create a wide and varied range of vegetation that opens itself up to hiking, walking, canoeing and rafting opportunities.

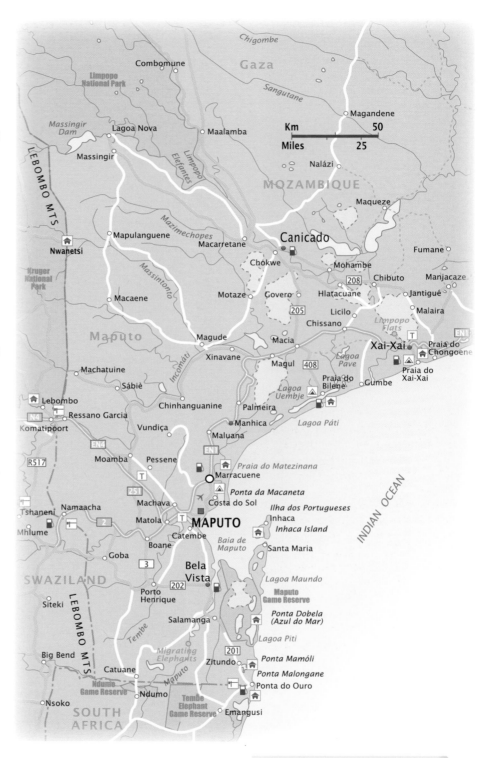

The mighty Zambezi River flows through the Cahora Bassa Dam and runs across the central parts of the country, emptying into the Mozambique Channel and the Indian Ocean at the 100km-wide (62-mile) Zambezi Delta.

The country's highest point is the 2436m (7993ft) Binga Peak, found in the Chimanimani mountain range, on the border with Zimbabwe (Mozambique shares a border with six other countries).

LAND MINES AND MALARIA
This tourist paradise carries with it a number of downsides, notably the risk of AIDS, bilharzia, malaria, and the abundant buried land mines that dot the countryside. This scourge of the civil war has taken a massive toll on thousands of civilians.

INHACA ISLAND

An idyll of beautiful beaches whose shores are dotted with stands of mango trees and lined with brightly coloured offshore reefs, Inhaca Island is about 24km (15 miles) from the mainland and easily accessible via the ferries departing from the capital. It is the largest island in the Gulf of Maputo and its pretty village presents a fascinating look at island life. Dominated by the upgraded Inhaca Hotel, the narrow streets have a good selection of restaurants and cafés interspersed with the odd (laid-back) attraction. Situated in extraordinarily rich waters, the island's popular coastal attractions have proven to be its most magnetic drawcard. Apart from the marine research centre, which offers a different perspective to the conventional island idyll, Inhaca's shores have striking beaches and a fascinating reef that makes for some of the finest diving, snorkelling and underwater explorations on Africa's east coast.

EXPLORING MAPUTO PROVINCE

Readily accessible by road from South Africa, Maputo province has everything: well-stocked reserves, historic towns and magical beaches, outstanding diving and miles of endless road that create a memorable adventure playground. For most 4x4 enthusiasts – and this is the only real way to explore the south – the departure point is Komatipoort in South Africa's Mpumalanga province, and entry is via Ressano Garcia in the far south. Life here centres on the capital that, although dilapidated, is well thought out and charming in character and mood. The war-ravaged streets remain much as they were during the civil war, but are now peopled by laughing children, earnest street vendors and sarong-clad women.

MAPUTO PROVINCE IN A NUTSHELL

Best times: The climate is hot and humid, but cool weather and coastal breezes can be had from June to August.

Risk factor: Experienced mechanics specialising in 4x4 maintenance are hard to come by; language is an obstacle. Roads are navigable but are generally in poor condition and best suited for 4x4 vehicles.

Health: Malaria is rife and AIDS is a real threat. Waterborne diseases include hepatitis, typhoid, cholera and dysentery. Water is not drinkable.

Pack: Lightweight summer clothing and sunscreen. Bottled water is vital. Be familiar with your vehicle's needs and bring your own spares! Beach driving requires a permit.

GETTING AROUND MAPUTO

Despite the tourist traffic, communication remains an obstacle even in the capital, and Portuguese (the official language) is spoken only by a few. Lined by groves of cashew trees and a series of villages of bamboo-and-palm huts, the scarred roads in the south are generally in poor condition, making 4x4 vehicles preferable to sedans. Be on the lookout for potholes – a reliable warning sign is sandy patches gouged into the grass on the sides of the tarred roads, an indication that vehicles have been compelled to scramble off the road. Off-road, the sand is as fine as castor sugar and travellers reluctant to break a sweat are advised to pack up and go home. Even in the best-maintained areas, driving can be demanding and the slightest falter can end in spinning wheels and flying sand. This is especially true on the shoreline, where beach sand is very fine. The coast is extremely fragile, and a permit is required to drive along the beach. Edge forward very slowly, with diff-locks engaged and tyres deflated, and drive on the compact sand below the high-water mark.

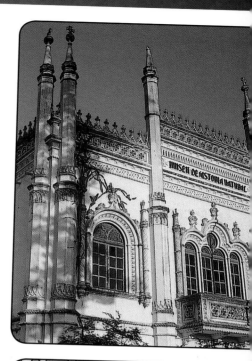

Top to bottom: Natural History Museum in Maputo; mural depicting Samora Machel; the ferry crossing from Catembe to Maputo.

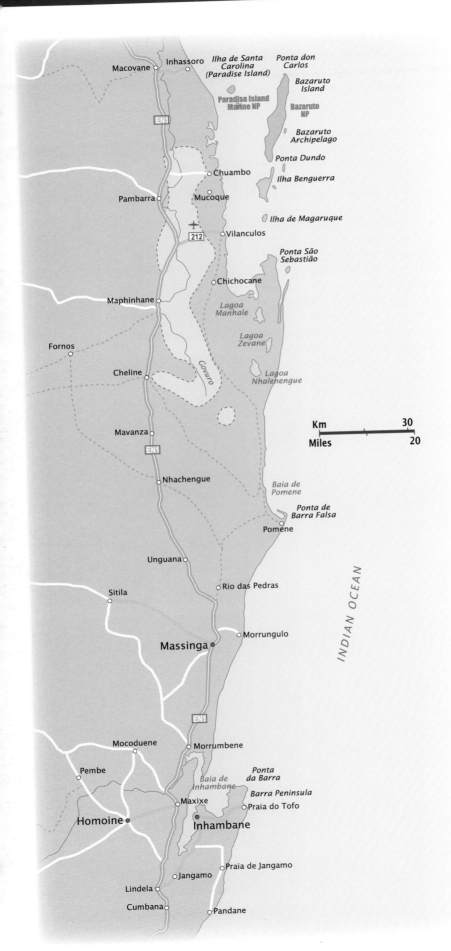

HISTORY AND MYSTERY

Mozambique has done duty as a Portuguese outpost, and numerous Portuguese and Arab traders and colonists settled along the coast over the centuries since Vasco da Gama 'discovered' this land in 1497. The country's history is shrouded in mystery, including the legend of King Solomon's Mines – explorers have yet to stumble upon this vast stash of gold – and the myth of a fabulously wealthy empire, Monomotapa.

The country saw massive slave trading in the 1800s as well as pirate attacks on the mainland and islands. More recently, the brutal civil war decimated much of the land, infrastructure and wildlife until peace was declared in the early 1990s.

TRIBAL LIFE

Mozambique features eight major tribal groups, the largest of which is the Makua-Lomwe (accounting for close to half the population). The next largest is the Tsonga (a quarter of the population), and other groups include the Shona and the Zambezi Valley tribes (the Chuabo, Sena and Nyungwe), as well as the Yao.

INHAMBANE

The Inhambane area is rich with a fabulous marine life, almost two million coconut palms, and interesting local diversions such as dhow taxis and roadside stalls. The town itself provides a fascinating glimpse back in time and is known for the hundreds of dhows that float on Inhambane Bay's tranquil waters. Reed baskets at the Mercado Municipal (municipal market) make a fine purchase, along with hats and mats. The bell tower at the 200-year-old Cathedral of our Lady of the Conception offers magnificent views of the town and surrounding bay.

BAZARUTO ARCHIPELAGO

The Bazaruto Archipelago is a chain of tiny islands roughly 20km (12 miles) off

> ### GREAT SOUTHERN AFRICAN BEACH HOLIDAY RESORTS AND HOTELS
> · Mnemba Island Lodge (Zanzibar, Tanzania)
> · Beacon Island Resort (Plettenberg Bay, South Africa)
> · Pestana Bazaruto Lodge (Bazaruto, Mozambique)
> · The Bay Hotel (Cape Town, South Africa)
> · Benguerra Lodge (Benguerra Island, Mozambique)

the Mozambique coast, which have been incorporated into the Bazaruto National Park. Its unique and isolated ecosystem ensures near-pristine diving conditions in warm waters heated by the Benguela Current, with an amazing tropical sea life of brightly coloured corals, anemones, fish and turtles, while saltwater fly-fishing is growing in popularity throughout the archipelago.

Rehabilitated after the Mozambican conflict, Bazaruto Archipelago comprises four principal islands – Bazaruto Island, Magaruque, Benguerra and Santa Carolina, perhaps better known as Paradise Island – and several smaller reef-lined islands, which make up the national park. Bazaruto, Magaruque and Benguerra are the largest of the group.

DIVING BAZARUTO

Buffeted by fluctuating sea levels, powerful currents and strong winds, the unique ecosystem is relatively isolated and, as such, remains untouched by development. The waters are crystal clear and splashed with colour in the form of tropical sea life that makes for a magnificent underwater experience with wonderful spots to explore. The diving, outstanding beaches, up-market accommodation, and fishing and birding opportunities have earned the archipelago a reputation as a favourite tourist spot. Idyllic Bazaruto is most popular among fly-in travellers, but only visitors with reservations at one of the lodges are permitted to overnight on the islands themselves. Access to these protected waters is via boat from Vilanculos, approximately 500km (300 miles) south of Beira. Camping is permitted but is not recommended, as there are so many choices for more comfortable lodgings on the magical islands.

CAST AWAY

Mozambique is an angler's paradise with world-class catches up for grabs. Black marlin, sailfish and a host of game fish draw marine anglers, while freshwater angling offers great bass as well as tiger fish (notably at Cahora Bassa). Tourists and locals find spear fishing, snorkelling, scuba diving, sailing and sea kayaking (as well as many other water activities) highly rewarding here. Mozambique's numerous habitats and over 600 bird species should make 'twitchers' happy.

After the internal strife and deterioration, national parks and reserves are being upgraded while 4x4 routes are abundant, as are hiking and climbing trails.

BARRA PENINSULA

Barra is the site of the province's capital, Inhambane. It is understandably among Mozambique's most popular holiday Meccas: the azure waters, coves, bays and sands perfectly characterise the leisurely pace of beach holidays. The landscape of Barra and the adjoining Cape Inhambane are dotted with coconut plantations and mangrove swamps, and the wave-washed shores are a powerful lure to the marine wonderland. Beware though: the waters are warm but unpredictable, and powerful rip currents and volatile waves make it an exhilarating but not particularly safe adventure experience.

Top to bottom: local fishermen hauling in their catch; lighthouse on Bazaruto Island; a young boy contemplates the next catch.

99

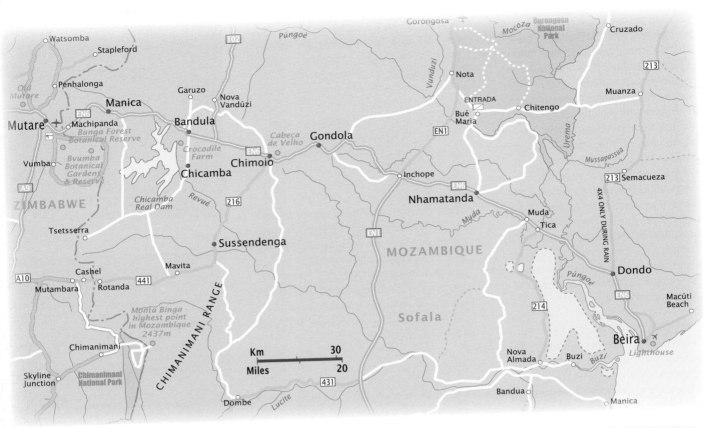

BEIRA

Mozambique's second-largest city, Beira operates as a busy port yet is somewhat shabby and chaotic. It has, however, achieved fame for its lip-smacking prawns and inviting white-sand beaches, many of which offer excellent swimming. Beira's architecture is varied, ranging from the beautiful Catedral de Nossa Senhora de Rosário (1915, a functioning church), the neoclassical Clube des Chinês (1917, now the city archives), and Casa Infante Sagres. Colonial structures include the Casa Portugal, Banco Standard Totta, and the avant-garde exhibition hall, Casa dos Bicos. The 1200-seater Cinema São Jorge is one of Africa's largest and most ornate cinemas. Beira also offers a clutch of interesting art galleries, and a municipal market offering excellent seafood and fruit and vegetables bigger than you've ever seen before. The best place to buy prawns is from the fishermen on Macúti Beach: the beach was named after the wrecked ship that was towed in front of the lighthouse to act as a breakwater.

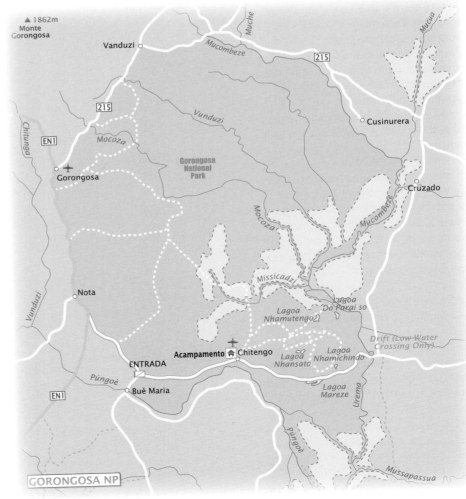

GORONGOSA NP

BEIRA CORRIDOR AND RAILWAY

The Beira Corridor is a 32km-wide (20-mile) corridor of land that follows the railway line from Mutare in Zimbabwe to Beira in Mozambique. The corridor and the railway line provide landlocked Zimbabwe with a vital trade and tourist link to the Indian Ocean. Closing the line was once used as a means of stifling the former Rhodesian government, and it has been repeatedly opened and closed over the years as a result of decades of civil war and armed conflict.

GORONGOSA NATIONAL PARK

Following decades of liberation fighting and bloody civil war, Mozambique's wildlife – elephant, buffalo, blue wildebeest, hippo, Burchell's zebra and waterbuck all previously numbering in the thousands – was all but obliterated. The legacy of the armed conflict saw these species dip into the low hundreds, or disappear completely. Once considered one of the continent's greatest legacies, Gorongosa was originally set aside as a hunting area with the goal of providing game meat to thousands of workers on the burgeoning sugar and coconut plantations.

Gorongosa's tourist appeal is its magnificent vegetation, which includes grasslands along Lake Urema, as well as vibrant forests of fever trees lining seasonal pans, and woodland and dense palmveld, all filled with a vibrant diversity of wildlife species. Gorongosa is a vital sanctuary for the Sofala zebra (a subspecies of the Burchell's zebra), whose numbers have plummeted from 30,000 down to around 50 over the last three decades. The park is also an attraction for birders, with the spotting of the Palm-nut Vulture a major feather in any twitcher's cap. Hundreds of other species include the Collared Palm-thrush, Racket-tailed Rollers, Rufous-bellied Herons, Martial Eagles and Silvery-cheeked Hornbills.

Some of the park's favoured activities are guided canoe trips and walks (both organised and run by park management), as well as the 350km (217-mile) trip to Inchope, which can be done by two-wheel-drive bakkies out of the rainy season.

FLORA AND FAUNA

Mozambique has a tropical to subtropical climate, and its landscape is dressed in temperate rainforest, mopane woodland, old baobab trees, woodland mahogany and the unique mangroves with their root systems running above and below the earth. Animals include masses of birds (over 900 species) and an abundant marine life (including the walrus-like dugong). The country's mammal populations are now increasing among species such as elephant, buffalo, lion and leopard as well as roan and sable antelopes.

GORONGOSA IN A NUTSHELL

Climate: The cool months (May–Sep) are the best for visitors, rather than the hot and humid months (Oct–Dec) when early rains can make mudbaths out of dirt roads and tracks.
Risk factor: Summer rains can make large areas treacherous or totally inaccessible.
Pack: You'll need to ensure you're self-sufficient, so bring your own food (stock up at supermarkets in Beira or Chimoio). Manage your fuel reserves carefully as fuel is not available at Inchope or Gorongosa village. Be sure to fill up at Save Bridge, Chimoio or Beira.
Facilities: Some basic facilities exist in the park, mainly camp sites with all the basics for weary travellers.

Top to bottom: a local woman busy in her outdoor kitchen; Mount Gorongosa under cloud; sunset over Mount Gorongosa.

CAHORA BASSA

The grand Cahora Bassa Dam is situated around 500km (310 miles) northwest of the Mozambique coast. Built during the heady days of the 1970s, the grand dam represented one of Africa's largest-ever civil engineering projects, and is one of the larger dams on earth.

Although the dam is a major producer of hydroelectric power for Southern Africa, it has admittedly become something of a white elephant – it operates way below its capacity as a result of damage incurred during the civil war. The dam has in effect created Lago de Cahora Bassa

(Lake Cahora Bassa), a monstrous 270km (170-mile) body of water that reaches all the way back to the confluence of the Zambezi and Luangwa rivers on Zambia's border. The dam lies in a magnificent gorge and amid glorious scenery. It's not a surprise, then, that the dam itself has developed into something of a tourist attraction with its superb scenery and views. There are tours of the dam and the impressive turbine room, although the facilities and amenities for visitors are rather basic. Visitors can get to the dam by car or by bus from nearby Songo, which acts as the dam's service town.

Chapas (converted minivans) also run a few times a day from Songo to the dam, but the more energetic can take the high road and walk the 6km (3.7 miles).

POWER ON TAP
The 2700km-long (1678-mile) Zambezi River starts as a mere trickle in the northwest of Zambia, yet gathers enormous momentum as it winds through six Southern African nations. Dams at Cahora Bassa and Kariba provide vast amounts of valuable hydroelectric power to the region.

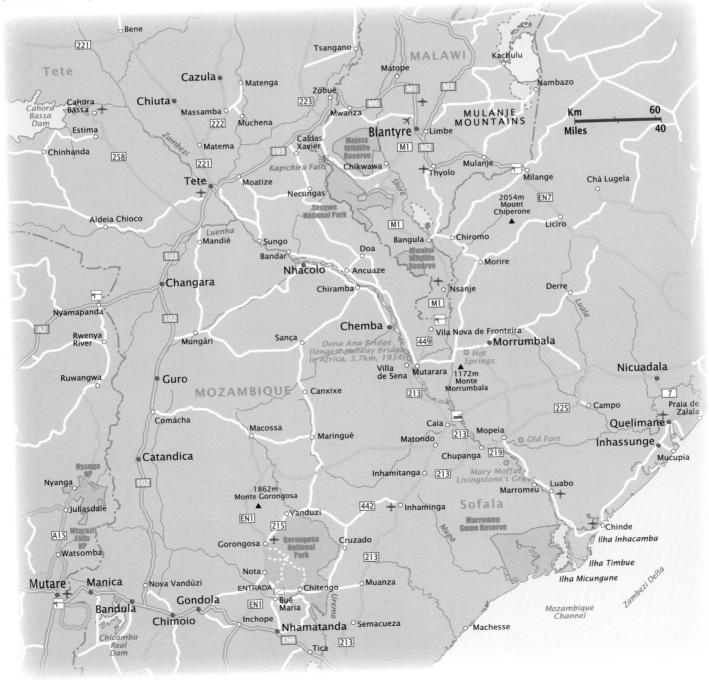

TETE

The nearest town of any decent size to Cahora Bassa is Tete, located southeast down the Zambezi, roughly 150km (95 miles) from the dam. A former vital trading outpost from the days before Portuguese 'rule', Tete remains a major cog in Mozambique's transport wheel. Its position on the Zambezi aside, Tete is also on the A2 from Zimbabwe through to Malawi. The town has an impressive suspension bridge that straddles the Zambezi River.

THE ZAMBEZI DELTA

The 3000km (1860-mile) Zambezi River winds for 820km (510 miles) of its route across Mozambique before reaching the ocean. Its broad valley slices the country in two, beginning at Feira and ending, after having accumulated run-off waters from five other countries, in the wetlands of the delta. By the time the waters reach Mozambique they have been tamed by Zimbabwe's Lake Kariba and are again dammed by the 160m (525ft) walls of the 270km-long (170-mile) Cahora Bassa, Mozambique's most ambitious dam. Having coursed through the hinterland, its waters guarded by crocodiles and hippos, the Zambezi begins to disperse about 600km (373 miles) downstream on the buffalo plains of Marromeu, where it spreads into a network of streams, channels and tributaries covering 4,000km^2 (1544 sq. miles).

Today, the delta spans only 100km (62 miles), but is nevertheless a visual delight – especially from the air – and is home to big game such as elephant, buffalo, rhino and roan antelope.

CHIMOIO AND MANICA

The capital of Manica province, Chimoio has plenty to offer travellers. The Cabeca do Velho (a large rock that bears an uncanny resemblance to an old man's face) sits 5km (3 miles) out of town and provides marvellous views for anyone who takes the relatively short trip to the top. Roughly 35km (21 miles) west of Chimoio is Chicamba Real Dam, a popular weekend getaway and angling spot, while to the southwest on the border with Zimbabwe is Monta Binga, at 2436m (7993ft) the highest peak in Mozambique and a popular target for climbers (although it's best approached from Zimbabwe's Chimanimani National Park).

Manica is a small settlement 70km (43 miles) to the west of Chimoio and has a rich history as a gold-trading area. Nearby attractions include the Chinamapere rock paintings, Vumba's mineral water springs and the Penha Longa Mountains (on the border with Zimbabwe).

CLIMBING MOUNT NAMULI

Climbers intent on tackling Mozambique's second-highest peak – the 2419m (7934ft) Mount Namuli – kick off their journey at Gurúè, in lush surrounds and amid tea plantations. The local Makua people regard the mountain as sacred, and hikers should respect local customs and traditions, which can include presenting the local chief with a gift of sorghum flour (from which beer will be made) along with offerings to the tribal ancestors.

IS THERE A DOCTOR?

Mozambique is the third-worst country in the world in terms of providing doctors for patients. For every 36,000 people in the country there is just one doctor. Malawi is by far the worst, with almost 50,000 people queuing for each doctor. In terms of deaths per 1000 members of the population, Mozambique ranks second in the world with 23 deaths per 1000 people, behind Angola on 25.

	DOCTOR RATE		DEATH RATE
1	Malawi	1	Angola
2	Eritrea	2	Mozambique
3	Mozambique	3	Niger
4	Niger	4	Malawi
5	Ethiopia	5	Zimbabwe
6	Chad	6	Botswana
7	Burkina Faso	7	Zambia
8	Rwanda	8	Rwanda
9	Liberia	9	Swaziland
10	Ghana	10	Sierra Leone

Top to bottom: Cahora Bassa dam wall; woman drying and sorting kapenta; kapenta rigs on Cahora Bassa.

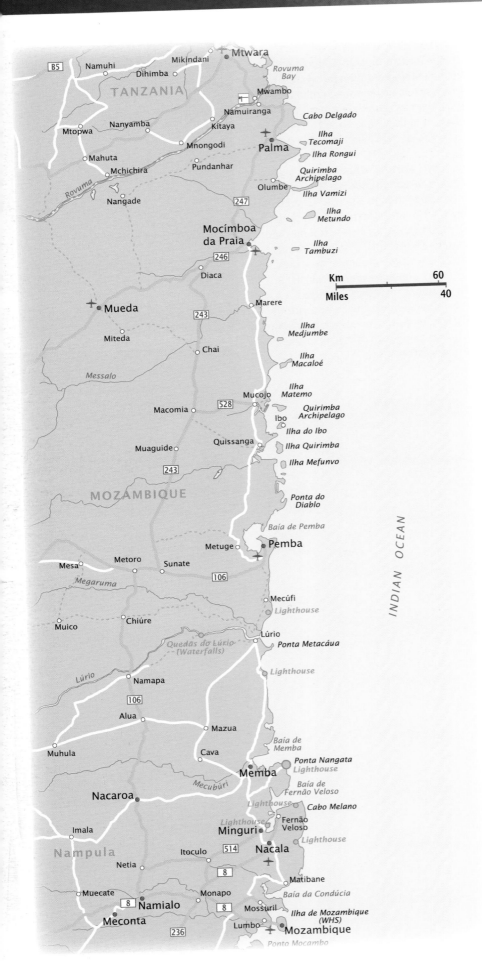

MOZAMBIQUE ISLAND

Also known as Ilha de Mozambique (or simply Ilha), Mozambique Island is a fascinating historical site that served the Portuguese and Arabs as a major fortified port city. It was declared a World Heritage Site in 1991 due to its rich seafaring history and architectural heritage. The island is just 2500m (8202ft) long and its widest point measures 600m (1969ft), yet its size belies the rich and varied range of cultures, languages, religions and historical influences that occupies the island, all of which have earned it the label of Africa's 'meeting point of civilisations'.

WALKING ILHA DE MOZAMBIQUE

Picture-perfect Ilha de Mozambique is linked via a bridge to the mainland 3km (2 miles) away, its coastline offering unsurpassed views across the Indian Ocean. Unfortunately, the waters here are severely polluted – a contrast to the diving spots further along the shore. Like much of Mozambique, the island that shares its name is impoverished, and conditions on parts of Ilha de Mozambique are no better than some of the worst on the mainland. Although most islanders in the southern reaches of the island live in small, tightly packed shelters in shack towns, the rest of the island – particularly the northern parts – comprises splendid colonial buildings, mosques, forts, palaces and churches. A reflection of its historic past, the streets and alleyways of the Old Town are edged by quaintly dilapidated structures that appear to have been standing here for millennia.

ILHA DE MOZAMBIQUE IN A NUTSHELL

Climate: Generally hot and humid, with cooler weather from June to August.
Risk factor: Petty crime may be a problem in the south of the island. Vandalising historic sites in any way is punishable by law.
Health: Malaria is rife on the mainland and AIDS is a real threat. Waterborne diseases include hepatitis, typhoid, cholera and dysentery. Be sure to drink only bottled water.
Pack: Lightweight clothing should be sufficient, but be sure to pack good walking shoes. The Muslim community will frown on skimpily clad female travellers. Sunscreen is recommended.
Facilities: Very, very basic to adequate.

WELL FORTIFIED

Although the urban heart is slowly losing its colonial atmosphere to the ambience of the traditional Muslim community that is reclaiming its stronghold on the island, there are still many remnants of yesteryear to be seen. The best preserved is the 16th-century Fort of São Sebastião, erected around a spring that remains the island's only reliable source of drinking water. Within its confines is the impressive Church of Nossa Senhora Baluarte, erected in 1522 and thus the southern hemisphere's oldest European building still standing. Also notable in their exquisite detail and historical significance are the Palace and Chapel of São Paulo (which served as the governor's residence in the 18th century) and the Jesuit College of São Paulo, with its almost Gothic pulpit dating back to the days when Portuguese Catholics held the island.

QUIRIMBA ARCHIPELAGO

Many of the islands on this vast archipelago have been settled for centuries, yet they remain somewhat removed from the mainstream tourist route, as access to the islands is not particularly easy and neither are facilities terribly impressive. Getting to and from the islands requires a bit of planning and help – boating in and out is heavily tide-dependent, and navigating the mangrove swamps that link many of the islands does require the help of someone with previous experience. Ibo is the most popular of the islands, but others worth visiting include Quirimba (a mission station and later a large coconut plantation), Matemo and Quisiva islands (both housing large Portuguese plantation houses), while Ilha das Rolas (Rolas Island) is a tiny speck in the ocean which serves as a useful seasonal settlement for local fishermen.

ILHA DO IBO

Heavily fortified during its Portuguese occupation, Ibo has a history as the region's most important supplier of slaves to the sugar plantations of Île de France. The island has seen better days, but its wide streets are lined with quaint Mediterranean-style buildings. Many of these stately structures were erected in the 1800s and, although the white-washed walls of the once grand but long abandoned Portuguese villas and palaces are fading, it is the very isolation that is the island's charm. The centuries-old churches and ancient bulwarks that fringe the streets and line the waterfront are but half the attraction — the other is the surrounding ocean, alive with turtles and dolphins that can easily be spotted from the dhows that ferry visitors around Ibo's romantic coastline.

Top to bottom: Ghost crab; snorkelling in crystal-clear water; coconut plantation.

105

Zambia

QUICK FACTS

Capital: Lusaka
Area: 752,610km² / 290,584mi²
Population: 12,9 million
Main ethnic groups:
· Bemba (36%)
· Maravi (18%)
· Tonga (15%)
Main languages:
· Bemba
· Tonga
· Nyanja
· Lozi
· Lunda
· English
Main religions:
· Christian (63%)
· Traditional beliefs (37%)
Currency: Zambian kwacha (100 ngwee)

IN THIS CHAPTER

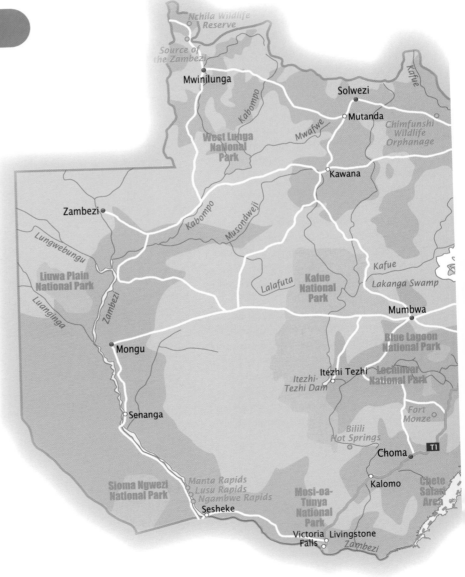

Top to bottom: microlighting over the Zambezi; a leisurely boat cruise; abseiling.

Zambia

Each activity is rated as 'To do', Mild or Wild based on intensity

TO DO	MILD	WILD
1	**2**	**2**

10 TOP ADVENTURES

1. Walking safaris
2. Walk with lions
3. Game viewing
4. Jet boating
5. Fishing
6. Whitewater rafting
7. Houseboating
8. Canoeing
9. Bungee jumping
10. Microlight and helicopter flips

Walking safari.

ON LAND

Walking safaris

WILD

Heading out into the wilderness on foot is exhilarating. Particularly when it's Big Five country. There are few places to beat the remote North Luangwa National Park, where the emphasis is on an exclusive wilderness experience, but you can also walk from camp to camp on elephant and hippo paths on the Chikoko Trails in South Luangwa.

The Bushcamp Company Ltd.
www.bushcampcompany.com
+260 624 5051
Robin Pope Safaris
www.robinpopesafaris.net
+27 11 021 9272
Remote Africa Safaris
www.remoteafrica.com
+260 332 4024

Walk with lions

Take a bush stroll with lion cubs in the Mosi-oa-Tunya National Park.

MILD

Wild Horizons
www.wildhorizons.co.za
+263 134 4571

Game viewing

MILD

Zambia's outstanding game viewing is world renowned, yet the parks are usually uncrowded. Top spots include the North and South Luangwa, Kafue and Mosi-oa-Tunya national parks, as well as Lake Mweru, Lake Bangweulu and Lake Tanganyika. The little-known Liuwa Plain experiences Africa's second-biggest migration of game (after that of the Serengeti/Masai Mara), with vast herds of wildebeest, antelope and the accompanying predators swarming the plains.

Robin Pope Safaris
www.robinpopesafaris.net
+27 11 021 9272
Remote Africa Safaris
www.remoteafrica.com
+260 332 4024
Wilderness Safaris
www.wilderness-safaris.com

+27 11 883 0747
Tongabezi Lodge
www.tongabezi.com
+260 21 332 7450
Flame of Africa
www.flameofafrica.com
+27 31 762 2424

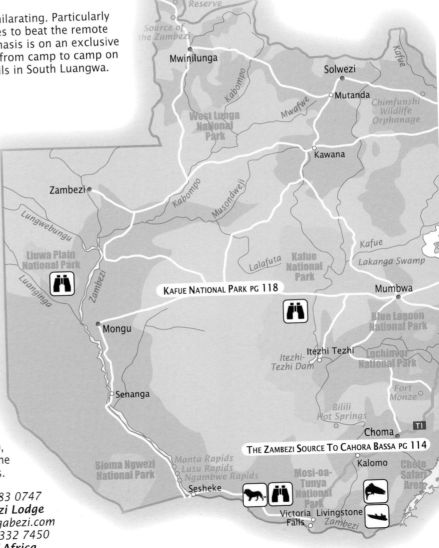

Map labels:
Nchila Wildlife Reserve
Source of the Zambezi
Mwinilunga
Solwezi
Mutanda
Chimfunshi Wildlife Orphanage
Kabompo
Mwafwe
Kafue
West Lunga National Park
Musondwei
Kawana
Zambezi
Kabompo
Lungwebungu
Lalafuta
Kafue
Lakanga Swamp
Liuwa Plain National Park
Kafue National Park
Luanginga
Zambezi
KAFUE NATIONAL PARK PG 118
Mumbwa
Blue Lagoon National Park
Mongu
Itezhi Tezhi
Itezhi-Tezhi Dam
Lochinvar National Park
Senanga
Fort Monze
Bilili Hot Springs
Choma
THE ZAMBEZI SOURCE TO CAHORA BASSA PG 114
Kalomo
Manta Rapids
Lusu Rapids
Ngambwe Rapids
Sioma Ngwezi National Park
Mosi-oa-Tunya National Park
Chete Safari Area
Sesheke
Victoria Falls
Livingstone
Zambezi

Jet Boating

Speed though rapids, spin on flat water or flash past the walls of the Batoka Gorge. Scary but safe!

WILD

Wild Horizons
www.wildhorizons.co.za
+260 312 3456
Maplanga Africa
www.maplanga.co.za
+27 11 794 1446
Cansaf
www.cansaf.com
+263 134 3352

Fishing

Get hooked on the Zambezi. Take a tranquil excursion to explore the waterways and try your hand at fly-fishing. Yellow belly bream, banded bream and several species of catfish are your targets.

TO DO

Tongabezi Lodge
www.tongabezi.com
+260 213 327 450
Maplanga Africa
www.maplanga.co.za
+27 11 794 1446
Chiawa Camp
www.chiawa.com
+260 126 1588

One-stop shop
Maplanga Africa
www.maplanga.co.za
+27 11 794 1446
Zambia Tourism
www.zambiatourism.com

One-stop operators at Livingstone/ Victoria Falls
Safari Par Excellence
www.safpar.com
+260 213 320 606
Shearwater Adventures
www.shearwateradventures.com
+263 134 4471
Wild Horizons
www.wildhorizons.co.za
+260 213 322 765

NB: Many activities listed around Livingstone/Victoria Falls can be organised from both the Zimbabwean and Zambian side of the Falls.

Sunset over the water.

THE COPPER BELT PG 119

LUANGWA NATIONAL PARK PG 116

Zambia

Each activity is rated as 'To do',
Mild or Wild based on intensity

TO DO	MILD	WILD
1	**2**	**2**

ON WATER

Whitewater rafting

No trip to Zambia or Zimbabwe is complete without an exhilarating trip down the Zambezi. Face rapids with names that say it all – Overland Truck Eater, Surprise, Devil's Toilet – and, on the flat sections, enjoy the dramatic Batoka Gorge.

WILD

Frontiers Adrenalin
http://frontiersadrenalin.com
+263 474 8391
Safari Par Excellence
www.safpar.com
+260 213 320 606

Shearwater Adventures
www.shearwateradventures.com
+263 134 4471
Wild Horizons
www.wildhorizons.co.za
+260 213 322 765

Canoeing

Sign up for a canoe safari on the Lower Zambezi River, sleeping out on islands and checking out the big game – or take a gentle paddle above Victoria Falls.

MILD

Chundukwa AdventureTrails
www.maplanga.co.za
+27 11 794 1446
**Cansaf Adventures and
Canoeing Safaris**
www.cansaf.com
+263 134 3352
Chiawa Camp
www.chiawa.com
+260 126 1588
Safari Par Excellence
www.safpar.com
+260 213 320 606
Shearwater Adventures
www.shearwateradventures.com
+263 134 4471
Wild Horizons
www.wildhorizons.co.za
+260 213 322 765

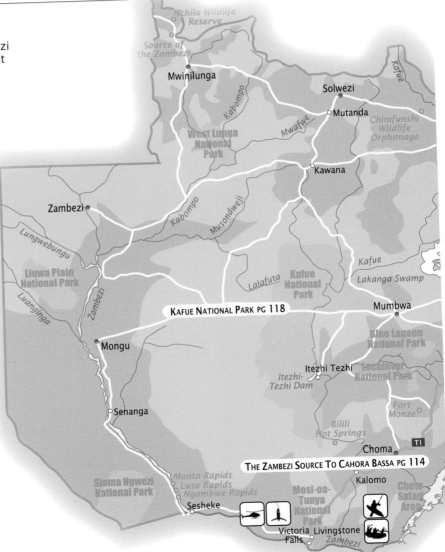

Houseboating on Lake Kariba.

Houseboating

Chill out on Lake Kariba, enjoying the peace, the birds and a spot of fishing.

TO DO

Flame of Africa
www.flameofafrica.com
+27 31 762 2424

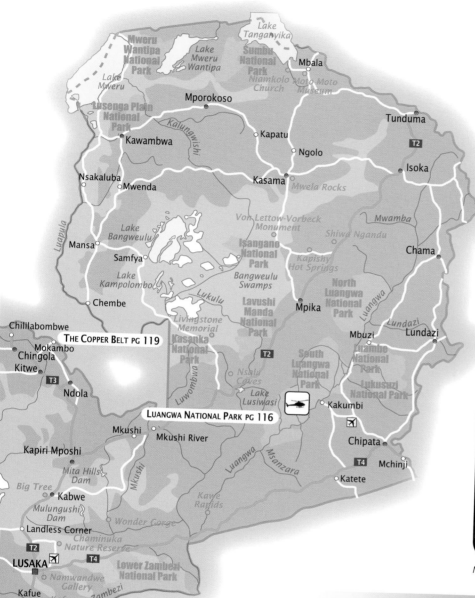

Canoeing up close to an elephant.

Microlighting over Victoria Falls.

IN THE AIR

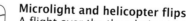

Microlight and helicopter flips

A flight over the thundering Victoria Falls, or Mosi-oa-Tunya, the 'Smoke that Thunders', is an absolute must-do. Adventurous sorts should sign up for a microlight trip – the more sedate option is a helicopter flip. A dawn microlight flight is also on offer in South Luangwa. Tafika Camp owner and mad keen pilot, John Coppinger, will swoop low over the river as he points out the Luangwa River's distinctive oxbow lakes and hippo pods.

MILD

Remote Africa Safaris
www.remoteafrica.com
+260 332 4024
Livingstone's Adventure
www.livingstonesadventure.com
+260 213 323 587
Shearwater Adventures
www.shearwateradventures.com
+263 134 4471

Bungee jumping

The ultimate adrenalin rush is the 111m plunge from the Victoria Falls bridge with only a piece of elastic round your ankles.

WILD

Shearwater Adventures
www.shearwateradventures.com
+263 134 4471

ON LAND

View Victoria Falls
Whichever way you look at it, Victoria Falls, one of the seven 'Natural Wonders of the World', is absolutely spectacular. Gaze your fill from the rim, or if you're feeling energetic take the steep trail down to the riverbank.

Elephant safaris
Become one with nature as you meander beside a small herd of habituated elephants through the Mosi-oa-Tunya NP. Trained guides explain the behaviour patterns of the majestic creatures as they feed on succulent foliage or, if you're lucky, take a wallow in the Zambezi.

Safari Par Excellence
www.safpar.com
+260 213 320 606

Mountain biking
Half-day mountain bike safaris in South Luangwa usually result in up close and personal encounters with game.

Remote Africa Safaris
www.remoteafrica.com
+260 332 4024

Quad biking
Hop on an all-terrain vehicle and head into the bush to spectacular viewpoints overlooking the Batoka Gorge.

Livingstone's Quad Company
www.livingstonesadventure.com
+260 213 323 587

Train trip
All aboard for a night of fine dining and some exciting game viewing in the Mosi-oa-Tunya National Park – take a trip on a historic steam train.

Royal Livingstone Express
www.royal-livingstone-express.com
+27 11 469 0484

Steam train trip.

Visit Livingstone Island
Take a boat trip through the channels of the Zambezi to the place where David Livingstone first viewed Mosi-oa-Tunya 'the Smoke that Thunders'. If you're feeling brave you can peer down the 103m from the Devil's Pool – a natural bathing pool right on the rim of the mighty waterfall.

Thongabezi Lodge
www.tongabezi.com
+260 213 327 450

Birding
Zambia is a twitcher's paradise, with all the major parks offering superlative guiding and sightings. The diversity of the habitat at Chaminuka makes it a premier bird-watching location, and the little-known Lochinvar NP is another popular spot.

Chaminuka
www.chaminuka.com
+260 211 254 140
Bushtracks Africa
www.gotothevictoriafalls.com
+27 11 469 0484

Horse riding
Choose between horse riding in the Shiwa Hills or checking out the game on a horseback safari in Kafue NP. And if that's not your style you can always ride in a horse-drawn carriage at Victoria Falls.

Shiwa Horse Safaris
www.shiwangandu.com
+260 95 314 814
Chaminuka
www.chaminuka.com
+260 211 254 140
Victoria Carriage Company
www.livingstonesadventure.com
+260 213 323 587

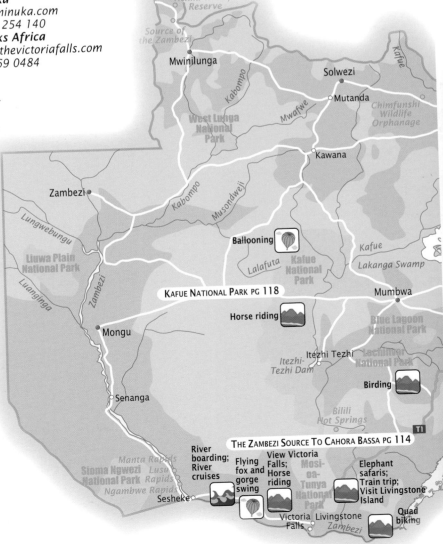

ON WATER

River boarding
The Zambezi has big waves and play spots where you can surf and ride whirlies to your heart's content.

Frontiers Adrenalin
http://frontiersadrenalin.com
+263 474 8391
Safari Par Excellence
www.safpar.com
+260 213 320 606

River cruises
A sunset cruise through the channels of the Zambezi River on an elegant safari boat is the stuff of romance. And when the Luangwa River overflows and floods the South Luangwa NP in emerald season, game viewing is done by boat – an exciting adventure that takes you through the channels and tranquil lagoons.

Livingstone's Adventure
www.livingstonesadventure.com
+260 213 323 587
Robin Pope Safaris
www.robinpopesafaris.net
+27 11 021 9272
Remote Africa Safaris
www.remoteafrica.com
+260 332 4024

OTHER ADVENTURES

1. View Victoria Falls
2. Elephant safaris
3. Mountain biking
4. Quad biking
5. Train trip
6. Visit Livingstone Island
7. Birding
8. Horse riding
9. River boarding
10. River cruises
11. Flying fox and gorge swing
12. Ballooning

Zip line.

IN THE AIR

Flying fox and gorge swing
If you crave an adrenalin rush, head to Fifth Gorge, a tributary of the main Batoka Gorge, and brave the terrifying swing or zip line. Abseiling and rap jumping are offered at the same site.

Abseil Zambia
www.thezambeziswing.com
+260 332 1188

Ballooning
Start the day in style with a hot-air balloon safari over Kafue National Park.

Africa A-Z
www.africaa-z.co.za
+27 11 462 8857

LUSAKA

Having originated as little more than a single general store serving workers building a railway siding in the early 1900s, the modern city of Lusaka – succeeding Livingstone as the nation's capital in 1930 – has mushroomed into a hub of activity conveniently situated at one of the most important crossroads in Southern Africa.

Lusaka is every inch a modern urban settlement with all the charm and scourges that entails: open-air markets, tree-lined boulevards and dusty side streets lurking with muggers and less innocuous criminals. In reality, apart from a network of travel-oriented facilities such as the airport, bus terminals and tourist offices, there is little to attract the casual sightseer. Lusaka's citizens are nevertheless widely acknowledged as the friendliest and most hospitable on the continent.

ON THE WATERS OF THE ZAMBEZI

The Zambezi River is the favourite playground of water-sport adventurers in Southern Africa. While the river can be gentle and tranquil in parts, it can also be venomously fearsome in others and, as a result, offers something for everyone. As it is the focal point of river adventure in both Zambia and Zimbabwe, tour operators abound. The gentler option is canoeing or kayaking the way local inhabitants have done for centuries. The

AFRICA'S LONGEST RIVERS		
Nile River	6695km	4160 miles
Congo River	4700km	2920 miles
Niger River	4184km	2600 miles
Zambezi River	2574km	1660 miles
Ubangi-Uele	2300km	1429 miles
Orange River	2200km	1367 miles

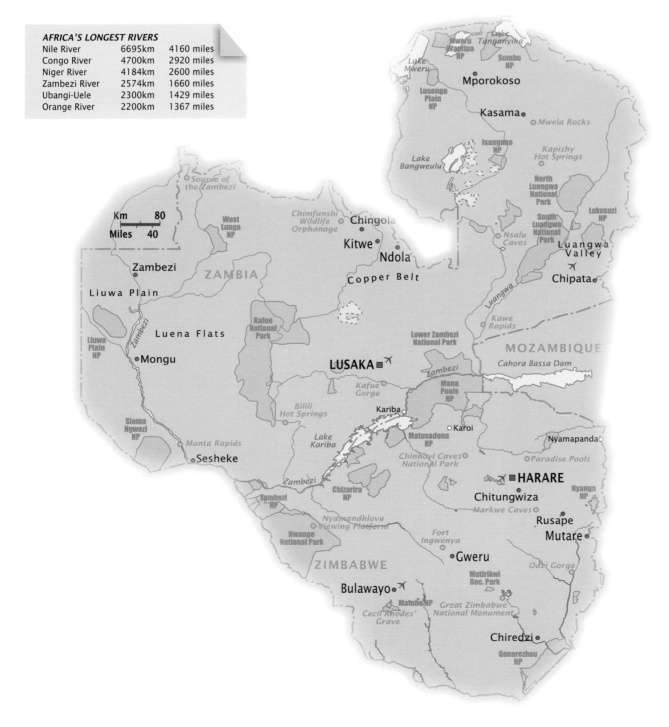

level of skill required is basic and, as long as you don't have a fear of water, this can be enjoyed by all. Canoeing and kayaking the gentler waters above the famed Victoria Falls is the most popular choice, and several adventure companies are based here. Excursions last from a few hours on the water to four days or even more than a week, covering about 20km (12 miles) a day. A number of Zimbabwe-based trips launch from the Kariba vicinity, and may take you as far as Chirundu, with a further three days to Mana Pools and another three days to Kenyamba.

A more daring option would be to tackle the whirlpools at Mupata Gorge, but these demand considerably more skill to negotiate and can be very hazardous for the inexperienced.

DRIVING THE ZAMBEZI

The land through which the 2700km (1700-mile) Zambezi River cuts is some of Africa's finest wilderness area, but can also be among the most treacherous, especially when navigating the shores of the river. For the most part, the tracks and roads are lined with trees, and the escarpment on both the Zimbabwean and Zambian sides can be steep and dangerous. Some roads and paths have been forged along the river, but certain sections have fallen prey to erosion and, occasionally, flooding. All 4x4 drivers should take precautions and ensure they have vehicle spares. During the arid season, flood plains are dry, grass cover minimal, and a fine dust covers much of the land. Although the area is lush after the rains, the rushing waters can be hazardous, and the wildlife present their own risks, while armed poachers may follow in their tracks. The route of the Zambezi is not an easy drive, but areas such as the Mana plains may be less challenging. Mana is renowned for its hiking and foot safaris under the protection of armed guards. The region is well developed, so facilities are good, with regular opportunities to refuel, restock and repair vehicles. Also en route are

fishing camps and other tourist activities.

While the section below Kariba is one of the least tamed, much of the hospitality industry centres on Mana Pools NP. The terrain varies from the rocky Zambezi escarpment to plains, and although it may be explored on foot, it is closed to the public from May to October. An alternative route is the Zambian wilderness between Mongu and Mwinilunga. Known as the Source of the Zambezi, the veld varies from a relatively comfortable drive over level ground to some extremely demanding stretches that require considerable driving skill.

Top to bottom: the Victoria Falls bridge over the Zambezi River connects Zambia and Zimbabwe; Burchell's zebra; Zambezi river boarding.

AFRICA'S GREAT RIVER SOURCES				
RIVER	FROM	TO	DISTANCE	
Nile	Lake Victoria	Mediterranean Sea	6695km	4160 miles
Congo	Lualab and Luapula rivers	Atlantic Ocean	4700km	2920 miles
Niger	Guinea	Gulf of Guinea	4184km	2600 miles
Zambezi	Zambia	Mozambique Channel	2574km	1600 miles
Orange	Drakensberg	Atlantic Ocean	2200km	1367 miles

THE LUANGWA VALLEY

The Luangwa Valley follows the course of the Luangwa River; one side is wild, unpredictable and remote, the other a picturesque expanse of nature reserve where wild animals abound. The northern reaches of the valley, occupied mostly by the Bemba people, are dominated by the untamed wilderness of North Luangwa National Park. Nature reigns supreme in the park, which is difficult to access.

Predators and scavengers lurk in murky waters and scour the plains. It is from the fauna-rich miombo woodlands of the Zambian plateau that the escarpment dips 1000m (330ft) to the floor of the Luangwa Valley. Hippo and crocodile still inhabit the Luangwa River, but along the 200km (124 miles) that separate North Luangwa from its southern counterpart there is a noticeable change. South Luangwa National Park is one of Africa's

best reserves and is far more developed than the north. Although no 'walk in the park', it is much more accessible, with dry riverbeds and hard-baked soils opening into woodland and grassy plains populated with lion, leopard, elephant, buffalo, zebra and Thornicroft's giraffe. The Save the Rhino Trust continues to combat the poaching of elephant and rhino in the area.

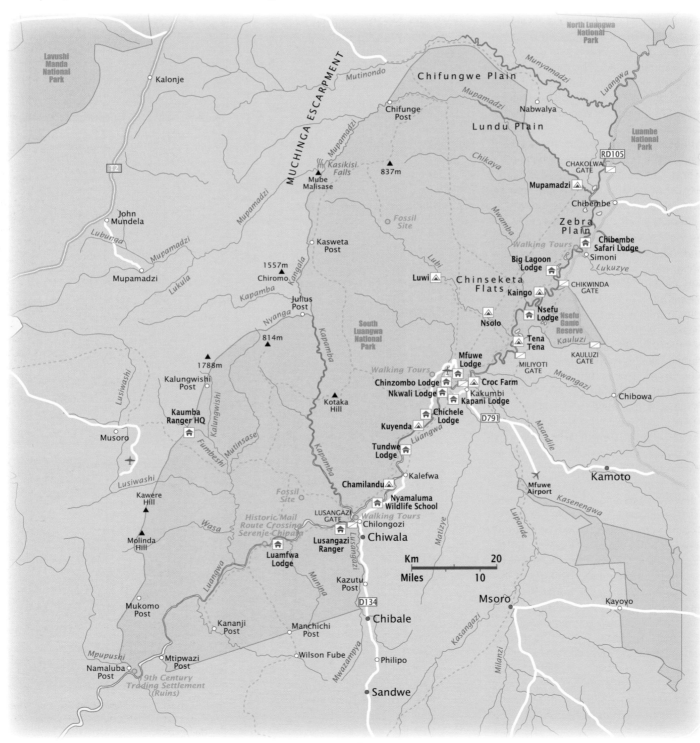

WALKING SOUTH LUANGWA

More easily reached than its northern neighbour, South Luangwa National Park is most popular among fly-in visitors, but may also be accessed by road, from Malawi via Chipata or from Lusaka along the Great East Road. The latter is worthy of its name, but certain areas remain tricky to navigate and, despite the repair work, are riddled with potholes. For hikers on walking safaris, this poses few problems, but the undulating roads offer some suggestion as to what the wilderness may offer. The ground varies from soft sand to hard-baked stretches that can take their toll on the legs on five-day guided walks or even shorter excursions. Hikers and self-drivers will have to cross stretches of scrubby veld and dry river-beds and, because there are no accessible bridges, this takes some stamina (and, for drivers, considerable skill behind the wheel). Generally, guides stick to open areas, where it is easier to spot predators and where escape routes are open.

Both the vegetation and the wildlife vary enormously, and South Luangwa is rightfully renowned for its lion, leopard, elephant, buffalo, zebra, puku, crocodile and hippo. The park has seen some development and is no longer as pristine as before. Increasingly, visitors are focused on experiencing the bird life, including herons, storks, Goliath Heron, egrets, marabou, jacana and ibis. There are a number of simple lodges and camp sites, but most safari-goers head for the lodges on the Luangwa River's eastern banks on the park's outskirts. Most have isolated fly camps within the park, which have been set up to cater for guests on walking safaris.

SHIWA NGANDU

Virtually hidden in the miombo woodland, this 9350ha (23,000-acre) grand private estate near Mpika is astonishing. In 1914 Stuart Gore-Brown, ex-soldier, mentor and explorer, laid claim to 4900ha (12,000 acres), later adding 4450ha to the property. He went on to play a pivotal role in the story of Zambia and remains the only European settler to have been honoured with a state funeral and to be buried according to the ritual reserved for a tribal chief. The grand old Shiwa House is in a sad state of disrepair, but the surrounding wilderness is quite beautiful.

BAROTSELAND

Fiercely independent and devout followers of tradition, the people of Barotseland remain one of the most authentic indigenous groups in Zambia. Barotseland once extended far and wide, but now centres on the Zambezi's flood plains. The most engrossing feature of the region is the rituals of its people, epitomised in the Kuomboka, a lavish parade that sees the Lozi king take to the waters in an ornate barge in his ceremonial evacuation of the flood plain in favour of higher ground. The ritual is repeated every year as a highlight of the ceremonial calendar.

Top to bottom: Kuomboka ceremony; a herd of buffalo in the southern region; sunset over the Luangwa River.

WALKING SAFARI DESTINATIONS

Zambia	North Luangwa
Zimbabwe	Mana Pools
Tanzania	The Serengeti, Selous and Ngorongoro
South Africa	Kruger National Park and Hluhluwe-iMfolozi Park
Kenya	Aberdare NP
Botswana	Okavango Delta

SOUTH LUANGWA IN A NUTSHELL

Climate: Sep–Nov can be unbearably hot in the valley, but the dry months, from Jun–Nov, are pleasant and provide the best game viewing.
Risk factor: Distances are vast and may be challenging in parts, with the usual risks posed by wilderness safaris, so it is best to take a pre-arranged tour with guides.
Health: Malaria is rife all year round, as are waterborne diseases.
Pack: Anti-malarial medication, water purification tablets, protective clothing and good hiking shoes.
Facilities: Facilities are good (even impressive) in the lodges, but some hiking stopovers can be quite basic.

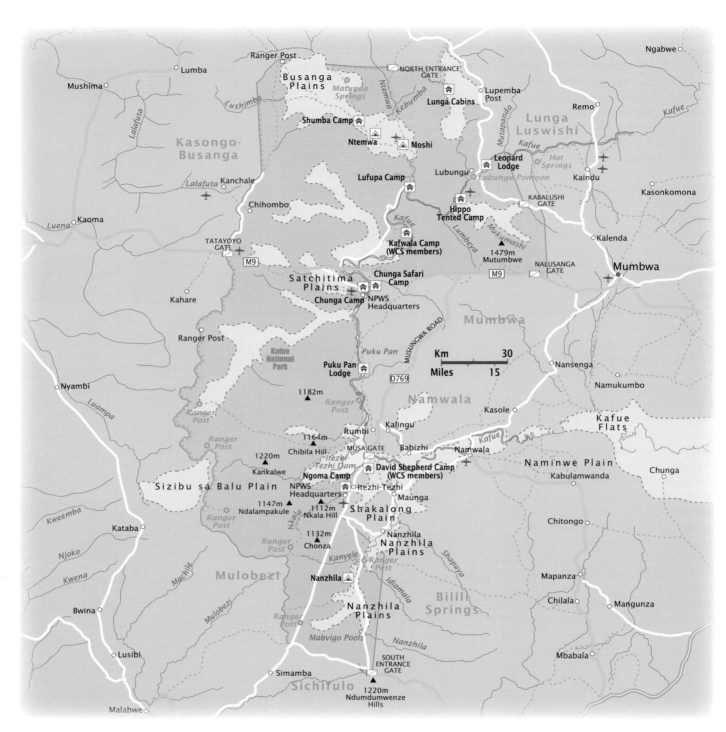

AMAZING NATIONAL PARKS

With kilometre after endless kilometre of wide, open plain, vast stands of indigenous woodland and lush riverine vegetation – most of which remains mercifully unblemished and packed with enormous herds of game and an abundance of predators – it is no surprise that Zambia enjoys much acclaim as one of Africa's finest wildlife destinations. Not only are its national parks and game management areas set in what may well be some of Africa's most authentic wilderness areas, but the backdrop of Zambia's landscape is arguably the most breathtaking in Southern Africa. Zambia covers an impressive 750,000km² (290,000 sq. miles) and has about 20 national parks, more than 30 game management areas and countless numbers of small private and state-run reserves. Perhaps because most are separated from each other by vast distances and, in some cases, are virtually inaccessible or difficult to get to, they represent some of Southern Africa's most pristine wilderness areas.

KAFUE NATIONAL PARK

Zambia's top parks include some of Africa's finest, such as South Luangwa and Kafue (the most accessible of the parks), Lower Zambezi and Mosi-oa-Tunya. These most popular parks have seen considerable development in the way of roads and other infrastructure, with the establishment of a number of camp sites and exclusive private lodges, most of which are affiliated to safari operators. The superb wilderness areas harbour massive herds of game, including Africa's most recognised wildlife species such as lion, leopard, buffalo and elephant. Throughout the history of Zambia, wildlife resources were traditionally controlled by tribal laws and custom; however, with the settlement of Europeans and the increase in poaching, game reserves were set aside to control hunting, poaching and the growth of population numbers.

Kafue itself lies around 200km (124 miles) west of Lusaka and is one of the world's largest parks with an astounding expanse of 22,000km^2 (12,400 sq. miles). Wildlife is prolific and Kafue offers fantastic walks and drives to see the diverse flora and fauna. The park is richly laced with rivers and lakes, but be careful, as they shelter large groups of hippo and crocodile. The wetlands are home to numerous small buck as well as more than 400 species of bird.

THE COPPER BELT

Steeped in a long and erratic history of colonial occupation, Zambia and Zimbabwe were once known as Northern and Southern Rhodesia respectively. Both countries are ethnically diverse and culturally extremely rich. Zambia's greatest asset is its copper reserves and even though these are gradually declining, copper exports still account for in the region of 80 per cent of the nation's foreign income. Zimbabwe, on the other hand, has historically relied almost entirely on the harvest of its cash crops, most notably tobacco, which once created one of the most broadly based economies of the region.

Top to bottom: Luangwa River Lodge; greater kudu in Kafue National Park; the sleek African Darter.

119

Malawi

QUICK FACTS

Capital: Lilongwe
Area: 118,480km² / 45,745mi²
Population: 14,9 million
Main ethnic groups:
· Maravi (55%)
· Lomwe (17%)
· Yao (13%)
· Ngoni (7%)

Main languages:
· English
· Chewa
Main religions:
· Protestant (34%)
· Catholic (32%)
· Traditional beliefs (18%)
Currency: Malawian kwacha (100 tambala)

IN THIS CHAPTER

Activities:

Fun on Lake Malawi.

Malawi

10 TOP ADVENTURES

1. Game viewing
2. Climbing and mountaineering
3. Hiking
4. Mountain biking
5. Flower viewing
6. Birding
7. Scuba diving
8. Sailing
9. Kayaking
10. Fishing

Mountain biking with spectacular views.

ON LAND

MILD

Game viewing

Although often overlooked by travellers who fall for the better-publicised attractions of Tanzania or South Africa, Malawi offers stunning, good value safari opportunities with big animals aplenty. The rugged Nyika NP in the north is home to mountain elephant, lion and huge herds of eland and roan antelope. You can step out of your tent at nearby Vwaza Marsh to a lakeside alive with hippo, crocs and elephant, or take your game viewing to a new level at Liwonde by signing up for a bush skills course on which you learn to identify and track the prolific wildlife.

Rift Valley Safaris
www.riftvalleysafaris-mw.com
+265 995 286 898
Wilderness Safaris
www.wilderness-safaris.com +27 11 883 0747
Jambo Africa Tours

www.jambo-africa.com
+265 182 3709
Land & Lake Safaris
www.landlake.net
+265 175 7120
Robin Pope Safaris
www.robinpopesafaris.net
+265 179 4491

Climbing and mountaineering

WILD

The magnificent granite domes of Mt Mulanje, known to the locals as the 'Island in the Sky', rise steeply from the lush tea plantations on the lower slopes, with the west face offering intrepid rock climbers one of the biggest walls in Africa. The range boasts the country's highest peak, Mt Sapitwa (3002m/9850ft), great huts, well-marked trails, forests of cedar trees and many endemic species, so is also popular with mountaineers and hardy trekkers.

Mountain Club of Malawi
www.mcm.org.mw
Mulanje Mountain Conservation Trust
www.mountmulanje.org.mw
+265 146 6282 or 146 6179

Hiking

MILD

Malawi has wonderful trails for hikers of all ages and abilities. Top spots include the foothills of the Mulanje Massif, the Zomba Plateau and the Nyika Plateau, home to the guided three-day Livingstonia Trail. Great short hikes include that up through the forests of the Mtsongololo Mountain in the Dzalanyama mountain range.

Active Escapes
www.active-escapes.co.za
+27 33 330 6131
Land & Lake Safaris
www.landlake.net
+265 175 7120

Mulanje Mountain Conservation Trust
www.mountmulanje.org.mw
+265 146 6282 or 146 6179

Mountain biking

MILD

Malawi is a fun country to explore on two wheels. Daredevils will find plenty of steep hills and some challenging single tracks on the Nyika and Zomba plateaux, while those who prefer more leisurely tours can cruise the national parks and back roads, enjoying game sightings, spectacular views and local interaction.

Active Escapes
www.active-escapes.co.za
+27 33 330 6131
Wilderness Safaris
www.wilderness-safaris.com +27 11 883 0747
Kaya Mawa
www.kayamawa.com

+265 999 318 359
Land & Lake Safaris
www.landlake.net
+265 175 7120
Bike & Saddle
www.bikeandsaddle.com
+27 21 813 6433

Flower viewing

TO DO

The wildflowers of the Nyika Plateau are one of the region's best-kept secrets.

Rift Valley Safaris
www.riftvalleysafaris-mw.com
+265 995 286 898
Wilderness Safaris
www.wilderness-safaris.com
+27 11 883 0747

Game viewing on foot.

Chitipa
Kaporo
Karonga
Chisenga
Uledi
M1
Nyika NP
Mkondowe
Nyika Plateau
Katumbi
Vwaza Marsh Wildlife Reserve
Rumphi
Kesitu

LAKE MALAWI-NORTH PG 128

Mzuzu
Euthini
Nkhata Bay
Chintheche
Mzimba
Chizumulu Island
Historic Mission
Likoma Island
Rupashe
Jenda
Dwangwa
Dwangwa
M1
Kasungu NP
Kasungu
Nkhotakota Game Reserve
Nkhotakota
Rusa
Bua
Ntchisi
Mponela
Lake Malawi
Mchinji
Senga
Makanjila
LILONGWE
M12
Lilongwe
LAKE MALAWI-SOUTH PG 130
Lake Malawi NP (WHS)
Monkey Bay
M1
Dedza
Chiponde
Mangochi
Fort Mangochi
Livulezi
Lake Malombe
Lake Chiuta
Ntcheu
Liwonde NP
Nayuchi
Liwonde
Lake Chilwa
M1
Shire
Zomba
M3
Nambazo
M6
Tedzani Falls
Mwanza
Majete Wildlife Reserve
Blantyre
Kapichira Falls
Mulanje
M2
Lengwe NP
Mwabvi Wildlife Reserve
Bangula
Nsanje

Birding
With its high mountain plateaux, broad-leaved miombo forests, huge wetlands and lake, Malawi is a twitcher's paradise.

TO DO

Active Escapes
www.active-escapes.co.za
+27 33 330 6131

Wilderness Safaris
www.wilderness-safaris.com
+27 11 883 0747

The Makokola Retreat www.
clubmak.com
+265 158 0244

Land & Lake Safaris
www.landlake.net
+265 175 7120

Rift Valley Safaris
www.riftvalleysafaris-mw.com
+265 995 286 898

Robin Pope Safaris
www.robinpopesafaris.net
+27 11 021 9272

ON WATER

Scuba diving/snorkelling

MILD

Lake Malawi is one of the best places in the world to learn to dive. The water's warm, clear and, most importantly, fresh, so all those wretched mask clearings don't result in salt water stinging your eyes. All around you are colourful little cichlids, the cute little fish of the lake that are much prized in fish tanks.

Aqua Africa
www.aquaafrica.co.uk
+265 135 2284
Kayak Africa
www.kayakafrica.co.za
+27 21 783 1955
Kaya Mawa
www.kayamawa.com
+265 999 318 359

The Makokola Retreat
www.clubmak.com
+265 158 0244
Danforth Yachting
www.danforthyachting.com
+265 999 960 077

Sailing.

Sailing

TO DO

A great way to explore the lake is to charter a catamaran and sail off into the sunset on your own private fishing, diving or sailing safari. If you're of a competitive bent you need to be there for the Lake Malawi Marathon.

Danforth Yachting
www.danforthyachting.com
+265 999 960 077
Barefoot Safaris
www.barefoot-safaris.com
+27 78 630 9734
Kaya Mawa
www.kayamawa.com
+265 999 318 359
Lake Malawi Yachting Marathon
www.hobiesa.co.za

Kayaking.

Kayaking

MILD

An overnight kayak trip on the 580km (360km) long lake is the classic Malawi experience. And since there's a support boat, anyone can sign up for a Robinson Crusoe-style island adventure. Shorter paddling trips are offered from most of the resorts.

Kayak Africa
www.kayakafrica.co.za
+27 21 783 1955
Danforth Yachting
www.danforthyachting.com
+265 999 960 077
Kaya Mawa
www.kayamawa.com
+265 999 318 359

Fishing

MILD

Whether you want to fight a tiger or cast a fly, there are opportunities the length of Lake Malawi. Senga Bay, in the south of the lake, is a top spot for trophy hunters, while salmon are a prized catch in the rivers of the Nkhotakota Wildlife Reserve.

Danforth Yachting
www.danforthyachting.com
+265 996 0077
Kaya Mawa
www.kayamawa.com
+265 999 318 359
Wilderness Safaris
www.wilderness-safaris.com
+27 11 883 0747
Jambo Africa Tours
www.jambo-africa.com
+265 182 3709
Land & Lake Safaris
www.landlake.net
+265 175 7120

Chitipa
Kaporo
Karonga
Chisenga
Uledi
M1
Nyika NP
Nyika Plateau
Mkondowe
Katumbi
Vwaza Marsh Wildlife Reserve
Rumphi
LAKE MALAWI-NORTH PG 128
Kasitu
Mzuzu
Euthini
Nkhata Bay
Chintheche
Chizumulu Island
Mzimba
Historic Mission
Likoma Island
Rupashe
Jenda
Dwangwa
Dwangwa
M1
Nkhotakota Game Reserve
Kasungu NP
Kasungu
Nkhotakota
Rusa
Bua
Lake Malawi
Ntchisi
Mponela
Mchinji
Senga
Makanjila
M12
Lilongwe
LILONGWE
Lake Malawi NP (WHS)
LAKE MALAWI-SOUTH PG 130
M1
Dedza
Chiponde
Mangochi
Fort Maguchi
Lake Malombe
Lake Chiuta
Ntcheu
Liwonde NP
Nayuchi
Livulezi
Liwonde
Lake Chilwa
M1
Shire
Zomba
M3
Nambazo
M6
Tedzani Falls
Mwanza
Blantyre
Majete Wildlife Reserve
Kapichira Falls
Mulanje
M2
Lengwe NP
Mwabvi Wildlife Reserve
Bangula
Nsanje

One-stop shop
Malawi Tourism
www.malawitourism.com

OTHER ADVENTURES

1. Quad biking
2. Lake of Stars Festival
3. Riverboat safaris
4. Scenic flights

 ## ON LAND

Quad biking
Check out the ancient baobabs, Anglican cathedral and other sights of sleepy Likoma Island on a guided quad bike tour.

Kaya Mawa
www.kayamawa.com
+265 999 318 359

Lake of Stars Festival
If you're into partying, this fantastic live music and performing arts festival, complete with its exotic lakeside setting, is a must-do.

Lake of Stars
www.lakeofstars.org

 ## ON WATER

Riverboat safaris
Check out the vast hippo pods, crocs and bird life as you cruise down the Shire River.

Wilderness Safaris
www.wilderness-safaris.com
+27 11 883 0747
Jambo Africa Tours
www.jambo-africa.com
+265 182 3709
Land & Lake Safaris
www.landlake.net
+265 175 7120

Cruising on a riverboat.

 ## IN THE AIR

Scenic flights
Get a bird's-eye view of the Lake of Stars or enjoy a spot of game viewing on a scenic flight.

Ulendo Safaris
www.flyulendo.com
+265 179 4638

Zebra at Nyika National Park.

Chitipa
Kaporo
Karonga
Chisenga
Uledi
M1
Nyika NP
Nyika Plateau
Mkondowe
Katumbi
Scenic flights
Rumphi
Lake Malawi-North PG 128
Vwaza Marsh Wildlife Reserve
Kasitu
Mzuzu
Euthini
Nkhata Bay
Chintheche
Chizumulu Island
Historic Mission
Mzimba
Lake of Stars Festival
Likoma Island
Scenic flights
Quad biking
Rupashe
Jenda
Dwangwa
Lake Malawi
M1
Dwangwa
Nkhotakota Game Reserve
Kasungu NP
Kasangu
Nkhotakota
Rusa
Bua
Ntchisi
Mponela
Mchinji
Senga
Makanjila
Lake Malawi NP (WHS)
M12
Lilongwe
LILONGWE
Lake Malawi-South PG 130
M1
Dedza
Monkey Bay
Chiponde
Mangochi
Fort Mangochi
Lake Malombe
Lake Chiuta
Livulezi
Ntcheu
Liwonde NP
Nayuchi
Liwonde
Lake Chilwa
M1
Shire
Zomba
Riverboat safaris
Nambazo
M6
M3
Tedzani Falls
Mwanza
Majete Wildlife Reserve
Blantyre
Kapichira Falls
Mulanje
M2
Lengwe NP
Mwabvi Wildlife Reserve
Bangula
Nsanje

LAKE MALAWI

Lake Malawi is one of Southern Africa's most valuable assets, yet it remains one of its most threatened, at constant risk from human intervention. The 23,000km² (8900-sq.-mile) lake is the third-largest inland body of water on the continent and covers nearly half the country's territory. The 585km (364 miles) of its length comprise a diversity of habitats for an array of wildlife. As a result, the lake – encircled by mountain slopes – has formed the mainstay of the nation's economy and the nucleus of its tourism industry.

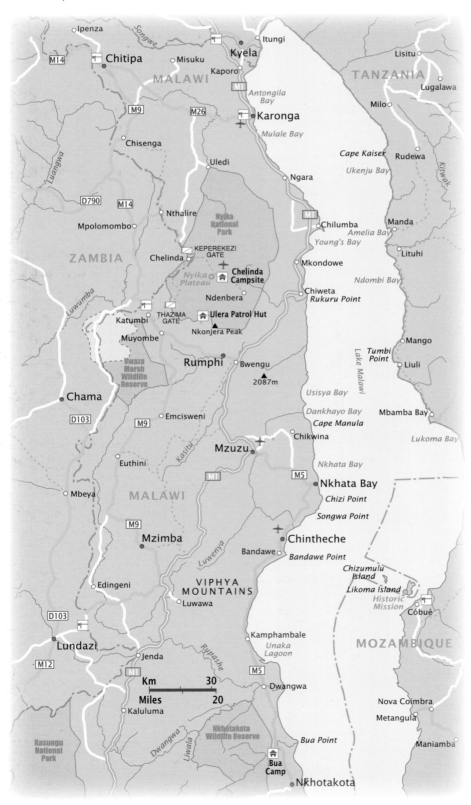

THE LIFE OF THE LAKE

The most important human settlement along the shore, blessed with tranquil beaches, is the fishing community at Chembe, who depend on Lake Malawi for their livelihood. Numerous dugout vessels ply the lake surface, netting fish which form the staple diet of Malawi. The lake has one of the world's richest populations of freshwater fish and many of the species found here are endemic. Casual angling is forbidden in areas, including Lake Malawi National Park and the surrounding islands, although water-based leisure activities are encouraged. Conservation remains a precarious occupation, even when tackled with the best of intentions and, sadly, Lake Malawi seems to be one such failure. The great lake, with about 350 endemic cichlid and some 650 other fish species, is home to a precious freshwater fish population faced with almost certain extinction if the situation on its shores is allowed to persist. The destruction of the ecosystem has been environmentally catastrophic, making education and environmental control a necessity if the lake is to be preserved.

THE COUNTRY

Malawi is a desperately poor nation, with the bulk of its rural people engaged in farming, and the majority of citizens living on the shores of Lake Malawi (Lago Niassa in Mozambique and Lake Nyasa in Tanzania) depending on its waters for their livelihood. Malawi is covered by large stretches of endless savanna and has proven remarkable in its resilience. The landlocked 'Warm Heart of Africa', Malawi is a traveller's dream: wild animals crossing an unspoiled wilderness easily accessible to visitors, and all very, very cheap.

NYIKA NATIONAL PARK

Almost hidden in the northwestern reaches of the country, Nyika is Malawi's greatest national park, certainly in terms of size. The wild, high-lying terrain comprises hill and valley virtually enclosed by the inclines of the surrounding escarpment.

Nyika's varied vegetation has given rise to an equally varied array of animal and plant species, from endemic orchids and chameleons to the highest number of leopards in southeast Africa. The park is home to zebra, reedbuck, roan antelope, eland, klipspringer, duiker, jackal and hyena, as well as 250 bird species.

THE NYIKA PLATEAU
At an altitude of about 2000m (6560ft) above sea level, the face of Nyika Plateau (part of Nyika National Park) is unlike anything you may see elsewhere in Malawi. Its flat, horizonless plains, waving with high savanna grasses interrupted only in the distance by the occasional forest grove and a lone hill, dip down into rugged gorges. A series of jagged mountain peaks neatly encircles the grassy plateau and lends the wilderness a quiet, even melancholy feel. Road access to Nyika is somewhat lacking, providing a rather uncomfortable journey to the national park along the more established route which, although short in distance, can take longer than five hours. Many roads – particularly those in, around and to the park – are impassable during the wet season, yet road travel is your only choice, and no visitors are allowed to enter the park on foot.

NYIKA'S WILDLIFE
Although there's plenty of wildlife at Nyika, hikers following the numerous walks and trails that cross the plateau tend to lose out on sightings of zebra, roan antelope, reedbuck, waterbuck, eland and kudu. The high, golden grasses provide ample camouflage for these animals and, in addition, provide shelter to about 450 bird species, among them Wattled Cranes and francolins. As a result, horseback safaris have proven to be the best way to spot the various game species scattered across Nyika National Park. Quite at home

here are herds of elephant, buffalo, kudu and plenty of roan antelope, plus the occasional lion and leopard.

RIDING NYIKA
Exploring Nyika on horseback is the most rewarding vantage point from which to experience the wide, open veld of the park and view the carpets of wildflowers that cover its spring landscape. Atop a steed, high above the tall grasses, the wilderness and its creatures are far more accessible to the eye and camera lens.

Private operators offer various routes and trails that include excursions to a number of different sites, among them Lake Kaulime, the plateau's only natural lake. Nyika's horseback trails can take a few hours, a few days, or even a few weeks to enjoy, provided your pocket and levels of endurance are up to the financial and physical limits. Most operators insist that you take a mounted guide: these scouts are friendly, knowledgeable, willing to assist with all requests and are invariably an enormous help.

LIKOMA ISLAND
Although Likoma lies just off Mozambique, the island remains the property of Malawi. Its coastline, dotted with lone baobabs alongside crystal waters, takes on the flavour of the motherland. The sandy 17km^2 (6.5-sq.-mile) island with its mango trees and rugged mountain peaks is otherwise flat and unprepossessing, but its languid beaches are lapped by clear waters. Lying in splendid isolation off the mountain-backed beach of Mozambique's mainland, Likoma can be difficult to reach and the only proper (albeit rather unreliable) way to get there is via the *MV Ilala*, the dilapidated but enchanting old lake steamer that ferries passengers between Likoma and Mozambique once a week. The island is tranquil and laid-back and, apart from the weekly performance of the malipenga dancers pandering almost exclusively to a tourist audience, there are few notable landmarks. The most significant is the cavernous St Peter's Cathedral, built along the lines of Winchester Cathedral by Anglican missionaries in the early 1900s. St Peter's remains the focal point of the island today, with many of the locals working virtually all year every year on maintaining the colossal remnant of Likoma's colonial past.

Top to bottom: Kaya Mawa beach; camping on Kande beach; a local fishing boat.

NYIKA IN A NUTSHELL
Climate: Moderately warm to hot, temperatures range from 20ºC (68ºF) to 27ºC (80ºF) throughout the year.
Risk factor: Risks are few, but most horseback safari operators will insist clients have some skill on horseback.
Health: Malaria is a real threat and water sources may contain bilharzia.
Pack: Drink only bottled water and keep a supply of purification tablets.
Facilities: A horseback safari means that you will be roughing it.

KAYAKING ON LAKE MALAWI

The shores of Lake Malawi have one of the worst records of malaria infection in the African interior, and bilharzia is a constant threat, yet the lake's waters remain the region's favoured leisure destination. The hospitality industry has established a home here: an ever-growing number of hotels, lodges and camp sites offer anything from windsurfing and kayaking to sailing, snorkelling and diving. The best way to experience the lake's varied habitat is by kayak, exploring the waters and shoreline caves and stopping to snorkel among the fish. Most of the lake's islands offer guided kayaking expeditions, and the sport is fast gaining popularity among adventurers. Private operators have, in recent years, been permitted to lead kayaking trips between the islands in the concession areas and basic camps have been established on some of the stopovers. There is little to beat the gentle sway of a hammock and the warm showers provided by water buckets well placed among the lower branches of trees. The camp sites at Domwe and Mumbo offer a welcome base for energetic kayakers returning from their demanding lake activities, hopping from island to island, and flitting from one pool or cove to the next, especially when the sun is high and the water bottle is nearly empty. Stopovers on the islands may be occupied by rock climbing, beachcombing, bird-watching, and even swimming. Be warned: there is the possibility of a chance encounter with a crocodile.

LILONGWE

Although Malawi's vast natural heritage is the country's enduring drawcard, the appeal of its large centres (in particular its capital at Lilongwe) should not be underestimated. Blantyre stretches for about 20km (12 miles) into Limbe, and is the social and commercial heart of Malawi. Lilongwe, on the other hand, is gentle, laid-back and utterly predictable in character. Although only of limited interest to the casual visitor, the sprawling city is home to about half a million Malawians and offers a refreshing mix of old and new, with little clutter, noise or commotion. The older sectors of Lilongwe have retained much of their original charm, while the modern parts are a surprisingly sedate collection of malls, tourist traps and official buildings merging well with the islands of green that form the residential districts. A notable example is Capital City, initiated by President Banda with the financial assistance of the South African government during the height of the latter's apartheid regime. Not only is the climate of the city moderately warm, but Lilongwe is very accessible, very cheap and, in the heart of Southern Africa, a convenient base from which to explore the region.

SHIRE RIVER

The 596km (370-mile) Shire, flowing from the lake through Malawi and Mozambique to the Zambezi, is the country's longest river. It winds through Malawi's Liwonde

National Park, crossing some of the country's most abundant wildlife territories and its wild open spaces. The waters are the hunting and grazing habitat of crocodile and hippo, while the surrounding wilderness supports a small but healthy population of elephant and even two black rhinos, introduced into the area in recent years. The shallows, wooded shores and expansive sky are home to numerous waders, waterfowl and various migrant birds during the summer months. Though much of the Shire offers boat rides for visitors, the southern valley remains largely undiscovered. Top attractions are the wild expanses of Majete Wildlife Reserve and Lengwe National Park.

LIWONDE NATIONAL PARK
The smallest, most accessible and most rewarding of Malawi's national parks, Liwonde is also the best managed. Drastic improvements in the training of rangers and other staff have meant that the park, once plagued by poaching and suffering rapidly declining wildlife populations, is better patrolled than ever. The ranging staff today encounters fewer and fewer traps, and the threat of poaching has been curtailed, although perhaps inevitably some subsistence poaching continues. There has been a discernible increase in mammal numbers, and elephant herds have more than quadrupled in under 30 years. Today the 548km^2 (212-sq.-mile) stretch of land is home to more than 600 elephant, 500 sable antelope and nearly 3000 hippo.

LIWONDE'S OTHER FAUNA
Liwonde boasts healthy herds of bushbuck, impala and waterbuck, along with troops of vervet monkeys and yellow baboons. There are leopards and there have been good sightings of the elusive spotted hyena, yet the numbers of predators seem to be declining; the lions that were once common prowlers on these plains have been eradicated. However, following the success of reintroduction programmes focusing on zebra, eland, reedbuck, buffalo and even black rhino, attempts will be made to reintroduce lion once officials are satisfied that they can be contained within park borders.

MOUNT MULANJE
The Mulanje region in the south of the country lies at the heart of Malawi's tea industry. The slopes of the Mulanje massif are covered with a patchwork of verdant plantations, yet the majestic highlands that stretch up from the Zomba Plateau are ideal hiking territory. Mulanje and Zomba towns offer spectacular views of the country's highest peak, Mount Mulanje, towering 3002m (9850ft) over the region.

CLIMBING MOUNT MULANJE
The network of walks and trails (with many undiscovered routes) provides endless opportunities to wonder at Malawi's natural heritage. All are accessed via well-marked and reliable paths, dotted intermittently with a good number of well-maintained and serviced small huts for overnight stops. The remarkable panorama and good facilities that characterise Mount Mulanje have made it the country's top hiking destination, as well as a reserve (hikers must obtain permission at Likabula Forest Station).

FAIRLY EASY GOING
The going is seldom too tough for even the moderately fit (certain sections require determination, rock-climbing skill and perseverance), and a number of short, relaxed meanders in the lower reaches of the montane forest will satisfy casual walkers. To reach the top will take a full day, but it is not too arduous and offers great rewards. Local weather is volatile and it is easy to get lost on the mountain. The peak is often wrapped in billows of cloud and can be virtually impenetrable on foot; thick mist, heavy cloud cover and relentless precipitation can cause drastic drops in night temperatures. Consult the officers at Likabula or knowledgeable climbers affiliated to local mountain clubs.

> **CONSERVATION IN MALAWI**
> Traditionally, Malawi placed much importance on protecting its wildlife heritage, and an impressive expanse of its land cover is designated as protected land. Reserves and parks cover about 20 per cent of the country, and yet Malawi's national parks have never really featured among its top attractions. Many of the country's wildlife areas are not particularly well developed, and a near disastrous combination of limited resources and lack of commitment from officials has meant that these parks failed to realise their potential. Until recently, poaching was a major concern as many wild species were hunted, poached or raided from traditional lands. Funds from donor countries have helped to reintroduce species to traditional roaming grounds, as well as establishing a better overall conservation climate and infrastructure.

Top to bottom: a local girl from the Ngoni tribe carrying a basket on her head; lodge overlooking the Shire River; children at Senga Bay.

Tanzania

QUICK FACTS

Capital: Dar es Salaam, Dodoma
Area: 945,087km² / 364,900mi²
Population: 43,2 million
Main ethnic groups:
· ±120 Bantu groups (99%)
Main languages:
· Swahili
· English

Main religions:
· Traditional beliefs (42%)
· Muslim (31%)
· Christian (27%)
Currency: Tanzanian shilling
(100 cents)

IN THIS CHAPTER

A dhow at sunset.

Hiking on Mt Kilimanjaro.

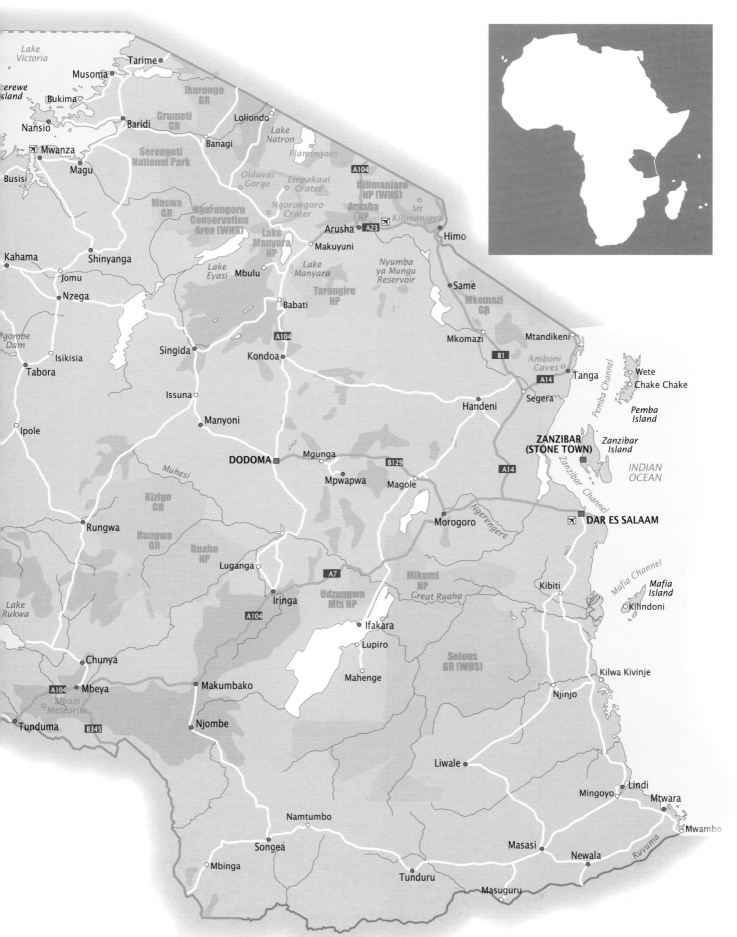

Lake Victoria

Tarime

Musoma

Ikorongo GR

Bukima

Kerewe Island

Nansio

Grumeti GR

Baridi

Loliondo

Banagi

Lake Natron

Mwanza

Serengeti National Park

Flamingoes

Magu

Busisi

Maswa GR

Olduvai Gorge

Empakaai Crater

A104

Kilimanjaro NP (WHS)

Kahama

Ngorongoro Conservation Area (WHS)

Ngorongoro Crater

Arusha NP

Mt Kilimanjaro

Himo

Shinyanga

Lake Manyara NP

Arusha

A23

Jomu

Lake Eyasi

Mbulu

Makuyuni

Nzega

Lake Manyara

Nyumba ya Mungu Reservoir

Samè

Ngombe Dam

Babati

Tarangire NP

Mkomazi GR

Isikisia

Singida

Kondoa

Mkomazi

Mtandikeni

Tabora

A104

Amboni Caves

Issuna

B1

Tanga

Wete

Ipole

Manyoni

Handeni

A14

Chake Chake

Pemba Channel

Pemba Island

Segera

DODOMA

Mgunga

ZANZIBAR (STONE TOWN)

Zanzibar Island

Muhesi

A14

INDIAN OCEAN

Mpwapwa

B129

Magole

Kizigo GR

Zanzibar Channel

Rungwa

Ngerengere

Rungwa GR

Morogoro

DAR ES SALAAM

Ruaha NP

Luganga

A7

Mikumi NP

Kibiti

Mafia Channel

Lake Rukwa

Iringa

Udzungwa Mts NP

Great Ruaha

Mafia Island

Kilindoni

A104

Ifakara

Selous GR (WHS)

Chunya

Lupiro

A104

Mbeya

Mahenge

Mbozi Meteorite

Makumbako

Kilwa Kivinje

Tunduma

B345

Njombe

Njinjo

Liwale

Lindi

Mingoyo

Mtwara

Namtumbo

Mwambo

Songea

Masasi

Newala

Mbinga

Tunduru

Ruvuma

Masuguru

133

Tanzania

10 TOP ADVENTURES

1. Mountaineering
2. Game viewing
3. Mountain biking
4. Hiking
5. Archaeological and cultural tours
6. Marathon running
7. Birding
8. Scuba diving/snorkelling
9. Dhow sailing
10. Ballooning

Mountaineering.

ON LAND

Mountaineering

WILD

Climbing Kilimanjaro, Africa's highest peak (5889m/19,322ft), is on most adventurer's lists. It's not cheap and it's a hard slog, but when you stand on the summit of the snowcapped volcano it certainly feels good. The cheapest, and easiest, way to go is the five-day, hutted, standard route, the Marangu (or Coca Cola) route, but this is by far the most crowded. If you have the time, opt for one of the longer camping routes. Not only are they less crowded but if you take an extra day you'll acclimatise much better and enjoy the experience more.

Neighbouring Meru is also a great three- to four-day climb. The scenic peak, which several operators offer as a warm-up climb for Kilimanjaro, involves more scrambling than on Kili and affords stunning views of the latter's icecap as well as plenty of game sightings on the lower slopes.

Wild Frontiers
www.wildfrontiers.com
+27 72 927 7529
Adventure Dynamics
www.adventuredynamics.
co.za

+27 11 447 7013
Zara Tours
www.zaratours.com
+255 784 451 000
Go to Mount Kenya
www.gotomountkenya.com

+254 518 010 691
Savage Wilderness Safaris
www.whitewaterkenya.com
+254 252 1590

Game viewing

MILD

The endless plains of the Serengeti, home to huge herds of wildebeest, zebra and plains game, are one of the prime game viewing areas in the world. Most visitors come with an eye on the annual migration, when thousands upon thousands of wildebeest and antelope, followed by their predators, cross the Masai River on their way to or from neighbouring Masai Mara in Kenya. The Ngorongoro Crater, a large extinct volcano about four hours from Kilimanjaro on the way to the Serengeti, is one of the wonders of the world – for many, the ultimate game-viewing experience. The soda lake at the base of the 600m deep depression is pink with flamingos and the surrounding plains and forests teem with game in a truly spectacular location. And then there's Selous, Ruaha ...

&Beyond
www.andbeyond.com
+27 11 809 4300
Singita Game Reserves
www.singita.com
+27 21 683 3424
Zara Tours
www.zaratours.com
+255 784 451 000

Selous Safari Company
www.selous.com
+255 222 128 485
Ruaha Ruaha River Lodge
www.ruahariverlodge.com
+255 754 237 422
Wild Frontiers
www.wildfrontiers.com
+27 72 927 7529

Mountain biking

MILD

Take a safari on two wheels through the game-filled plains of the Ngorongoro and Karatu area or enjoy the spectacular views of Kilimanjaro, the highest mountain in Africa, as you circumnavigate the peak. The route, 290k (180 miles) long and largely off-road, takes yo through dry savanna dotted with acacia trees, forests and Maasai villages. The fascinating sp island of Zanzibar, with miles of hard sand be and back roads, is a mountain biker's paradis Take your own bike and overnight in pre-arranged guesthouses and hotels.

African Bikers
www.africanbikers.com
+27 21 465 2018

Bike & Saddle
www.bikeandsaddle.c
+27 21 813 6433

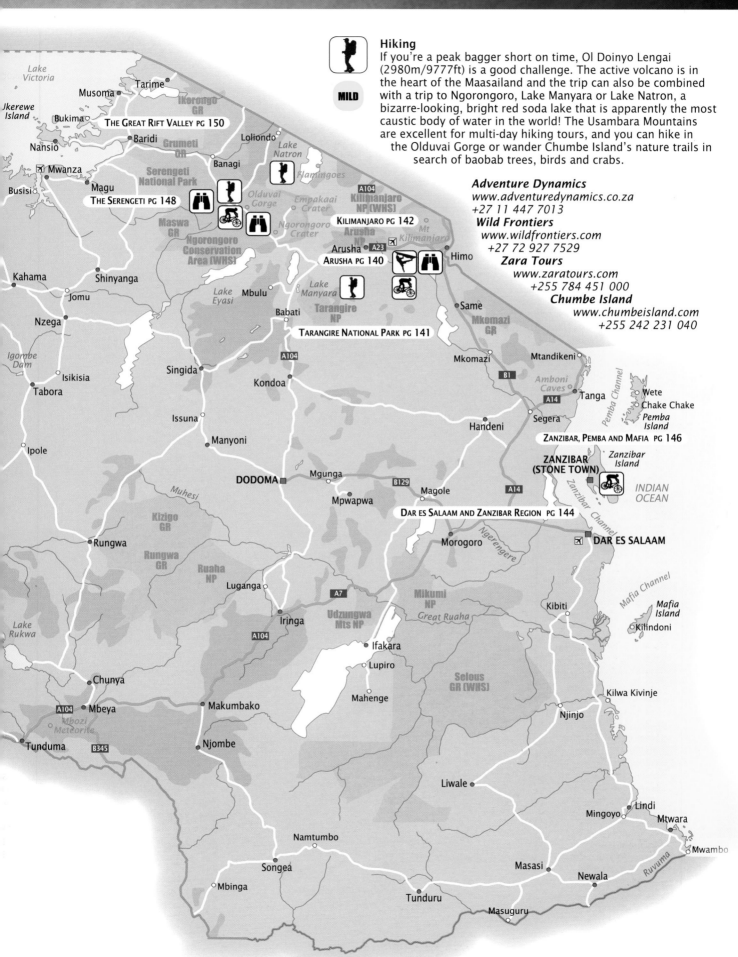

Hiking

If you're a peak bagger short on time, Ol Doinyo Lengai (2980m/9777ft) is a good challenge. The active volcano is in the heart of the Maasailand and the trip can also be combined with a trip to Ngorongoro, Lake Manyara or Lake Natron, a bizarre-looking, bright red soda lake that is apparently the most caustic body of water in the world! The Usambara Mountains are excellent for multi-day hiking tours, and you can hike in the Olduvai Gorge or wander Chumbe Island's nature trails in search of baobab trees, birds and crabs.

MILD

Adventure Dynamics
www.adventuredynamics.co.za
+27 11 447 7013

Wild Frontiers
www.wildfrontiers.com
+27 72 927 7529

Zara Tours
www.zaratours.com
+255 784 451 000

Chumbe Island
www.chumbeisland.com
+255 242 231 040

THE GREAT RIFT VALLEY PG 150

THE SERENGETI PG 148

KILIMANJARO PG 142

ARUSHA PG 140

TARANGIRE NATIONAL PARK PG 141

ZANZIBAR, PEMBA AND MAFIA PG 146

DAR ES SALAAM AND ZANZIBAR REGION PG 144

Tanzania

Each activity is rated as 'To do', Mild or Wild based on intensity

TO DO 4 **MILD** 1 **WILD** 1

 ## ON LAND

Archaeological and cultural tours

TO DO

Visiting 'The Cradle of Humankind' is a must-do. Fossils discovered in the deep canyon in the Great Rift Valley and at the Laetoli archaeological site provide convincing evidence that humans originated in Africa.
   Zanzibar's historical sites are also fascinating and can be explored on a Spice Island or Slave Tour.

Tanzania Adventure
www.tanzania-adventure.com
+255 786 013 994
Eco & Culture Tours Zanzibar
www.ecoculture-zanzibar.org
+255 242 233 731

Marathon running

WILD

East Africa is the home of some of the world's top marathon runners. Join them in Moshi, at the foot of Kilimanjaro, for one of the most scenic marathons in the world.

Kilimanjaro Marathon
www.kilimanjaromarathon.com
+27 72 927 7529

Birding

TO DO

If you are a serious twitcher, take a specialist birding safari to Selous, Lake Manyara or Lake Natron. Otherwise enjoy the bird life as part of a general game-viewing experience, particularly at Lake Manyara, famous for its numerous migratory and resident bird species.

Birding & Beyond Safaris
www.tanzaniabirding.com
+255 754 286 058
Foxes Safari Camps
www.tanzaniasafaris.info

+255 754 237 422
&Beyond
www.andbeyond.com
+27 11 809 4300

 ## ON WATER

Scuba diving/snorkelling

MILD

The calm, clear waters and professional dive schools make Zanzibar the perfect place to learn to scuba dive, while deep wrecks, and dives off the world-famous Mnemba and Pemba islands, provide a variety of challenges for experienced divers seeking an adrenalin rush.
   Snorkellers can hop on board the dive dhows or simply wade out from the beach on the mainland. But for a real spoil head to Chumbe Island Coral Park.

One Ocean Diving
www.zanzibaroneocean.com
+255 784 750 161
&Beyond
www.andbeyond.com
+27 11 809 4300
Chumbe Island
www.chumbeisland.com
+255 242 231 040

Dhow sailing

TO DO

There are few more romantic experiences than a sundowner trip on a traditional wooden dhow. One of the best trips, from Stone Town in Zanzibar, includes a visit to Chonguu (Prison Island) to see the colony of giant tortoises, imported from the Seychelles in the 18th century.

One Ocean Diving
www.zanzibaroneocean.com
+255 784 750 161
Bluebay Beach Resort and Spa
www.bluebayzanzibar.com
+255 242 240 240/1/2/3/4
&Beyond
www.andbeyond.com
+27 11 809 4300

Diving.

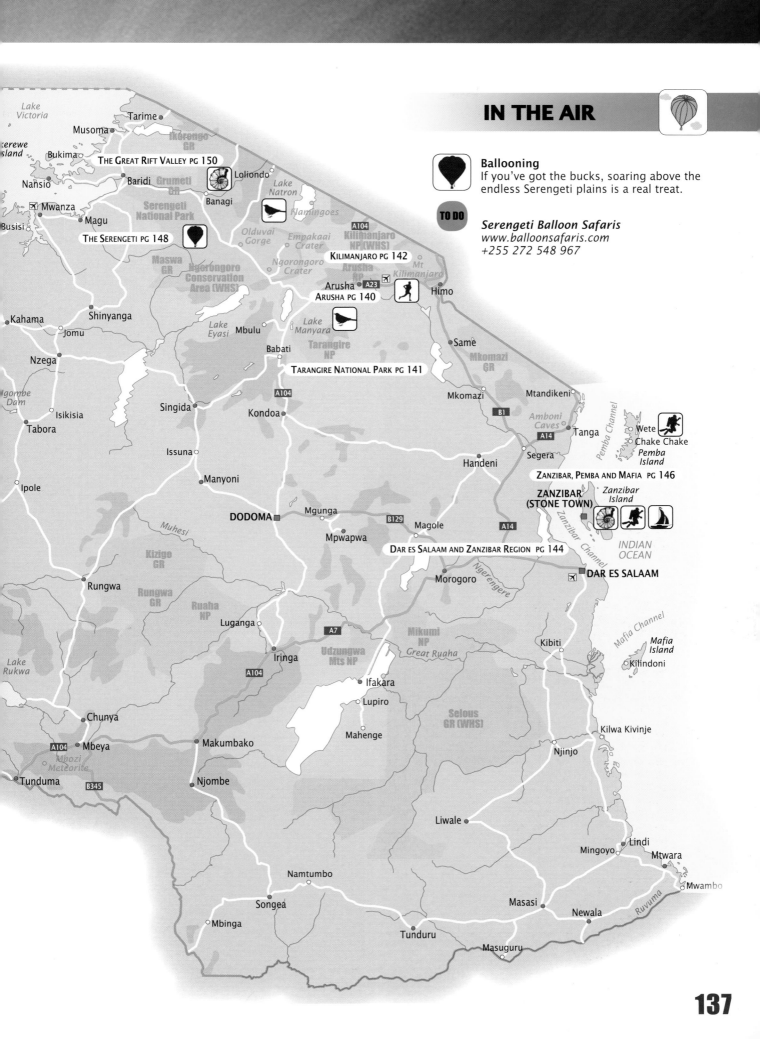

Ballooning
If you've got the bucks, soaring above the endless Serengeti plains is a real treat.

TO DO

Serengeti Balloon Safaris
www.balloonsafaris.com
+255 272 548 967

THE GREAT RIFT VALLEY PG 150

THE SERENGETI PG 148

KILIMANJARO PG 142

ARUSHA PG 140

TARANGIRE NATIONAL PARK PG 141

ZANZIBAR, PEMBA AND MAFIA PG 146

DAR ES SALAAM AND ZANZIBAR REGION PG 144

Map labels: Lake Victoria, Kerewe Island, Tarime, Musoma, Bukima, Nansio, Baridi, Mwanza, Magu, Busisi, Ikorongo GR, Grumeti GR, Loliondo, Banagi, Serengeti National Park, Lake Natron, Flamingoes, Olduvai Gorge, Empakaai Crater, Kilimanjaro NP (WHS), A104, Maswa GR, Ngorongoro Conservation Area (WHS), Ngorongoro Crater, Arusha NP, Mt Kilimanjaro, Himo, Kahama, Shinyanga, Jomu, Nzega, Lake Eyasi, Mbulu, Babati, Arusha, A23, A104, Same, Mkomazi GR, Lake Manyara, Tarangire NP, Tabora, Isikisia, Singida, Kondoa, Mkomazi, Mtandikeni, B1, Amboni Caves, A14, Tanga, Pemba Channel, Wete, Chake Chake, Pemba Island, Ngombe Dam, Ipole, Issuna, Manyoni, Handeni, Segera, Zanzibar Island, ZANZIBAR (STONE TOWN), Zanzibar Channel, DODOMA, Mgunga, B129, Magole, A14, Muhesi, Mpwapwa, INDIAN OCEAN, Rungwa, Kizigo GR, Rungwa GR, Ruaha NP, Morogoro, Ngerengere, DAR ES SALAAM, Mafia Channel, Mafia Island, Luganga, A7, Mikumi NP, Great Ruaha, Kibiti, Kilindoni, Lake Rukwa, Iringa, A104, Udzungwa Mts NP, Ifakara, Lupiro, Selous GR (WHS), Chunya, Mahenge, Kilwa Kivinje, A104, Mbeya, Makumbako, Mbozi Meteorite, Njinjo, Tunduma, B345, Njombe, Liwale, Lindi, Mingoyo, Mtwara, Namtumbo, Songea, Mbinga, Tunduru, Masasi, Newala, Ruvuma, Mwambo, Masuguru

137

Tanzania

OTHER ADVENTURES

1. Horse riding
2. Marine safaris

ON LAND

Horse riding
Saddle up and explore the game-filled plains of northern Tanzania on a one- or multi-day horse-back safari.

Singita Game Reserves
www.singita.com
+27 21 683 3424
Wild Frontiers
www.wildfrontiers.com
+27 72 927 7529

Zebra and wildebeest grazing.

ON WATER

Marine safaris
A boat trip from Fumba out to Menai Bay gives you time to view the dolphins, swim through the mangroves of Kwale Island and laze around on an empty sandbank.

Safari Blue
www.safariblue.net
+255 777 423 162

One-stop shop
Wild Frontiers
www.wildfrontiers.com
+27 72 927 7529

Dolphins.

Lake Victoria

Tarime

Musoma

Ikerewe Island

Bukima

THE GREAT RIFT VALLEY PG 150

Nansio

Baridi

Grumeti GR

Loliondo

Mwanza

Banagi

Lake Natron

Busisi

Magu

Serengeti National Park

Flamingoes

Olduvai Gorge

Empakaai Crater

A104

Kilimanjaro NP (WHS)

THE SERENGETI PG 148

Horse riding

Maswa GR

Ngorongoro Crater

Ngorongoro Conservation Area (WHS)

Arusha NP

KILIMANJARO PG 142

Mt Kilimanjaro

Kahama

Shinyanga

Arusha

A23

Himo

Jomu

Lake Eyasi

Mbulu

Lake Manyara

ARUSHA PG 140

Nzega

Babati

Tarangire NP

Same

Mkomazi GR

Igombe Dam

Isikisia

Singida

Kondoa

TARANGIRE NATIONAL PARK PG 141

Mkomazi

Mtandikeni

Tabora

A104

Amboni Caves

B1

Pemba Channel

Wete

Issuna

Tanga

Chake Chake

Ipole

Manyoni

Handeni

A14

Segera

Pemba Island

ZANZIBAR, PEMBA AND MAFIA PG 146

ZANZIBAR (STONE TOWN)

Zanzibar Island

DODOMA

Mgunga

Muhesi

Magole

B129

A14

Marine safaris

Mpwapwa

Kizigo GR

Zanzibar Channel

INDIAN OCEAN

Rungwa

Rungwa GR

DAR ES SALAAM AND ZANZIBAR REGION PG 144

Ruaha NP

Ngerengere

Morogoro

DAR ES SALAAM

Luganga

A7

Mikumi NP

Great Ruaha

Kibiti

Mafia Channel

Iringa

Udzungwa Mts NP

Mafia Island

A104

Kilindoni

Lake Rukwa

Ifakara

Lupiro

Chunya

Mahenge

Selous GR (WHS)

Kilwa Kivinje

A104

Mbeya

Makumbako

Njinjo

Mbozi Meteorite

Tunduma

B345

Njombe

Liwale

Lindi

Mingoyo

Mtwara

Namtumbo

Mwambo

Songea

Masasi

Newala

Ruvuma

Mbinga

Tunduru

Masuguru

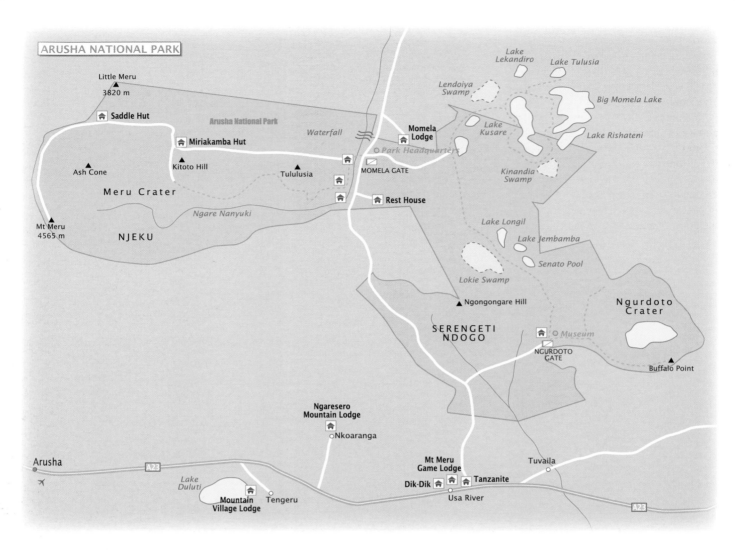

ARUSHA NATIONAL PARK

- Little Meru 3820 m
- Saddle Hut
- Arusha National Park
- Waterfall
- Momela Lodge
- Lake Lekandiro
- Lake Tulusia
- Lendoiya Swamp
- Big Momela Lake
- Miriakamba Hut
- Park Headquarters
- Lake Kusare
- Lake Rishateni
- Ash Cone
- Kitoto Hill
- MOMELA GATE
- Kinandia Swamp
- Meru Crater
- Tululusia
- Rest House
- Mt Meru 4565 m
- NJEKU
- Ngare Nanyuki
- Lake Longil
- Lake Jembamba
- Senato Pool
- Lokie Swamp
- Ngongongare Hill
- Ngurdoto Crater
- SERENGETI NDOGO
- Museum
- NGURDOTO GATE
- Buffalo Point
- Ngaresero Mountain Lodge
- Nkoaranga
- Arusha
- A23
- Lake Duluti
- Mountain Village Lodge
- Tengeru
- Mt Meru Game Lodge
- Tuvaila
- Dik-Dik
- Tanzanite
- Usa River
- A23

ARUSHA TOWN

The centre of trade and commerce in northern Tanzania, Arusha is one of Africa's fastest-growing cities. Not blessed with marvellous sightseeing opportunities, Arusha is, however, a great base for kick-starting your Tanzanian safari adventure. Located around 1540m (5053ft) above sea level, it is surrounded by fertile lands that yield marvellous crops of coffee, maize, flowers and bananas. The city is watched over by nearby Mount Meru (popular with

ARUSHA TOWN'S SIGHTS AND SOUNDS

- Uhuru Monument
- Arusha International Conference Centre (AICC)
- The clocktower roundabout
- The bustling city market bursting with fruit and vegetables
- The National History Museum with its exhibition on the evolution of humankind
- The Cultural Heritage Complex (on the Dodoma road out of Arusha)
- Meserani Snake Park, 25km (15 miles) outside of Arusha

climbers): on clear days you can see snow-capped 'Kili' in the distance.

ARUSHA NATIONAL PARK

To the northeast of Arusha town is Arusha National Park, a relatively tiny conservation area spread over just 137km² (50 sq. miles). It preserves a unique and individual natural world. Named after the Warusha people who have inhabited the area for generations, the park offers impressive game viewing and natural environments, ironically 'surrounded' by fairly densely populated areas. A lot of the park's interesting natural formations are a result of former volcanic activity in the region. There are three distinct landscapes within the park: Ngurdoto Crater, the Momela Lakes and Mount Meru. Ngurdoto is an extinct volcano, and the Momela Lakes came about following volcanic activity on the now dormant Mount Meru, a popular three-day climb (although it is possible to do it in a day).

Arusha offers great day-tripping safaris and expeditions, with plenty of observation hides and picnic sites, although there are good overnight facilities in the form of lodges and camp sites. There are truly magnificent views from the rim of Ngurdoto Crater. Early risers will get the best views in the morning light, the eye feasting on the crater, the surrounding areas as well as Mount Kilimanjaro.

TARANGIRE NATIONAL PARK

Tarangire offers 2600km² (1000 sq. miles) of rolling hills, riverine forests, acacia woodlands and ancient baobabs. The Tarangire River provides the only permanent water in southern Maasailand, and this makes the park a wildlife-spotter's paradise during the dry season (from June to September). The park's ecosystem is based on patterns of annual migration and it plays a big part in preserving the country's wildlife, which includes an abundance of bird life.

KINGS OF CONSERVATION

Tanzania can justifiably claim to have one of the most remarkable conservation records in Africa. Approximately 30 per cent of its land is dedicated to conservation efforts concentrated in wildlife sanctuaries made up of more than 35 parks, reserves and conservation areas. These range from the tropical coast to the semi-arid central plateau, and the semi-temperate highlands to forested woodlands. Tourists and safari-goers bring sought-after foreign currency into the country and, by visiting the reserves, help to preserve vital habitats such as the savanna grasslands and endless plains that are home to some of Africa's most recognised wildlife. Tanzania's tourist infrastructure is relatively sophisticated, and travel in and around the game reserves, national parks and World Heritage Sites (such as Arusha, Gombe, Kilimanjaro, Tarangire, Selous and the world-famous Serengeti and Ngorongoro) is generally a pain-free and quite luxurious experience.

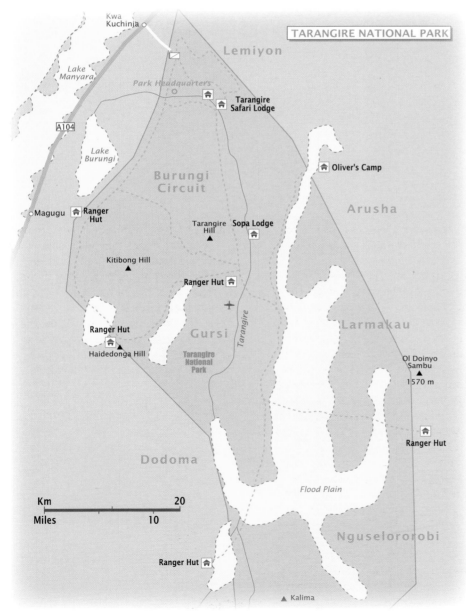

Top to bottom: camel safari; traditional dhow; a mighty buffalo.

MOUNT KILIMANJARO

Mighty Kilimanjaro, with an altitude of 5895m (19,340ft), emerged 750,000 years ago as a result of volcanic activity. 'Kili' is the world's highest freestanding mountain. The precise origin of Kili's name remains lost in time – the local word *kilima* (from which the name apparently stems) means 'hill' rather than 'mountain'. Rising from the plains of the Masai, the mountain peak – a dormant volcano – is snowcapped (although just 3 degrees south of the equator) and the make-up of the slopes varies enormously. From the foot to about 1800m (5900ft), the inclines comprise volcanic soils, and the vegetation up to 2800m (9200ft) is rainforest, which receives over 2000mm (79in) of rain. This is followed – to an altitude of 4000m (13,100ft) – by a moorland of heather and giant lobelias.

AFRICA'S HIGHEST MOUNTAINS

Kilimanjaro, Tanzania	5895m	19,341ft
Mt Kenya, Kenya	5199m	17,057ft
Stanley, Uganda-DRC	5110m	16,765ft
Ras Dashen, Ethiopia	4620m	15,158ft
Meru, Tanzania	4565m	14,977ft
Karisimbi, Rwanda-DRC	4507m	14,787ft
Tullu Deemtu, Ethiopia	4377m	14,361ft
Elgon, Kenya-Uganda	4321m	14,177ft
Toubkal, Morocco	4165m	13,655ft
Mt Cameroon, Cameroon	4095m	13,435ft

THE HIGHEST MOUNTAIN ON EARTH

Mauna Kea on Hawaii is 4207m (13,803ft) above sea level, but if measured from its base on the ocean floor, it's 10,200m (33,466ft) high.

KILIMANJARO IN A NUTSHELL

Climate: Avoid the rains in April, May and November.

Risk factor: Cheap package deals may be less reliable and less safe than those offered by established operators.

Health: Exhaustion, fatigue and altitude sickness are the most serious complaints. Be vaccinated against cholera, tetanus, hepatitis and polio. AIDS is prevalent.

Pack: Warm, waterproof and windproof clothes, sturdy hiking boots, a sleeping bag, sunscreen and water. Sweets help maintain energy. Also pack a head torch for the early-morning stretch and a kikoi (sarong) that can act as a scarf and pillow.

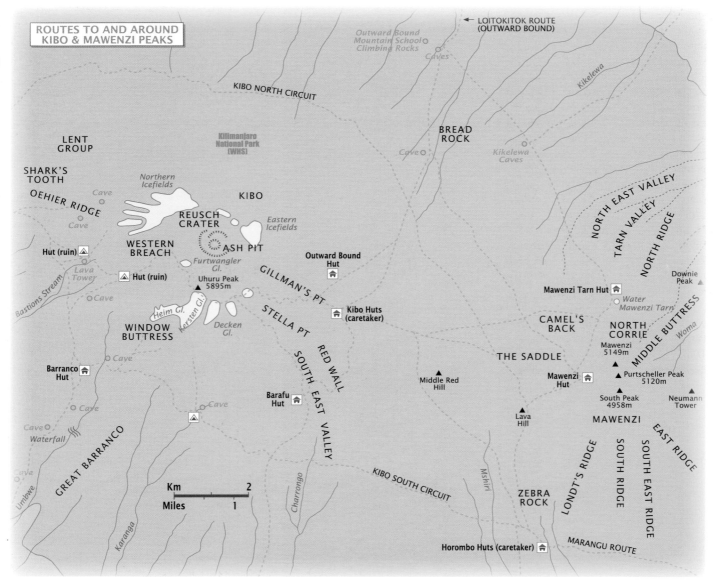

CLIMBING KILIMANJARO

Although there are difficult areas on Kili's slopes, it is unlikely you will need ropes, ice axes and picks, and the more followed routes are relatively trouble-free. In fact, the greatest challenge is overcoming the heat of the sun and the icy chill of the summit – the most reported danger is the altitude sickness that sets in at about 3500m (10,500ft). The only way to combat it is to climb slowly and stop often to allow your body to acclimatise. Climbing Kilimanjaro is an expensive exercise: although tour operators should see to transfers, accommodation and equipment, you need to hire registered guides and porters as well as pay the US$20 rescue fee. There are also park and camping fees, yet the standard five-day climb is so popular that it can be overbooked (the park sees 20,000 visitors pass through a year). On the first day of the ascent you depart from the park and take an undemanding three- or four-hour hike through rainforest to the A-frame huts at the first rest stop. You then plough on to the night stop at Mandara Hut, from where you will progress to Horombo on day two. Here, at 3720m (12,200ft), is where the first signs of altitude sickness strike. The day's five-hour trek will take you to the rim of Maundi Crater and up an incline to the highlands. The trek becomes tougher by the third day as you pass the Last Water and Zebra rocks and move onto The Saddle, the bridge connecting the peaks of Kibo and Mawenzi. The last stretch of the six-hour walk up to Kibo Hut at 4700m (15,440ft) can be arduous. Kibo is dreary and cold, and the last two days are mentally and physically demanding. In the icy morning, you head for Gillman's Point on the crater. Oxygen is very thin, making the walk tougher, but a mere 210m (700ft) further is the great reward: Kilimanjaro's true summit, Uhuru Peak.

Top to bottom: Mount Kilimanjaro; Kibo crater; ice cliffs on Kibo.

HIGHEST MOUNTAIN ON EACH CONTINENT

· Asia	Everest	8850m	29,028ft
· South America	Aconcagua	6959m	22,826ft
· North America	McKinley (Denali)	6194m	20,316ft
· Africa	Kilimanjaro	5895m	19,335ft
· Europe	Elbrus	5642m	18,505ft
· Antarctica	Vinson Massif	4897m	16,062ft
· Oceania	Carstensz Pyramid	4884m	16,024ft
· Australia	Kosciuszko	2228m	7307ft

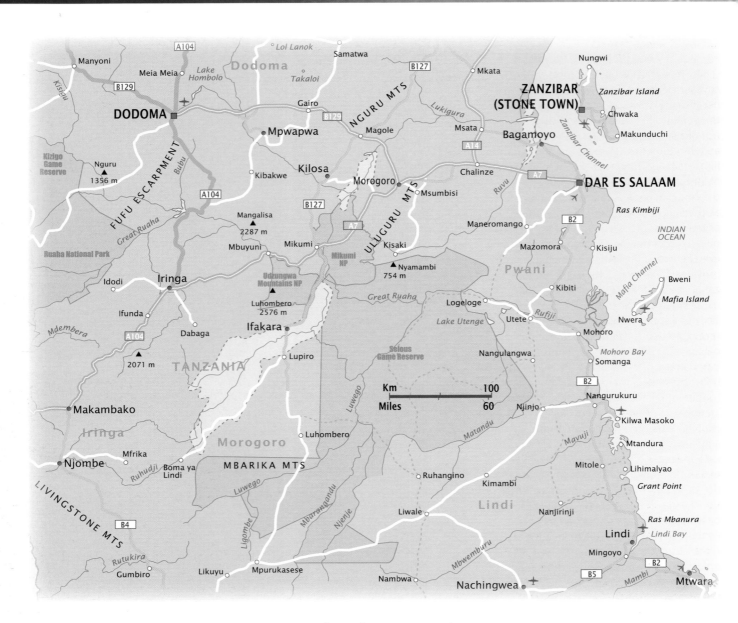

DAR ES SALAAM

Dar es Salaam (Dar) is a rather young city, yet it is Tanzania's most strategic harbour and the largest urban settlement in the country. While Dodoma and Dar es Salaam are both capital cities of the country, it is Dar es Salaam that is its very exciting heart. Established in 1870 as a 'Haven of Peace' by the Sultan Majid, to-day's thriving, modern city has remained true to its nature as a bustling African hub but also has the cosmopolitan flavour that seems to characterise so many of Tanzania's urban centres. Dar is the axis on which the national economy pivots. With its striking backdrop and string of breathtakingly beautiful (and famous) beaches, even the inner city is punctuated here and there with patches of emerald green. While the urban chaos that pervades so much of metropolitan Africa has not escaped Dar, there is an overriding sense of the quaint and the charming in the city centre. The city has a long legacy of colonial intervention but this, combined with the remarkable spirit and conviviality of its people, makes for an even more fascinating adventure. English and German colonists left behind a wonderful amalgamation of architecture that combines well with the indigenous flavour of the city. Dar plays host to a number of plush hotels, fine restaurants and up-market shopping haunts, but is also the home of an unusual collection of cathedrals and churches, museums and markets, galleries and boutiques – all haphazardly interspersed with many important cultural sites that are only decades old.

EXPLORING ZANZIBAR'S WATERS

Some 85km (53 miles) long and 25km (16 miles) wide, Zanzibar's coast of rocky coves, mangroves, lagoons, pristine beaches and astonishing coral reefs allows the pursuit of many leisure activities, from kayaking to deep-sea game fishing and, more recently, diving and snorkelling. Visibility from a kayak is virtually unobstructed and you will see right down to the corals and reefs. This area is known as the Sunrise Coast, and this is most true of Bwejuu and Makunduchi. There are numerous boat trips to offshore islets and even Pemba, and exploring these by boat provides a unique glimpse of coastal Tanzania. It also offers some of the best scuba diving and snorkelling in East Africa. The corals are virtually unscathed and the reefs teem with sea creatures. Although diving is extraordinary, few operators are based on the eastern shore so conditions here are better. Because it is so sheltered, too, visibility makes for excellent diving. The beach at Chumbe Island Coral Park is punctuated with 'eco-bungalows', and a network of walking and diving trails laces the coast. There are also wrecks to explore, and the Stone Town harbour is dotted with 200 of them. However, conditions in the harbour are poor and it is best to explore wrecks elsewhere on the coast. The east coast of Zanzibar Island remains undeveloped, and most lodgings are rustic, but tour operators offer some great attractions, including increasingly popular big-game fishing and deep-sea diving, as well as the magical opportunity to dive with dolphins and turtles – and even the occasional shark.

Top to bottom: Dar es Salaam sunrise; a palm weaver; spectacular diving off Zanzibar.

145

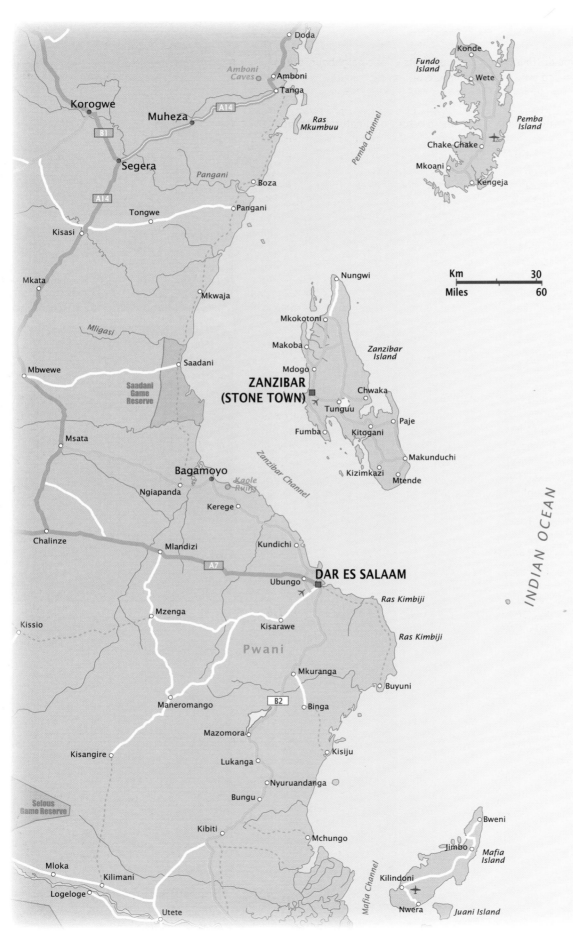

Doda

Amboni Caves
Amboni
Tanga

Korogwe
Muheza
A14

B1

Segera

A14

Pangani

Boza

Tongwe
Pangani

Kisasi

Mkata

Mkwaja

Mligasi

Mbwewe
Saadani
Saadani Game Reserve

Msata

Bagamoyo
Kaole Ruins

Ngiapanda

Kerege

Chalinze
Mlandizi
Kundichi
A7

DAR ES SALAAM
Ubungo

Mzenga

Kisarawe

Pwani

Kissio

Mkuranga
Buyuni

Maneromango
B2
Binga

Mazomora

Kisiju

Kisangire
Lukanga

Nyuruandanga

Bungu

Kibiti

Mchungo

Mloka
Kilimani

Logeloge

Utete

Ras Mkumbuu

Pemba Channel

Konde
Fundo Island
Wete

Pemba Island

Chake Chake
Mkoani
Kengeja

Km   30
Miles   60

Nungwi

Mkokotoni

Makoba
Zanzibar Island
Mdogo

ZANZIBAR (STONE TOWN)
Chwaka
Tunguu
Paje
Fumba
Kitogani
Makunduchi
Kizimkazi
Mtende

Zanzibar Channel

INDIAN OCEAN

Ras Kimbiji
Ras Kimbiji

Mafia Channel

Bweni
Jimbo
Mafia Island

Kilindoni

Nwera
Juani Island

ZANZIBAR

Although the name may conjure up romantic images of an exotic destination inaccessible to all but locals and only a handful of intrepid adventurers intent on discovering Africa's legendary city, Zanzibar is, in fact, one of East Africa's most significant tourist destinations. Spread across two separate islands some 40km (24.8 miles) from Tanzania's mainland, the most famous is the island of Zanzibar (Unguja). The other is Pemba, just kilometres to the northeast.

The word 'Zanzibar' is said to have originated from an early, all-encompassing name given to much of East Africa's coast by Arab traders. This stretch of shore, it is said, was once commonly known as Zinj el Barr, meaning the 'Land of the Black People'.

The slave trade in Zanzibar was abolished in 1907. Now called the Spice Island, Zanzibar is a tropical paradise, known for its spectacular beaches and the lingering ghosts of ancient Africa. At the island's centre stands Stone Town, the old quarter of Zanzibar Town. Most visitors agree that it is the heady aroma of spices and the tangible sense of history that is Stone Town's most alluring drawcard. The winding, mostly cobbled streets, alleys and footpaths criss-cross in a labyrinth not easily negotiated by the uninitiated, and the overriding buzz is a baffling combination of Arabic, Asian and European languages, led by a barrage of Swahili. The architecture is an endearing hotchpotch of the romantic and the practical: minarets and Gothic-like arches of palaces and forts frame markets and vibrant street stalls.

ZANZIBAR IN A NUTSHELL
Climate: Tropical and hot for most of the year; the best time to dive is during Oct–Nov.
Risk factor: Theft and mugging are becoming more frequent – keep an eye on equipment and accessories. Currents on the east coast may be dangerous. Zanzibar is Muslim, so exposed flesh is frowned upon beyond tourist spots.

PEMBA

The island of Pemba may not be as famous as its exotic neighbour, but it's more or less the same size, covering some 984km² (610 sq. miles) and is an equally picturesque beach idyll with plenty to offer, from natural splendour to a multitude of outdoor activities. Pemba is best known for the abundance of cloves harvested here annually, and the unsurpassed quality of its diving and snorkelling. Sweltering in the heat and alive with spice aromas, Pemba has also retained its centuries-old charm, remaining seemingly unchanged for hundreds of years – except for the tides and winds that continue to buffet the shores during seasonal monsoons. With a population of less than half a million, this tiny satellite of Tanzania also has a long and sometimes turbulent history of conquerors and colonists, and this has left an indelible mark on the island.

MAFIA

Mafia (not linked to the Italian Mob) is an ideal spot for adventurers, with magnificent diving (notably at Chole Bay, a protected deep-water anchorage), snorkelling, angling, dhow sailing, water sports and daydreaming on the beach.

Top to bottom: Swahili door in Stone Town; view of Stone Town; henna body art.

147

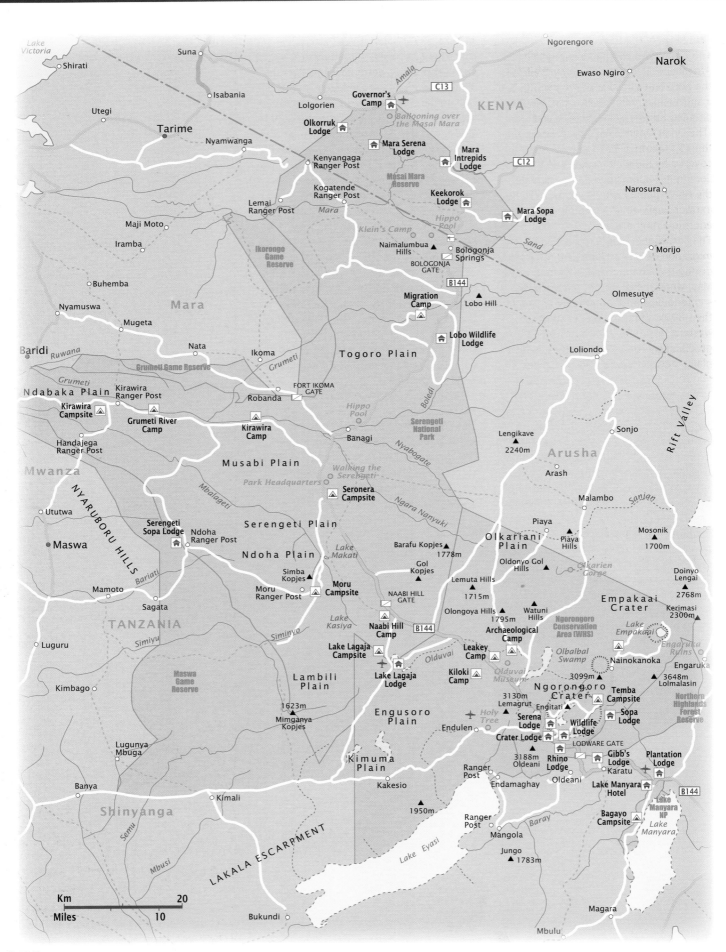

Lake Victoria
Shirati
Suna
Ngorengore
Narok
Utegi
Isabania
Lolgorien
KENYA
Tarime
Nyamwanga
Governor's Camp
Olkorruk Lodge
Ballooning over the Masai Mara
Ewaso Ngiro
C13
Mara Serena Lodge
Mara Intrepids Lodge
C12
Narosura
Kenyangaga Ranger Post
Maji Moto
Kogatende Ranger Post
Keekorok Lodge
Mara Sopa Lodge
Iramba
Lemai Ranger Post
Masai Mara Reserve
Mara
Klein's Camp
Hippo Pool
Sand
Morijo
Buhemba
Ikorongo Game Reserve
Naimalumbua Hills
Bologonja Springs
BOLOGONJA GATE
Olmesutye
Nyamuswa
Mara
Mugeta
Togoro Plain
Migration Camp
B144
Lobo Hill
Loliondo
Nata
Ikoma
Lobo Wildlife Lodge
Baridi
Ruwana
Grumeti
Grumeti Game Reserve
FORT IKOMA GATE
Boledi
Ndabaka Plain
Kirawira Ranger Post
Robanda
Hippo Pool
Serengeti National Park
Lengikave 2240m
Arusha
Kirawira Campsite
Grumeti River Camp
Kirawira Camp
Banagi
Nyabogate
Handajega Ranger Post
Musabi Plain
Walking the Serengeti
Arash
Mwanza
Mbalageti
Park Headquarters
Ngara Nanyuki
Malambo
Sanjan
Ututwa
Serengeti Sopa Lodge
Seronera Campsite
Piaya
Mosonik 1700m
Maswa
Ndoha Ranger Post
Serengeti Plain
Olkariani Plain
Piaya Hills
Ndoha Plain
Lake Makati
Barafu Kopjes 1778m
Oldonyo Gol Hills
Okarien Gorge
Doinyo Lengai 2768m
Luguru
Simba Kopjes
Gol Kopjes
Lemuta Hills 1715m
Empakaai Crater
Kerimasi 2300m
Mamoto
Moru Ranger Post
Moru Campsite
NAABI HILL GATE
Lake Empakaai
Sagata
Lake Kasiya
Olongoya Hills 1795m
Watuni Hills
Ngorongoro Conservation Area (WHS)
Engaruka Ruins
TANZANIA
Siminyo
Naabi Hill Camp
B144
Archaeological Camp
Olbalbal Swamp
Nainokanoka
Engaruka
Luguru
Lake Lagaja Campsite
Olduvai
Leakey Camp
Kiloki Camp
Olduvai Museum
3099m
3648m Lolmalasin
Kimbago
Lambili Plain
Lake Lagaja Lodge
Temba Campsite
Northern Highlands Forest Reserve
1623m
Mimganya Kopjes
Engusoro Plain
3130m Lemagrut
Ngorongoro Crater
Sopa Lodge
Lugunya Mbuga
Holy Tree
Endulen
Engitati
Serena Lodge
Wildlife Lodge
LODWARE GATE
Gibb's Lodge
Plantation Lodge
Banya
Kimuma Plain
Crater Lodge
3188m Oldeani
Rhino Lodge
Karatu
Kimali
Kakesio
Ranger Post
Endamaghay
Oldeani
Lake Manyara Hotel
B144
Shinyanga
1950m
Ranger Post
Bagayo Campsite
Lake Manyara NP
Semu
Mbusi
LAKALA ESCARPMENT
Lake Eyasi
Mangola
Jungo 1783m
Lake Manyara
Magara
Bukundi
Mbulu

Km   20
Miles   10

THE SERENGETI

The dramatic natural arena in which Africa's greatest display plays itself out, the horizonless plains of the Serengeti are a spectacular wildlife sanctuary without parallel. Known by the local Maasai as 'The Great Open Place', the plateau of the 15,000km² (5800-sq.-mile) plain is covered by the short grasses of the Serengeti National Park, acclaimed as the finest game reserve in Africa. This extraordinary ecosystem is home to enormous populations of mammals. The Serengeti's annual wildebeest migration begins on the southern plateau during the summer rains (December to May) when the herds of 100,000 animals – extending for 40km (25 miles) – begin their 800km (500-mile) trek to the western territories, only to make the gruelling return trip to the southern plains between October and November.

SERENGETI IN A NUTSHELL
Requirements: Travellers from South America and most of Africa must have yellow fever immunisation certificates.
Climate: Jun–Oct is coolest, but this is also the busiest and most expensive time of the year. Jan–Feb may be better; although hot, it is the best time to see migration in the southern park.
Risk factor: There is always a degree of risk involved when it comes to wildlife.
Health: Be vaccinated against cholera, tetanus, hepatitis and polio. Malaria is rife in the lowlands. AIDS is a threat.
Pack: Most operators supply basics; take light hiking gear, warm clothes, walking boots and sun protection.

WALKING THE SERENGETI

The Serengeti is home to some of the most impressive herds of wildlife on the continent; its landscape features valleys, rolling hills and patches of scrubby woodland. The plains are the most memorable and the easiest to cross. One way of avoiding the tourist trap is to explore the land on foot – almost within touching distance of more than a million wildebeest, hundreds of thousands of Thomson's gazelle, and tens of thousands of zebra, impala and topi. The prospect of walking this wild countryside is at once intimidating and enthralling. These herds are stealthily stalked by the great predators of Africa, including not only lion, cheetah and leopard, but also wild dog, jackal, spotted hyena and bat-eared fox. Given that even the best roads are poor and the distances are vast, it is best to opt for a tour company. Arusha has plenty of options, but only some hiking tours are based on responsible ecotourism. However, you do not want to end up in the middle of the Serengeti without shelter and without a guide. Reliable operators charge more, but the package includes park fees, camping fees, food and fuel costs, plus they provide drivers, cooks, porters and guides. By choosing to walk, you will be faced with limited facilities such as long-drop toilets and basic camp sites, and will not have at your disposal the luxuries offered by the exclusive lodges and tented camps.

Top to bottom: hot-air balloon over the Serengeti; a 4x4 vehicle tests the shifting sands; portrait of a Maasai girl.

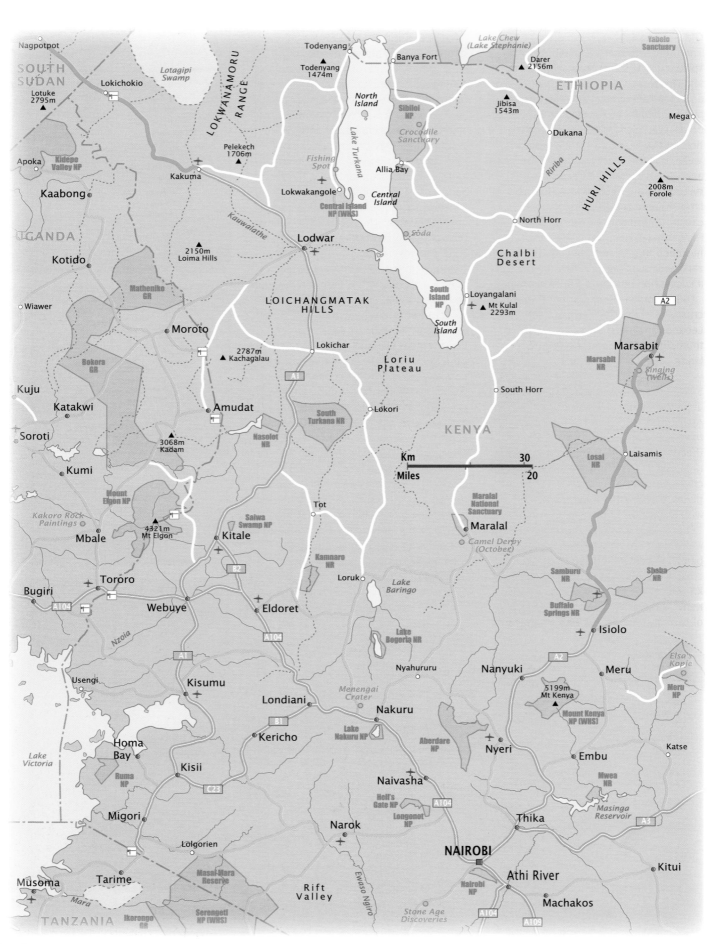

GREAT RIFT VALLEY

The Great Rift Valley is one of the most spectacular volcanic regions on earth, and the area's geology has given rise to an extraordinary diversity of landscape and faunal life, which reaches its pinnacle on the wild plains of Kenya. At its most dramatic in East Africa, the Great Rift Valley was formed some 20 million years ago when violent subterranean shifts resulted in the collapse of huge tracts of land situated along parallel fault lines, causing volcanic eruptions of molten rock. The length of this great scar that has been forged down one-sixth of the earth's circumference is characterised by a succession of great lakes.

Today, this massive fissure in the earth's crust stretches 9500km (6000 miles) from Lebanon to Mozambique, and no fewer than 800km (500 miles) between Lake Manyara and the Red Sea. The dramatic inclines of its valley walls cut between 50km (30 miles) and 500km (300 miles) across the width of the African landscape. Apart from Ethiopia on the Horn of Africa, the two countries that feature the most theatrical inclines of the great valley are Kenya and Tanzania, both of which are characterised by high-lying inland plateaus and fertile coastal belts dotted with tropical islands.

The valley's extraordinarily vertical walls loom up from the wide golden plain below, the cliff-like ramparts broken by cross fractures. In a region perhaps best known for the phenomenon of its wildlife, Kenya and Tanzania have, in the process of capitalising on their extraordinarily rich natural heritage, both achieved an enviable record of conservation.

NGORONGORO CRATER

The Ngorongoro Crater is the largest intact volcanic caldera in the world. The expansive tableland covers the 265km² (102 sq. miles) of the crater floor and forms the heart of the Ngorongoro Conservation Area. Hedged in by 600m (2000ft) walls that tower high above the open savanna, the crater is a sweep of untamed wilderness across which herds of zebra and wildebeest (with head counts numbering in the hundreds) charge. Huge flocks of pink flamingos wade the seasonal waters. The plains and montane forest are home to an astounding array of Africa's most recognised wildlife, with no fewer than a quarter million large mammals scattered across the emptiness. The abundance of antelope species means that this is also prime big-cat country, with cheetah, leopard and the world's densest population of over 100 lion. The rest of the Big Five have also settled here: elephant bulls, 3000 head of buffalo and roughly 20 black rhino.

Top to bottom: Ngorongoro crater wall; inside the crater; Olduvai Gorge.

VOLCANOES IN AFRICA
Africa is relatively quiet in terms of volcanic activity, yet it has its fair share of active and dormant 'blowers':

Cameroon	Mount Cameroon
Comoros	Le Kartala
DRC	Nyiragongo
Kenya	Mount Kenya
Réunion	Piton de la Fournaise
	Piton des Neiges
Rwanda	Mount Karisimbi
Tanzania	Kieyo
	Mount Kilimanjaro
	Meru and Ngurdoto
	Ngozi
	Ol Doinyo Lengai
	Rungwe
Uganda	Bufumbira
	Bunyaruguru Field
	Fort Portal Field
	Katunga
	Katwe-Kikorongo Field
	Kyatwa Volcanic Field
	Muhavura

NGORONGORO'S WILDLIFE STARS
Flora: Red thorn, nuxia congesta, crotons, strangler fig, mosses, orchids, ferns, old man's beard, umbrella trees, lichen, euphorbia, elephant ears, lion's mane, Sodom apple, wild bananas, yellow fever trees, Cape chestnut, a wide range of grassland and the poisonous red-and-yellow leopard lily.
Fauna: Squirrels, baboons, buffalo, cheetah, leopard, lion, elephant, black rhino, antelope such as duiker and bushbuck, genet, serval, African civet, and hundreds of bird species, including masses of flamingo, Martial Eagles, Blacksmith Plovers, Crested Guineafowl, shrikes, weavers, Narina Trogon, Livingstone's Turaco, kites and Marabou Storks.

151

Kenya

QUICK FACTS

Capital: Nairobi
Area: 592,747km² / 228,861mi²
Population: 43 million
Main ethnic groups:
 · Kikuyu (21%)
 · Luhya (14%)
 · Kamba (11%)
Main languages:
 · Swahili
 · English
 · Kikuyu
 · Luo
 · Kamba
Main religions:
 · Catholic (34%)
 · Protestant (32%)
 · Traditional beliefs (26%)
 · Muslim (6%)
Currency: Kenyan shilling
 (100 cents)

IN THIS CHAPTER

Snorkelling with whale sharks.

Climbers on Point Dutton, Mount Kenya.

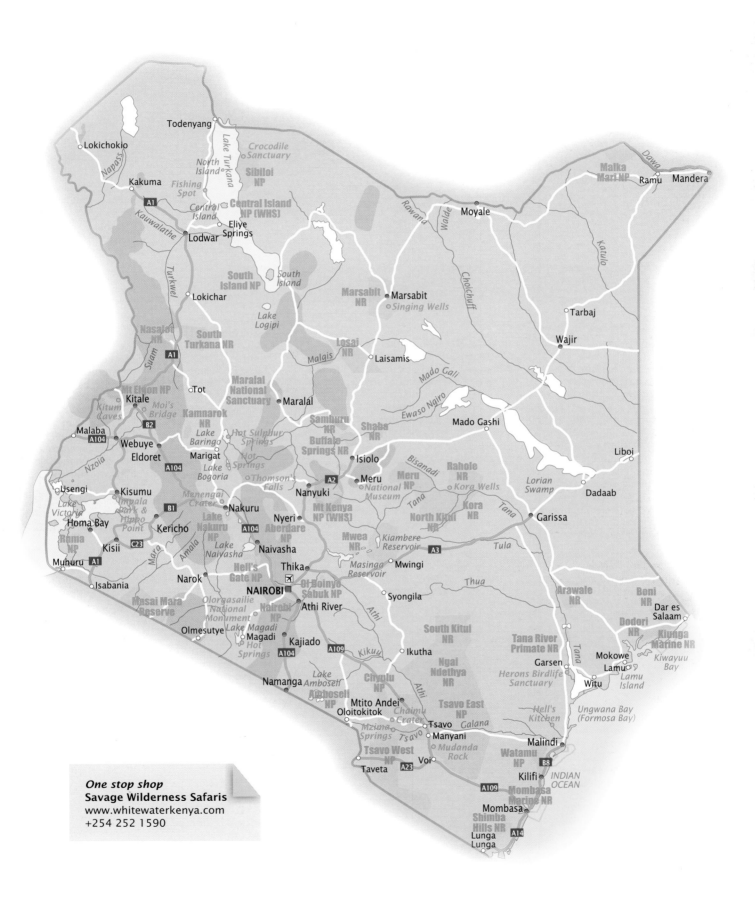

One stop shop
Savage Wilderness Safaris
www.whitewaterkenya.com
+254 252 1590

Kenya

10 TOP ADVENTURES

1. Game viewing
2. Mountain biking
3. Mountaineering
4. Horse riding
5. Rock climbing
6. Birding
7. Scuba diving/snorkelling
8. Whitewater rafting
9. Fishing
10. Ballooning

Horse riding across the game-filled plains.

 ## ON LAND

Game viewing

Kenya's best-known park is the Masai Mara, an extension of the great Serengeti plains of Tanzania. It's amazing at any time of year, but if you go between July and October you might be lucky enough to catch one of Africa's premier wildlife experiences, the wildebeest migration, when the plains fill with vast herds of wildebeest and their accompanying predators. If photography is your passion then you probably have your sights on Amboseli, famed for its elephant population and much photographed views of game silhouetted against the snowcapped peak of Kilimanjaro. Primate lovers should visit the Sweetwaters Chimpanzee Sanctuary in the Ol Pejeta Conservancy. And, if you're a list ticker, you can be tracking elephants, the biggest land mammal, at Chilu Hills, only 30 minutes' drive from Diani Beach, where you can swim with whale sharks, the biggest fish in the sea.

Serena Active
www.serenahotels.com
+254 202 842
Safaris Unlimited
www.safarisunlimited.com
+254 289 1168
Ol Pejeta Conservancy
www.olpejetaconservancy.org
+254 723 312 673

Diani Safaris
www.dianisafaris-kenya.com
+254 403 202 078 or
+254 775 691 800
Hartley's Safaris
www.hartleys.co.za
+27 11 467 4704
&Beyond
www.andbeyond.com
+27 11 809 4300

Mountain biking

There's no better way to experience Kenya's diverse landscapes and wildlife than on a bike. Hell's Gate, the Laikipia Plateau and the coastal Arabuko Sokoke Forest are popular with mountain bikers.

Karisia MTB Safaris
www.mountainbikesafaris.com
+254 721 836 792
Savage Wilderness Safaris
www.whitewaterkenya.com
+254 252 1590
Bike & Saddle
www.bikeandsaddle.com
+27 21 813 6433

Mountaineering

At 5199m (17,057ft), Mt Kenya is the second-highest mountain in Africa and a much cheaper – and quieter – experience than trekking on Kilimanjaro. You need specialised climbing skills and equipment to make it right to the summits of the highest peaks – Nelion and Batian – but the hike to the walker's peak, Point Lenana, is a worthy goal and you'll be blown away by the outsized lobelia, erica and the other flora of the surrounding national park. If that sounds too hardcore, Mt Logonot volcano (2780m/9121ft) is a great one-day climb on which you'll often spot game.

Go to Mount Kenya
www.gotomountkenya.com
+254 518 010 691
Savage Wilderness Safaris
www.whitewaterkenya.com
+254 252 1590
Peak High Mountaineering
www.peakhigh.co.za
+27 33 343 3168

Horse riding

Riding through the game lands of Kenya – getting really close to the animals and sleeping out in the great African plains – is one of the quintessential African adventures. The Chyulu Hills, Laikipia Plateau and Masai Mara are all popular destinations.

Best of Kenya
www.bestofkenya.com
+254 733 618 183
Safaris Unlimited
www.safarisunlimited.com
+254 289 1168

Rock climbing

TO DO

Unlike Kilimanjaro, the highest peaks of Mt Kenya are the preserve of rock climbers. The 'standard' route is a long but fairly easy climb up Nelion (the second-highest peak) followed by a descent to the often icy 'Gates of the Mist' and the final scramble to Batian's highest point. As long as they are fit and strong, novice climbers can make the ascent with guides, while for rock-jocks there are plenty more challenging routes to test their skills.

Savage Wilderness Safaris
www.whitewaterkenya.com
+254 252 1590

Peak High Mountaineering
www.peakhigh.co.za
+27 33 343 3168

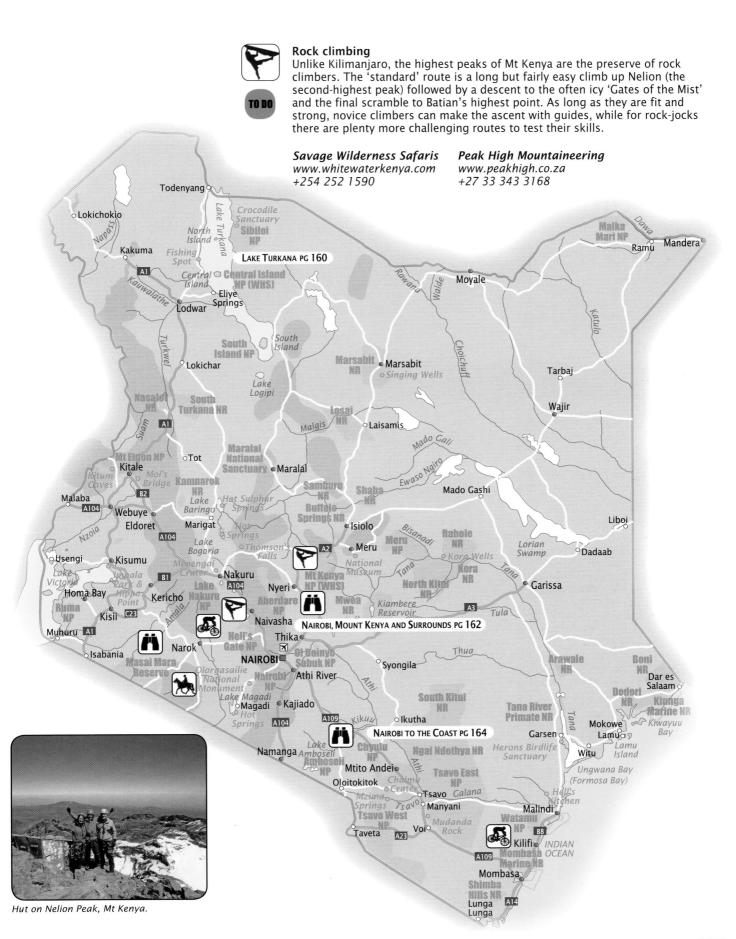

Hut on Nelion Peak, Mt Kenya.

Kenya

ON LAND

Birding

Boasting over 1100 bird species, Kenya is a twitcher's paradise, with most of the top spots also boasting big game. Gatamaiyu Forest in the Great Rift Valley – one of the world's most spectacular volcanic regions – is a must-do, as are Lake Jibe and the magnificent pink flamingos of Lake Nakuru. The mangrove forests of Mida Creek Reserve and nearby Arabuko-Sokoke Forest are superb coastal locations that can be enjoyed on self-guided walks.

TO DO

Best of Kenya
www.bestofkenya.com
+254 733 618 183
&Beyond
www.andbeyond.com
+27 11 809 4300
http://walkingtrailskenya.com/
your-birding-hotspots/

Diving.

ON WATER

Scuba diving/snorkelling

A coral reef runs almost the entire length of the Kenyan coastline, so scuba divers will be in their element. The Watamu/Malindi and Kisite marine parks offer some of the best diving on the African coast; for really out-of-this-world diving, get on a liveaboard and head for the Pemba Channel.

MILD

Aqua Ventures
www.diveinkenya.com
+254 422 332 420
Diani Marine
www.dianisafaris-kenya.com
+254 403 202 078
Buccaneer Diving
www.buccaneerdiving.com
+254 716 430 725 or +254 202 039 464
Serena Active
www.serenahotels.com
+254 202 842 000
Hartley's Oceans and Islands
www.hartleys.co.za
+27 11 467 4704

Fishing

Fishermen are spoilt for choice. Lake Victoria is home to one of the world's best-known trophy fish, the Nile perch, renowned for its fighting tenacity. Alternatively, you can try tickling a mountain trout in the high-altitude streams of Mount Kenya or the Aberdares, or head for the coast for a spot of saltwater fly-fishing. Kenya has some of the best, and most challenging, big-game fishing in the world, so if you've got the bucks, charter a boat from one of the coastal resorts between Mombasa and Malindi or from Lamu and head out for a tussle with a tuna, wahoo or, Hemingway's prized species, marlin.

MILD

Rusinga Island Lodge
www.rusinga.com
+254 202 531 314/5
Ocean Sports Resort
www.oceansports.net
+254 422 332 288
Serena Active
www.serenahotels.com
+254 202 842 000

Whitewater rafting

The Tana River, located just outside Nairobi, is an exhilarating day trip for novices, while the Athi River offers big water and the chance of sighting big cats. Multi-day trips can be tailored to include walking and caving in Chyulu.

TO DO

Savage Wilderness Safaris
www.whitewaterkenya.com
+254 252 1590

Whitewater action.

Balloning

Take to the dawn skies and float over the Masai Mara and other game-filled plains before coming down to earth with a slap-up bush breakfast and game drive.

TO DO

Governor's Camp Collection
www.governorscamp.com
+254 733 268 888
Hot Air Safaris
www.maraballooning.com
+254 702 999 278

Africa A-Z
www.africaa-z.co.za
+27 11 462 8857

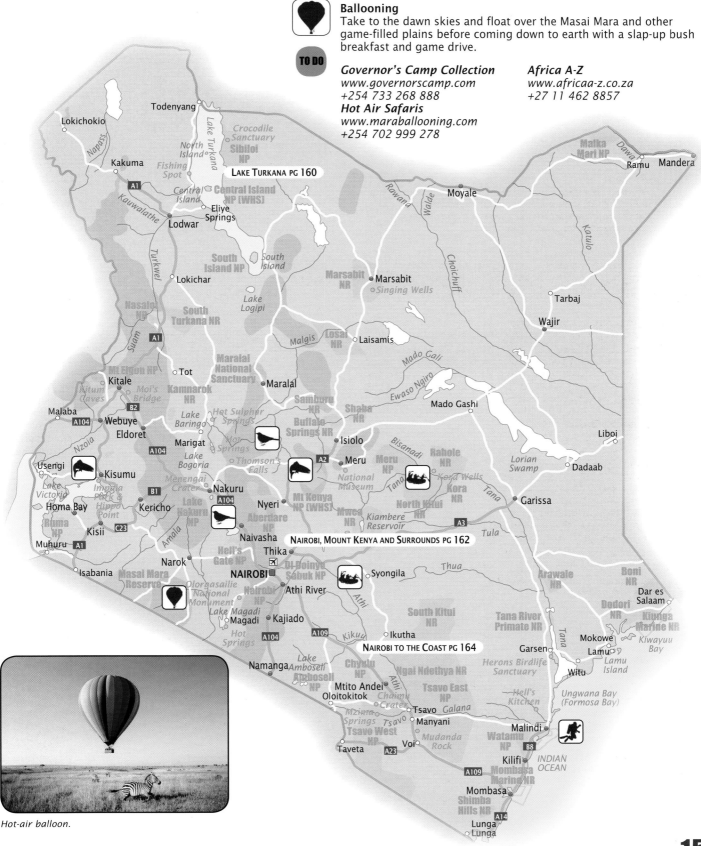

Hot-air balloon.

OTHER ADVENTURES

1. Trekking/hiking
2. Walking/camel safaris
3. Kitesurfing and windsurfing
4. Stand-up paddle boarding
5. Marine safaris
6. Sea kayaking
7. Skydiving
8. Bungee jumping and zip line

Walking and camel safari, Laikipia.

 ### ON LAND

Trekking/hiking
Trails and guided hikes abound throughout Kenya but top spots include the Loita Hills, Laikipia Plateau, Ol Njorowa Gorge in Hell's Gate NP and the boardwalk at Mida Creek. Check out http://walkingtrailskenya.com for up-to-date details.

Savage Wilderness Safaris
www.whitewaterkenya.com
+254 252 1590
Serena Active
www.serenahotels.com

+254 202 842 000
Safaris Unlimited
www.safarisunlimited.com
+254 202 087 296

Walking/camel safaris
Walking safaris in Laikipia are a bit unusual as your kit is carried by camels – as are you, if you tire!

Karisia Walking Safaris
www.karisia.com
+254 721 836 792

 ### ON WATER

Kitesurfing and windsurfing
One of the best kitesurfing beaches in the world, Diani Beach has the perfect conditions for this exciting new sport.

H2O Extreme
www.h2o-extreme.com
+254 721 495 876

Extreme Outdoors Africa
www.extremeoutdoorsafrica.com
+254 722 344 885

Stand-up paddle boarding
The warm, sheltered waters off the Kenyan coast are perfect for this family-friendly new sport. Local operator, H2O Extreme Kenya, is the only water-sports centre in East Africa to offer stand-up paddle boarding (SUP) courses and rentals.

H2O Extreme
www.h2o-extreme.com
+254 721 495 876

Marine safaris
During February and March you can join researchers on a whale shark tagging programme at Diani Beach and snorkel with the biggest fish in the sea, or act as a spotter from the accompanying light aircraft. The world's largest open-water whale shark enclosure, with its own natural coral reef, is due to open in March 2013 and will be both a tourist attraction and marine rehabilitation centre. Or take a dhow trip from Shimoni checking out the dolphins en route to the coral island of Wasini, a site of early Swahili civilisation.

East African Whale Shark Trust
www.giantsharks.org
+254 720 293 156

Diani Safaris
www.dianisafaris-kenya.com
+254 403 202 078 or
+254 775 691 800

Sea kayaking
The shallow reefs, with their magnificent little rock outcrops, are perfect for a gentle paddle. Pack a mask and snorkel and you can hop off to ogle the pretty corals and fish.

Ocean Sports Resort
www.oceansports.net
+254 422 332 288

Aqua Ventures
www.diveinkenya.com
+254 422 332 420

Sea kayaking.

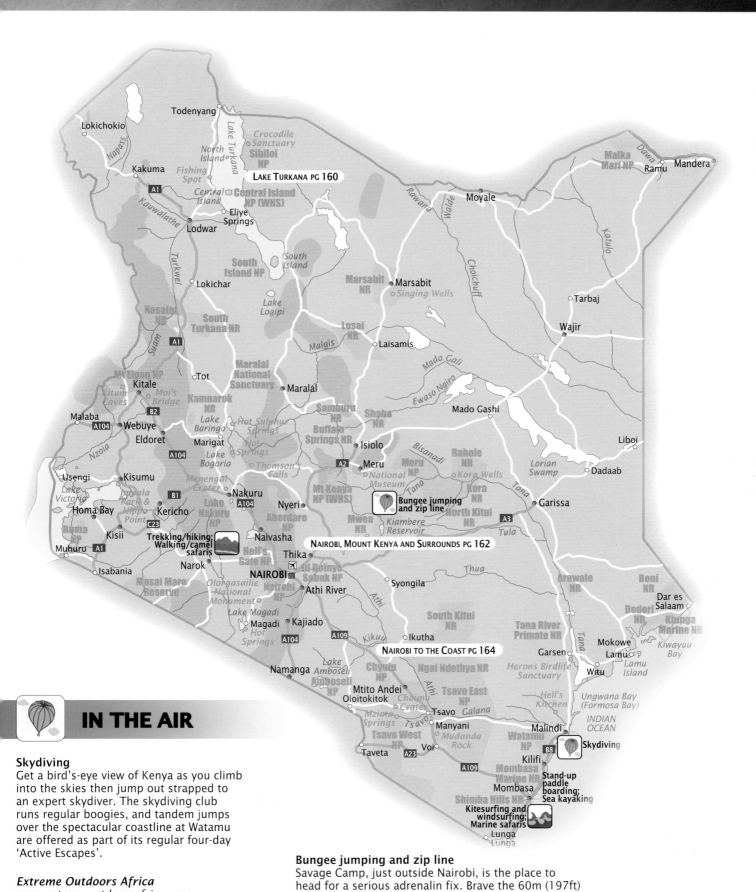

IN THE AIR

Skydiving

Get a bird's-eye view of Kenya as you climb into the skies then jump out strapped to an expert skydiver. The skydiving club runs regular boogies, and tandem jumps over the spectacular coastline at Watamu are offered as part of its regular four-day 'Active Escapes'.

Extreme Outdoors Africa
www.extremeoutdoorsafrica.com
+254 722 344 885
Active Escapes
www.active-escapes.co.za
+254 733 897 661

Bungee jumping and zip line

Savage Camp, just outside Nairobi, is the place to head for a serious adrenalin fix. Brave the 60m (197ft) bungee or fly across the Tana River on a zip line.

Savage Wilderness Safaris
www.whitewaterkenya.com
+254 252 1590

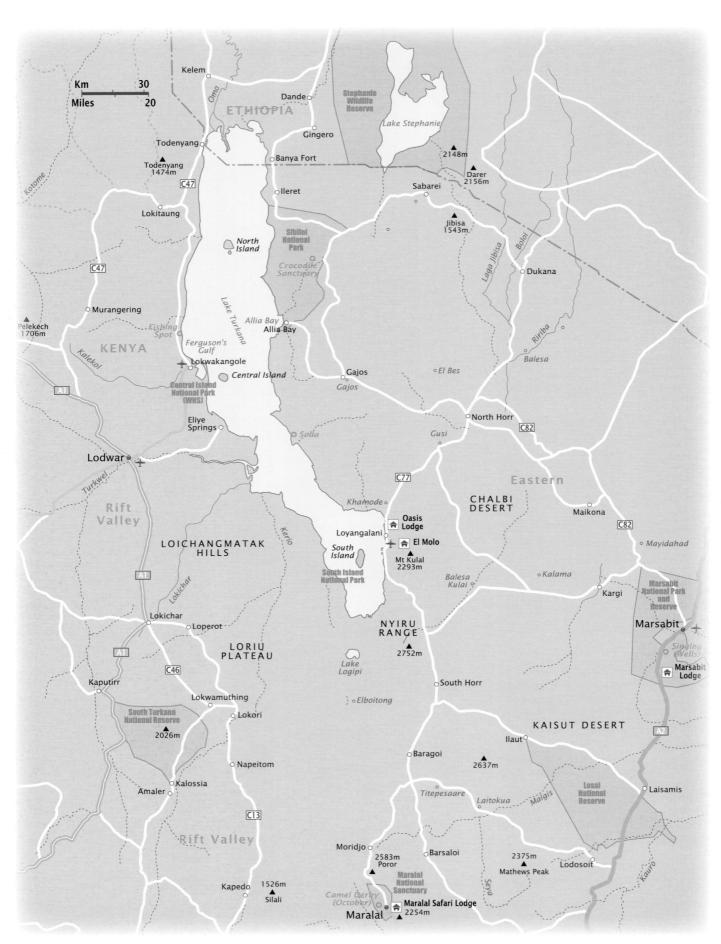

Km ——— 30
Miles ——— 20

Kelem
Dande
ETHIOPIA
Gingero
Stephanie Wildlife Reserve
Lake Stephanie
▲ 2148m
Todenyang
Banya Fort
▲ Todenyang 1474m
C47
Ileret
Sabarei
Darer 2156m
Lokitaung
Jibisa 1543m ▲
North Island
Sibiloi National Park
Crocodile Sanctuary
Dukana
Pelekech 1706m ▲
Murangering
Fishing Spot
KENYA
Allia Bay
Allia Bay
Lake Turkana
El Bes ○
Ririba
Kalekol
Ferguson's Gulf
Lokwakangole
Central Island
Gajos
Gajos
Balesa
Central Island National Park (WHS)
North Horr ○
C82
Eliye Springs
Solia
Gusi
Lodwar ○
Turkwel
Khamode
C77
Eastern
Rift Valley
Oasis Lodge
CHALBI DESERT
Maikona
C82
Kerio
Loyangalani
El Molo
Mt Kulal 2293m ▲
Mayidahad ○
LOICHANGMATAK HILLS
South Island
South Island National Park
Balesa Kulai
Kalama ○
Marsabit National Park and Reserve
Lokichar
Kargi
A1
NYIRU RANGE
▲ 2752m
Marsabit
Lokichar
Loperot
Singing (Wells)
LORIU PLATEAU
Lake Logipi
South Horr ○
Marsabit Lodge
A1
Kaputirr
Lokwamuthing
Elboitong ○
KAISUT DESERT
South Turkana National Reserve
Lokori
Ilaut
A2
▲ 2026m
▲ 2637m
Losai National Reserve
Napeitom
Baragoi ○
Kalossia
Titepesaare
Laitokua
Laisamis
Amaler
Seya
Malgis
C13
Moridjo ○
Barsaloi ○
2375m ▲
Lodosoit
Rift Valley
2583m ▲ Poror
Mathews Peak
Kapedo ○
1526m
Maralal National Sanctuary
Camel Derby (October)
Maralal Safari Lodge
Silali
Maralal ▲ 2254m
Kauro

LAKE TURKANA

Kenya's long, narrow lake covers 7104km² (2743 sq. miles) and is known by many locals as Basso Narok (Black Lake). It forms a ribbon of water 250km (155 miles) long and 56km (35 miles) wide, enclosed by the cliffs of the Rift Valley, and cuts through the parched northern reaches of endless horizons and volcanic outcrops. Fed by Ethiopia's Omo River and, to some degree, by the Turkwel, Lake Turkana is the world's largest desert lake and one of the largest alkaline lakes. Volcanic islands in the middle of the lake are the territory of hippos and some 22,000 crocodiles, while the waters shelter huge Nile perch. Migrant birds visit in such great numbers that their breeding sites on South and Central islands have been declared national parks.

THE SOURCE OF THE RIVER

Originating in the forests of the Eastern Mau Escarpment are the Njoro, Makalia and Enderit rivers, which drain into the great body of water that forms the heart of Lake Nakuru National Park, providing sustenance for half a million Kenyans. The lake now flows for only one-third of the year and has been reduced to dust six times in the last decade. The government's Fisheries Department has, fortunately, taken steps to help preserve the nation's marine life: it declared a short moratorium on trawling and also established a task force charged with investigating the status of marine resources for future generations.

AFRICA'S NATIONAL PARK PRIDE

Despite certain conservation problems and concerns, some of the world's finest national parks and reserves exist in Kenya. Parks such as Aberdare, Amboseli, Meru, Tsavo East and West, and Samburu provide, in the most part, an outstanding wildlife experience. Although the tourist trade has numerous drawbacks (Amboseli and Masai Mara are criss-crossed with tracks and trails carved by the caravan of tourists), in most cases a percentage of the revenue generated by safari operations and the entrance fees to government parks and reserves is allocated to local inhabitants and the establishment of wildlife research programmes and conservation education centres. Poaching, an ever-growing population and ever-

increasing land use create enormous pressure on wild spaces. The Masai Mara's wildebeest population has dropped from 120,000 to 22,000 in 20 years, their seasonal stomping grounds giving way to farmland and cattle pastures. Such situations are exacerbated by seemingly irresponsible and narrow-minded decisions made by non-aligned government officials.

THE WOOD AND THE TREES

Despite enormous opposition from local, international and non-governmental conservation organisations, the Kenyan government announced that it would excise about 67,000ha (165,500 acres) of the country's unique woodlands, including some 270ha of Nakuru, 1825ha of Mount Kenya, 2837ha of Marmanet and 900ha of Molo. Leading environmental groups have lashed out, pointing to the irreparable damage to the immediate environment, as well as the effect on the national economy and the ecology of the broader region. Felling these forests would alter local rainfall, thus affecting the water system and agriculture – not to mention the other industries dependent on hydroelectric power. In fact, Kenya's rivers are already suffering from natural deterioration.

Top to bottom: Lake Turkana at sunset; a child enjoying some fun in the lake; an abandoned boat on the shore.

161

NAIROBI

One of the most cosmopolitan and certainly one of the younger of Africa's capitals, Nairobi is a metropolis of museums and malls interspersed with boutiques and bars, curios and criminals, market stalls, galleries and even game reserves. Nairobi's three million inhabitants come from a variety of tribal cultures, and the noise, colour and squalor of the older portions of the city contrast greatly with modern structures such as the Kenyatta Conference Centre. Nairobi National Park lies on the city perimeter, with the Aberdare National Park nearby and river rafting on the Athi River.

NATIONAL PARKS AND RESERVES

With nearly 60 separate, officially designated conservation areas, including national parks, reserves, marine reserves and wetlands, covering 10 per cent of Kenya's land and waters, Africa's largest, best-stocked and most accessible protected areas belong to Kenya. The word 'safari' is taken from the local Swahili language and, appropriately, the safari industry is now one of the nation's most important income producers. Kenya's central plateau is divided by the Great Rift Valley. The varying geology of the region means that the wildlife areas cover an extraordinary range of landscapes, from open plains to densely wooded f orests and marine environments.

Sadly, wild Kenya remains under constant threat of numerous scourges.

MOUNT KENYA

Sacred Kirinyaga (Mount Kenya) on the central highlands is a playground for hikers, mountaineers and climbers. The snowcapped summit of its three-million-year-old bulk stands at 5199m (17,058ft), although glaciation has already hacked off 2000m (6500ft) from its original height. Topped by three main peaks (Batian, Nelion and Lenana), the slopes of this extinct volcano are covered in snow and ice, with 600km² (230 sq. miles) of protected land above the 3200m (10,500ft) forest line. The region is the traditional home to the Kikuyu people, and the park shelters birds, elephant, black rhino, buffalo, lion and bushbuck. Mount Kenya NP is one of the country's top safari spots (with more than adequate facilities) and a popular recreation destination for climbers eager to ascend Africa's second-highest peak. The three main hiking routes across Mount Kenya (Naro Moru, Sirimon and Chogoria) vary in distance and accessibility, demanding various degrees of fitness. Some of the climbs are relatively easy, while others demand all the skills and equipment (ice axes and ropes) of dedicated mountaineers. Trails, camps and huts on the trail circuit are accompanied by some fine hotels and plush safari lodges that offer excellent game viewing and night drives.

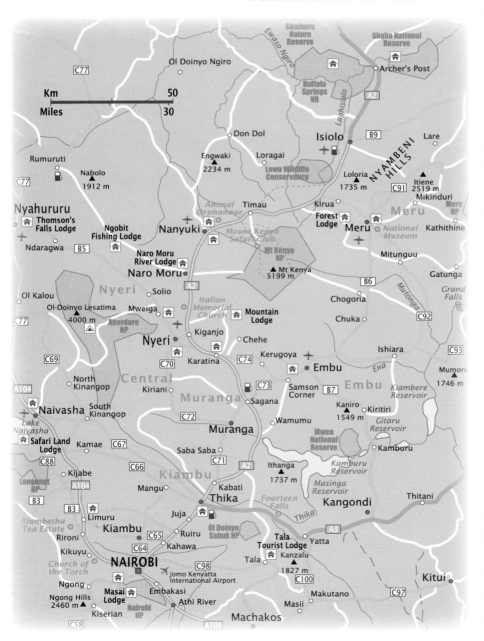

AFRICA'S GREAT MOUNTAIN ICONS

· Mount Kilimanjaro	Tanzania
· Mount Sinai	Egypt
· Table Mountain	South Africa
· Hand of Fatima	Mali
· Mulanje	Malawi
· Ol Doinyo Lengai	Tanzania
· Spitzkoppe	Namibia

ABERDARE NATIONAL PARK

Lying 100km (62 miles) north of Nairobi, Aberdare is a fairly small park of just 767km² (296 sq. miles), yet it boasts a wide diversity of fauna, partly owing to its mountainous terrain, which includes a highest point of 3995m (13,100ft) in the form of Ol-Doinyo Lesatima. Waterfalls are a natural accompaniment to such terrain, and one of the most accessible and widely photographed is the Chania Falls (Queen's Cave Waterfall, as Queen Elizabeth II once lunched here). The country's highest falls are the Gura Falls, which spill water down from a spectacular height of 457m (1500ft), although viewing can only be done from the top of the falls, which reduces the 'wow factor' for visitors. The waterfalls and streams are a rich source of trout for those who enjoy fly-fishing, but the high rainfall in the area makes a 4x4 essential. The rains also encourage a proliferation of wildlife as well as heavy vegetation, which serves to impede game viewing. Sometimes it's best to rise above it all, and a night (or more) at The Ark or Treetops lodges allows great game viewing after dark.

SAMBURU, BUFFALO SPRINGS AND SHABA RESERVES

Lying on the Ewaso Ngiro River ('river of brown water'), Samburu and Buffalo Springs create excellent conditions for predators such as lion, cheetah and leopard, as well as the delightful gerenuk ('standing buck'), Grevy's zebra, beisa oryx and the reticulated giraffe. Samburu is also a popular spot for camel safaris.

Shaba offers a totally different habitat from the nearby Samburu and Buffalo Springs reserves. Shaba's plains are dotted with springs, small swamps and rocky hills, and it was at Shaba that author and conservationist Joy Adamson lived, rehabilitated a leopard called Penny, and was eventually murdered.

CAMEL SAFARIS

Camel safaris provide a unique alternative to 4x4s. Escorted by an armed guide, you ride and walk alongside the camels throughout the day and get to see scores of wild animals. Although you get to travel through otherwise inaccessible areas, many 'camel safaris' may mean little more than hiking alongside the great beasts as they lumber across the veld. Yet this doesn't detract from the experience.

Most operators allow trekkers to hitch rides on the backs of the camels, which are constantly tended by expert handlers who are keen to help and are eager to please. Many local safari guides may don traditional dress for the benefit of tourists, but they are well versed in the lore and the lie of the land, and you would do well to trust their instincts. The pace of the walk is usually brisk, but the guides are able to point out all the wildlife, including countless bird species. At night, the caravan sets up camp on a riverbank or alongside a water hole ... where wildlife tends to congregate after dark. Nights are spent under a big, white mosquito net, or in one of the tents carried by the camels. Most camel treks will last at least five days and, although shorter safaris may be available, don't be tempted to take the one- or two-day options, even though it's easier on your body. Apart from the fact that it will give you a far better feel for the land and its people (a glimpse is never enough), the longer the safari, the cheaper the per-day rate. There is plenty of competition among the individual operators, but fees and costs are generally similar and, although there are always chancers, most of the larger, more established safari companies based in Kenya have sound track records and offer a variety of exciting options.

Top to bottom: high-rise buildings, Nairobi; Mount Kenya National Park; Mount Kenya.

163

TSAVO AND AMBOSELI NATIONAL PARKS

Kenya's most-visited wildlife and nature area, Amboseli National Park was reduced to almost one-tenth of its original size following a conflict of interest between the Maasai herds and the region's wildlife. Set over 392km² (151 sq. miles), Amboseli is famed for its elephant populations as well as its much-photographed views of Kilimanjaro. The drawcard for tourists is the chance to witness nature's great beasts from close range as they feed and bathe in the swamps.

Tsavo West is more scenic than its eastern counterpart, and safaris in the West are a popular attraction, particularly for the famous red elephants. Tsavo is a massive park set on over 20,000km² (8035 sq. miles), with an altitude ranging from 230m (755ft) to 2000m (6562ft).

BALLOONING OVER THE MASAI

The Masai Mara's 1680km² (650 sq. miles) is little more than an extension of Tanzania's Serengeti. It is also the traditional homeland of the Maasai nation, but much of the land has now been given over to the wildlife, which has made the Masai Mara Reserve one of the most highly regarded in the world. Thousands of visitors make their way here every year to witness, first-hand, the magnificence of Kenya's wildlife in what is acclaimed as the finest game-viewing experience in Africa. Visitors cross the great savanna plains on foot, on horseback, via 4x4 and, most memorably, in a hot-air balloon. At the crack of dawn, travellers converge around the deflated balloon and the roaring apparatus that will fill it up. As the sun emerges, the burners are ignited and passengers board for a brief lecture on the etiquette of ballooning, which is essentially a dangerous pastime if rules aren't followed. Looking down from the morning sky, the view is breathtaking – the wilds of the bushveld are stretched out below, dotted with an astonishing number of wild animals.

GREAT AFRICAN BALLOON TRIPS	
Egypt	The Nile's West Bank
	Valley of the Kings
	The Pyramids
South Africa	The Pilanesberg
Namibia	Sesriem Canyon
	Namib Desert
	Sossusvlei
Kenya	The Masai Mara
Tanzania	The Serengeti

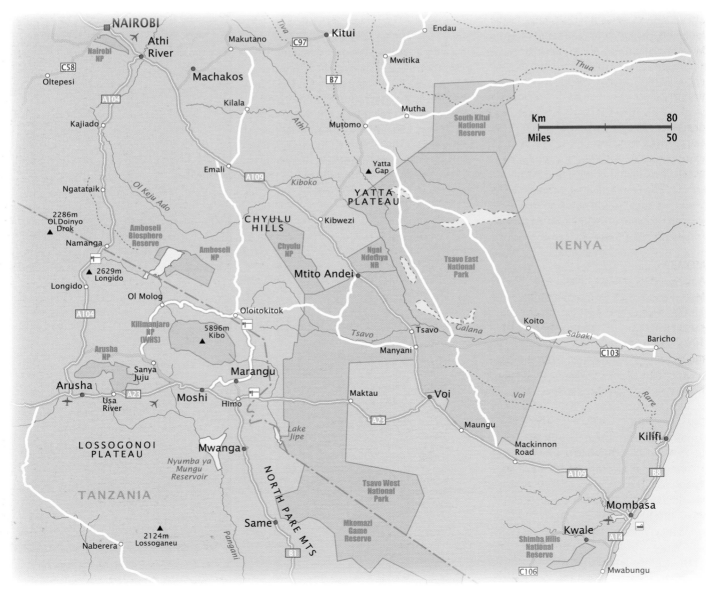

THE MASAI'S FAUNA

Scattered across the veld are the Big Five (elephant, lion, leopard, buffalo and rhino) as well as big-game species such as cheetah, giraffe and zebra. There are also wildebeest ranging the veld in their thousands, plus impala, hartebeest, bushbuck, waterbuck and reedbuck. Braving the wind-chill factor (even in Africa you'll feel this up in a hot-air balloon) will allow you an unparalleled view of the animals, as well as birds that number up to 500 species – among them hawks and falcons, bustards, vultures and sunbirds. Game viewing is outstanding almost all year, but especially good in January and February. The highlight of the year is the migration of wildlife (notably wildebeest) which cross from Tanzania between December and May in search of pasture. The one-hour aerial flit across the bushveld ends with a sumptuous champagne breakfast, after which you will be driven back to the lodge on an early-morning game drive. Memorable as the balloon safari is, you should expect to pay a lot for the experience. There is no budget accommodation in the park and, if you do decide to sacrifice the luxury of an up-market lodge or tented camp in order to rough it at the camp sites, be sure to budget for other expenses such as entry fees, guide fees, porter fees, camping fees, guard fees and firewood. The cheapest way is to tag onto an organised safari led by one of the many private operators working and competing in the region.

MOMBASA

A romantic port on a coral island, Mombasa has retained much of its 12,000-year charm. Like Zanzibar, it has remained virtually unchanged for about 100 years, with its floating market skirting the shores of Mombasa Island. With a population of half a million, old Mombasa has a long history of conquerors and colonists. Historic Fort Jesus guards the Old Harbour, with spectacular reefs 640m (2000ft) offshore. These reefs are lined with white, pebble-free beaches such as Tiwi and Diani, circled by dhows and schools of tropical fish, and offer excellent snorkelling and scuba diving adventures.

LAMU ARCHIPELAGO

The islands of Lamu, Manda and Pate form the Lamu Archipelago, site of some of the best diving off East Africa. Lesser-known isles include Manda (best known for its Takwa Ruins covering 5ha or 12 acres) and Pate Island, home to the mystical 8ha (20-acre) Swahili state of Shanga. Most prominent of the trio is Lamu Island, a 9th-century settlement of cobbled streets and flagstoned courtyards. The island, 19km (12 miles) long, is a mix of traditional Islam and Swahili and offers a fascinating glimpse into old Africa. The lively harbour front is the hunting ground of the island's feral cats.

DHOW SAILING ON THE COAST

Most of Kenya's offshore islands offer dhow day trips. The wind-powered craft offer a tempting alternative to the dusty roads of coastal villages. Whether you are taking an extended overnight journey along the Kenyan coast, an afternoon excursion into the bay, a pleasure cruise, or simply using the dhow 'to get from A to B', there will inevitably be plenty of opportunities to weigh anchor anywhere along the shore. Dhow taxis are simple affairs with no frills and they line up for trade along the docks of the main harbour towns, where others from as far afield as Arabia and India may lie at anchor. Impromptu excursions with a party of half a dozen passengers sharing the cost may result in a delay, as skippers often wait until the dhow is full. There are comfortable vessels for more leisurely trips, although these are still quite basic, with few facilities on board.

> ### DHOW SAILING IN A NUTSHELL
> Climate: Conditions are usually hot and humid along the tropical coast.
> Health: Dehydration can be a risk; drink only bottled water.
> Pack: You will need little more than light cotton clothing, sunscreen and a sun hat, as well as some form of cover if you will be cruising at night.
> Facilities: Lodges, resorts and up-market hotels take good care of clients, but dhow taxis and small businesses offer few 'creature comforts'.

Top to bottom: maiden of the Samburu tribe; Lamu's central market; elephant at Amboseli.

165

QUICK FACTS

UGANDA
Capital: Kampala
Area: 236,036km² / 91,134mi²
Population: 35,9 million
Main ethnic groups:
· Buganda (18%)
· Banyoro (14%)
· Teso (9%)
Main languages:
· English
· Luganda
· Nkole
· Chiga
· Lango
· Acholi
· Teso
Main religions:
· Catholic/Protestant (66%)
· Traditional beliefs (18%)
· Muslim (16%)
Currency: Ugandan shilling
  (100 cents)

RWANDA
Capital: Kigali
Area: 26,340km² / 10,170mi²
Population: 10,7 million
Main ethnic groups:
· Hutu (90%)
· Tutsi (9%)
· Twa pygmy (1%)
Main languages:
· Kinyarwanda
· French
· Kiswahili
Main religions:
· Catholic (65%)
· Traditional beliefs (25%)
· Protestant (7%)
Currency: Rwandan franc
  (100 centimes)

IN THIS CHAPTER

Golden monkey.

Local boy and fishing boat.

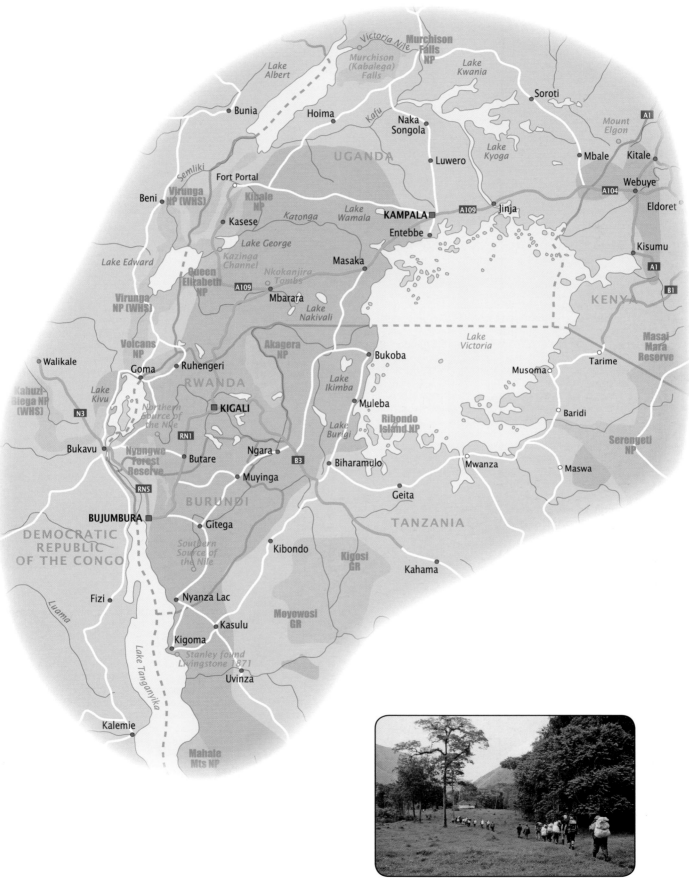

Lake Albert

Bunia

Hoima

Victoria Nile

Murchison Falls NP

Murchison (Kabalega) Falls

Lake Kwania

Soroti

A1

Mount Elgon

Kafu

Naka Songola

Luwero

Lake Kyoga

Mbale

Kitale

UGANDA

Webuye

A104

Eldoret

Semliki

Fort Portal

Virunga NP (WHS)

Beni

Kibale NP

Kasese

Katonga

Lake Wamala

KAMPALA

A109

Jinja

Entebbe

Kisumu

A1

Lake George

Lake Edward

Kazinga Channel

Queen Elizabeth NP

A109

Masaka

Nkokanjira Tombs

Mbarara

Lake Nakivali

Lake Victoria

KENYA

B1

Virunga NP (WHS)

Volcans NP

Walikale

Goma

Ruhengeri

RWANDA

Bukoba

Musoma

Tarime

Masai Mara Reserve

Kahuzi-Biega NP (WHS)

N3

Lake Kivu

Northern Source of the Nile

KIGALI

Lake Ikimba

Muleba

Ribondo Island NP

Baridi

Bukavu

Nyungwe Forest Reserve

RN1

Butare

Ngara

B3

Lake Burigi

Biharamulo

Mwanza

Serengeti NP

Maswa

RN5

Muyinga

BURUNDI

Geita

TANZANIA

Fizi

BUJUMBURA

Gitega

Kibondo

Kigosi GR

Kahama

DEMOCRATIC REPUBLIC OF THE CONGO

Southern Source of the Nile

Nyanza Lac

Luama

Kasulu

Moyowosi GR

Kigoma

Stanley found Livingstone 1871

Lake Tanganyika

Uvinza

Kalemie

Mahale Mts NP

Trekking in the Rwenzoris.

Uganda and Rwanda

10 TOP ADVENTURES

1. Gorilla tracking
2. Trekking/hiking
3. Mountaineering
4. Game viewing
5. Mountain biking
6. Chimp viewing
7. Paddling (rafting/kayaking/river boarding)
8. Fishing
9. Jet boating
10. Bungee jumping

Climbing on Mt Speke.

ON LAND

Gorilla tracking

WILD

The endangered mountain gorillas are only found in a tiny corner of Africa – the triangle of mountains where Uganda, Rwanda and the DRC converge – and Uganda's Bwindi Impenetrable Forest and Mgahinga Gorilla national parks offer some of the best and most accessible viewing. Permits are pricey and the trek often involves a strenuous, muddy hike through the jungle for an hour with one of the troops. But it's worth every penny and bead of sweat. This is one adventure you simply must not miss.

Rwanda is home to one-third of the world's remaining mountain gorillas, and the Virunga Volcanoes NP (Volcans NP), where legendary primatologist Dian Fossey spent decades studying the rare primates, is tops for gorilla tracking and for viewing cute golden monkeys.

Mgahinga Gorilla and Bwindi Impenetrable NPs
www.ugandawildlife.org
+256 414 355 405
Wild Frontiers
www.wildfrontiers.com
+27 72 927 7529
Abacus African Vacations
www.abacusvacations.com

+256 414 232 657
Flame of Africa
www.flameofafrica.com
+27 31 762 2424
Rwanda Development Board
www.rwandatourism.com
+250 252 580 388

Trekking/hiking

MILD

The seven-day circuit of the fabled 'Mountains of the Moon' is an incredible, but tough, adventure through boggy, high-altitude terrain. An easier option is the one- to 10-day Kilembe Trail. Mt Elgon, a beautiful volcano on Uganda's eastern border, is unspoilt and virtually unknown. There are self-guided short walks and guided overnight hikes to the summit. Alternatively, hike the Virunga volcanoes or in Mgahinga Gorilla National Park.

In Rwanda, visit the grave of primatologist Dian Fossey, climb the Bisoke volcano or explore the lava caves and tunnels of the Volcans NP. If you fancy an elevated view, take a canopy walk among the butterflies and birds of the Nyungwe Rainforest – contact ITT Travel.

Rwenzori Trekking
www.rwenzoritrekking.com
+256 774 114 499
Wild Frontiers
www.wildfrontiers.com

+27 72 927 7529
ITT Travel
www.itt.co.rw
+250 252 578 831

Mountaineering

WILD

Climbing the snowcapped, glaciated peaks of Marguerita, Speke and Baker in the Rwenzori Mountains of Uganda offers similar, and arguably even more dramatic, scenery than on the better-known peaks of Mt Kilimanjaro and Mt Kenya.

Summiting 4507m (14,787ft) Mt Karasimbi in Rwanda's Volcans NP is a tough but rewarding two-day outing with no technical difficulties, making it accessible to inexperienced mountaineers.

Rwenzori Mountaineering Services
www.rwenzorimountaineeringservices.com
+256 483 444 936 or 414 237 497
Rwenzori Trekking
www.rwenzoritrekking.com
+256 774 114 499
Wild Frontiers
www.wildfrontiers.com
+27 72 927 7529

Game viewing

TO DO

With the backdrop of the Rwenzori Mountains to the north and the Virunga volcanoes to the south, there are few places on earth to rival the scenery in the Queen Elizabeth NP. Large herds of elephant, buffalo, Uganda kob and topi are often seen, as well as 'tree-climbing' lions, which favour the park's big fig trees. Murchison Falls NP is renowned for excellent sightings of antelope, hippo, buffalo and elephant.

In Rwanda, Akagera NP, on the border with Tanzania, is the place to check out big game.

Abacus African Vacations
www.abacusvacations.com
+256 414 232 657
Flame of Africa
www.flameofafrica.com
+27 31 762 2424

Uganda Wildlife Authority (UWA)
www.ugandawildlife.org
+256 414 355 405
Akagera Game Lodge
www.akageralodge.co.rw
+250 567 805

Mountain biking

Ride through Bwindi NP checking out the monkeys and other wildlife, cruise the foothills of Mt Elgon or head out on the maze of dirt roads and tracks along the banks of the River Nile around Jinja.

The seven-day Congo Nile Trail along the eastern shores of Lake Kivu is a classic, and there are plenty other multi-day and short trails throughout Rwanda as well as bikes for hire.

MILD

Bwindi Impenetrable NP
www.ugandawildlife.org
+256 414 355 405
Rwandan Adventures
www.rwandan-adventures.com
+250 786 571 414
African Bikers
www.africanbikers.com
+27 21 465 2018

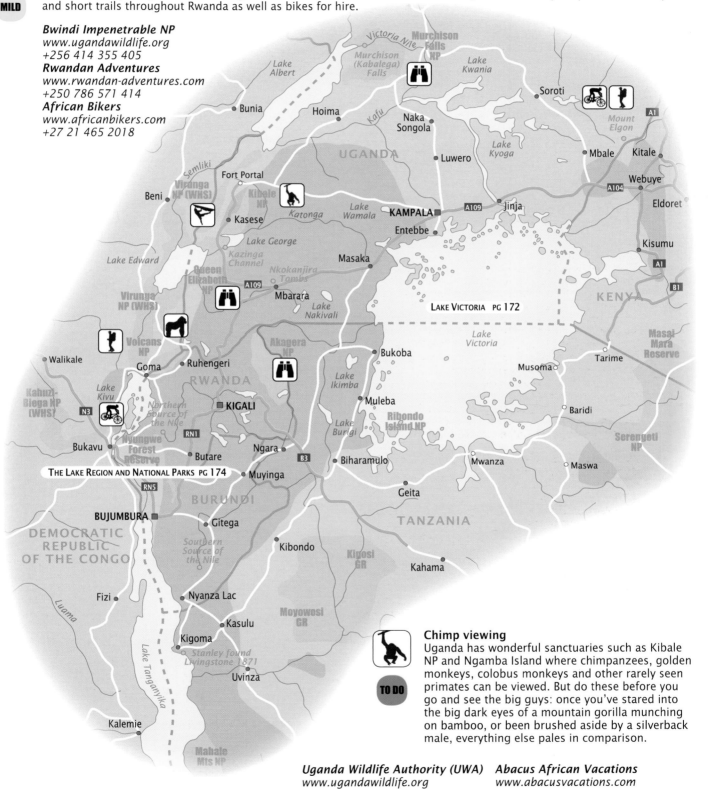

THE LAKE REGION AND NATIONAL PARKS PG 174

LAKE VICTORIA PG 172

Chimp viewing

Uganda has wonderful sanctuaries such as Kibale NP and Ngamba Island where chimpanzees, golden monkeys, colobus monkeys and other rarely seen primates can be viewed. But do these before you go and see the big guys: once you've stared into the big dark eyes of a mountain gorilla munching on bamboo, or been brushed aside by a silverback male, everything else pales in comparison.

TO DO

Uganda Wildlife Authority (UWA)
www.ugandawildlife.org
+256 414 355 405
Wild Frontiers
www.wildfrontiers.com
+27 72 927 7529

Abacus African Vacations
www.abacusvacations.com
+256 414 232 657
Flame of Africa
www.flameofafrica.com
+27 31 762 2424

ON WATER

Paddling (rafting/kayaking/river boarding)
The rapids on the Nile are big and intimidating, so whitewater rafting and kayaking is on a par with that on the mighty Zambezi. You can also learn to kayak or surf the waves on a river board.

WILD

Adrift
www.surfthesource.com
+256 312 237 438

Jet boating.

Fishing
Lake Victoria is famous is for its mean Nile perch. Hire a local fishing boat and you've a good chance of hooking a big one. Alternatively cast a line at Murchison Falls or on Lake Mburo.

MILD

UWA
www.ugandawildlife.org,
+256 414 355 405
Wild Frontiers
www.wildfrontiers.com
+27 72 927 7529

Mweya Safari Lodge
www.mweyalodge.com
+256 312 260 260
Abacus African Vacations
www.abacusvacations.com
+256 414 232 657

Jet boating
Race up the rapids at breathtaking speeds then sit quietly enjoying the magical scenery.

WILD

Wild Nile Jet
www.surfthesource.com
+256 312 237 438

IN THE AIR

Bungee jumping
The Nile High Bungee is one of the most impressive bungee jumps in the world. Kites and African Fish Eagles circle overhead as you plunge 44m down to the source of the Nile.

WILD

Adrift
www.surfthesource.com
+256 312 237 438

Nile High bungee jump.

OTHER ADVENTURES

1. Horse riding
   Mihingo Lodge
   www.mihingolodge.com
   +256 752 410 509
2. Birding
   Mweya Safari Lodge
   www.mweyalodge.com
   +256 312 260 260
   Birding & Beyond Safaris
   www.tanzaniabirding.com
   +255 744 286 058
   Uganda Wildlife Authority (UWA)
   www.ugandawildlife.org
   +256 414 355 405
   Rwanda Development Board
   www.rwandatourism.com
   +250 252 580 388

3. Tours of the genocide sites
   ITT Travel
   www.itt.co.rw
   +250 252 578 831
4. Sailing/cruising
   Uganda Wildlife Authority (UWA)
   www.ugandawildlife.org
   +256 414 355 405
   Abacus African Vacations
   www.abacusvacations.com
   +256 414 232 657
   Wild Frontiers
   www.wildfrontiers.com
   +27 72 927 7529
5. Flying
   Kampala Aero Club
   www.flyuganda.com
   +256 772 706 107

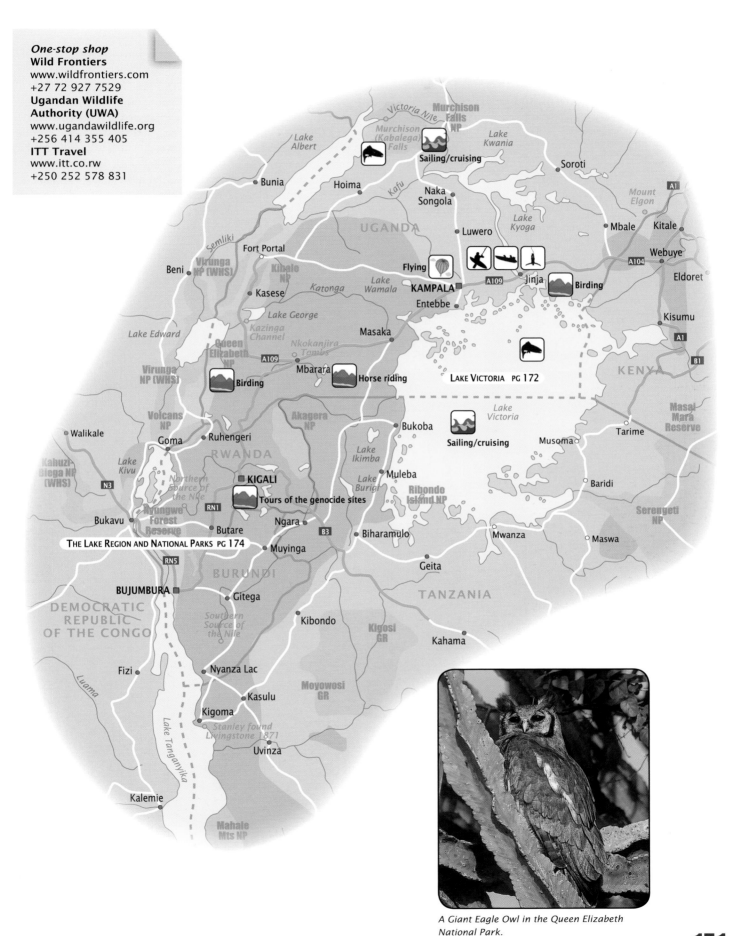

Lake Albert

Victoria Nile

Murchison Falls NP

Murchison (Kabalega) Falls

Sailing/cruising

Bunia

Hoima

Kafu

Naka Songola

Soroti

Lake Kwania

UGANDA

Lake Kyoga

Luwero

Mount Elgon

A1

Mbale   Kitale

Semliki

Fort Portal

Beni

Virunga NP (WHS)

Kibale NP

Flying

Webuye

A104

Kasese

Katonga

Lake Wamala

KAMPALA

A109

Jinja

Birding

Eldoret

Entebbe

Kisumu

Lake George

Kazinga Channel

Masaka

A1

Lake Edward

Queen Elizabeth NP

A109

Mbarara

Nkokanjira Tombs

Horse riding

LAKE VICTORIA PG 172

KENYA

B1

Virunga NP (WHS)

Birding

Volcans NP

Walikale

Goma   Ruhengeri

Akagera NP

Bukoba

Lake Victoria

Sailing/cruising

Musoma

Tarime

Masai Mara Reserve

RWANDA

Lake Kivu

Lake Ikimba

Kahuzi-Biega NP (WHS)

N3

Northern Source of the Nile

KIGALI

Tours of the genocide sites

RN1

Muleba

Lake Burigi

Ribondo Island NP

Baridi

Serengeti NP

Bukavu

Nyungwe Forest Reserve

Butare

Ngara

B3

Biharamulo

Mwanza

Maswa

THE LAKE REGION AND NATIONAL PARKS PG 174

RN5

Muyinga

BURUNDI

Geita

TANZANIA

Kahama

DEMOCRATIC REPUBLIC OF THE CONGO

BUJUMBURA

Gitega

Southern Source of the Nile

Kibondo

Kigosi GR

Fizi

Nyanza Lac

Moyowosi GR

Luama

Kasulu

Kigoma

Stanley found Livingstone 1871

Uvinza

Lake Tanganyika

Kalemie

Mahale Mts NP

A Giant Eagle Owl in the Queen Elizabeth National Park.

AFRICA'S AMAZING LAKES

- Africa's largest lake is Lake Victoria, which is also the second-largest fresh-water lake in the world. Victoria covers almost 70,000km² (26,830 sq. miles) and sits proudly 1130m (3720ft) above sea level. Its deepest known spot lies at a depth of around 82m (270ft).
- Africa's deepest lake is Lake Tanganyika, stretching down 1436m (4710 ft). It is the world's second-deepest freshwater lake after Lake Baikal in Russia.
- With over 500 species, Lake Malawi boasts the largest number of fish species in the world.

LAKE VICTORIA

The papyrus-fringed shores and inter-mittent swamps along Lake Victoria have contributed considerably to its image as one of the most striking in all of Africa. The largest of the continent's great lakes, Lake Victoria is a vast, gentle and tranquil body of water that borders Kenya, Tanzania and Uganda, and is a relatively short distance from Rwanda and Burundi. It is into this great lake that the beginning of the mighty Nile empties, and then leaves again at Jinja as the Victoria Nile.

Together with the Victoria Nile, Lake Victoria is at the heart of some of the best-watered lands on the African continent and is home to a great variety of wildlife, such as the black-and-white Pied Kingfishers (at home in the many shore-line bird sanctuaries), and the common Nile perch (which was introduced into the lake). Locals harvest the waters by casting fishing nets from small handcrafted row-boats to eke out a living: Lake Victoria is a place for the people of Uganda, offering little evidence of the tourist market.

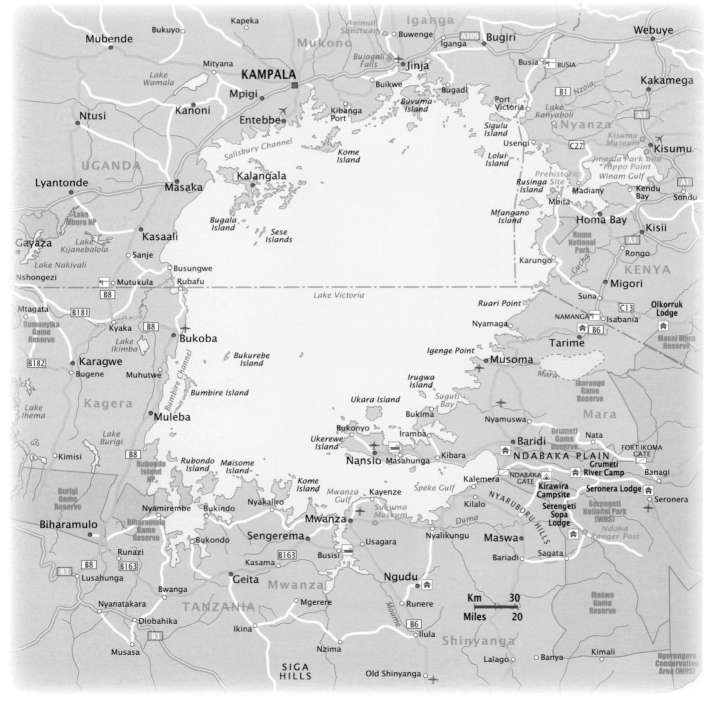

BURUNDI'S WHITE RIVERS

River rafting in Central Africa (with its abundance of water sources and undulating terrain) is one of the great whitewater experiences. Despite the enormous power of many of the rivers, the section of the Nile that makes its way across the Burundi landscape is far from impressive and, although it does offer at least some opportunity for leisurely exploration, it is not the Nile that provides thrilling whitewater rafting. Burundi's claim to fame is the Luvironza River in the far south of the country. The lay of the land here is rugged and bumpy, yet it is delightfully green in places and surprisingly hospitable to the traveller, especially given the isolated location. A few operators have established themselves in the region and many of the waterways are largely uncharted, making for some invigorating (but potentially hazardous) rafting that demands careful planning and nerves of steel. While some sections may be misleadingly gentle in appearance, others are clearly the playgrounds of only the most skilled, with one potentially disastrous series of rapids after another, accompanied by masses of frothing water.

KAMPALA

Despite the crumbling walls of the ghetto areas, what was once considered the Pearl of Africa is re-emerging as one of the gems in Africa's crown. Located on the undulating landscape so typical of Central Africa, the seven hills on which Kampala stands are lush and fertile, and the city is becoming a burgeoning modern centre, with an impressive National Museum and the enthralling Kasubi Tombs. The city is peopled with an eclectic mix of colourful characters, a parade of lively vendors and an avian population of Marabou Storks, which consistently alight on every conceivable vantage point.

AFRICA'S GREAT LAKES			
Lake Victoria	Tanzania/Uganda	68,800 km²	42,750 sq. miles
Lake Tanganyika	Tanzania/Burundi/DRC	32,900 km²	20,443 sq. miles
Lake Nyasa	Malawi/Mozambique	29,600 km²	18,392 sq. miles
Lake Turkana	Kenya	6400 km²	3977 sq. miles
Lake Albert	Uganda/DRC	5300 km²	3293 sq. miles
Lake Edward	Uganda/DRC	2325 km²	1445 sq. miles
Lake Chad	Chad/Nigeria	1350 km²	839 sq. miles

Top to bottom: Nile monitor eating a crab; Mkusi Falls; dugout canoe on the shore.

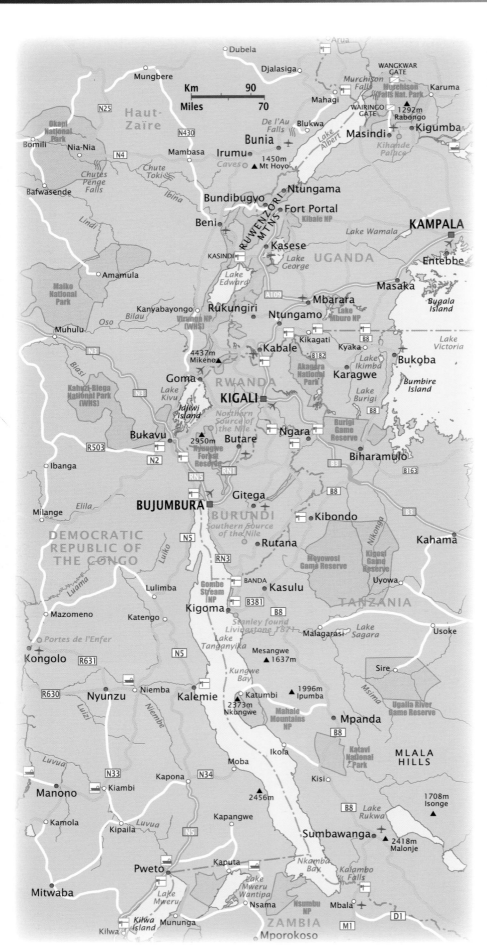

KIGALI

Kigali lies in the centre of a country that has seen devastating conflict in recent times. Yet, the capital is an important cultural, economic and academic centre, and attempts are being made to resurrect its beauty and heal the scars of war.

LAKE KIVU

Lake Kivu covers 2698km² (1042 sq. miles) and is 475m (1558ft) deep. It is navigated by small vessels and shallow barges, many of which service the tea and cotton processing industries around Kamembe. The surrounds are dotted with Rwanda's natural gems, including the 100m (330ft) Les Chutes de Ndaba, the waterfalls on the Rusizi River, Nyakabuye's hot springs and the Rugege Forest.

WONDERFUL WATERWAYS

Volcans National Park in the far north and Nyungwe Forest in the south are the most popular attractions, but the waterways that lead to and from Lake Kivu in the far west, Lake Bulera in the north and Lake Muhazi in the east provide some of the finest adventure thrills. Only a small section of the Nile falls within Rwanda's borders and the best whitewater is found in Uganda on the portion of the Nile known as the Victoria Nile, around Lake Victoria and Lake Mobutu (Lake Albert). Much of the land is terraced (both naturally and to accommodate the plantations), creating a succession of rapids and waterfalls, ranging from a mere step in the river's course to towering (and unrideable) falls.

MURCHISON FALLS

One of Uganda's icons, the Murchison (Kabalega) Falls lies in 3900km² (1,500 sq. miles) of natural splendour, divided by the waters of the Victoria Nile as it snakes from Lake Kyoga to Lake Albert. A three-hour boat trip from Paraa takes visitors to the foot of the falls. Another diversion is to catch the vessel that featured in *African Queen*. Unearthed on the banks of the Victoria Nile during the reclamation of the park, it continues to ply the river.

The countryside comprises mostly savanna and grassland; along the river-banks dense forest is interspersed with acacia trees and papyrus reeds. Here you find lion and leopard, elephant, giraffe, bushbuck and waterbuck, crocodile and hippo. Waterfowl are common, and you may spot shoebills, African Skimmers, Red-throated Bee-eaters, herons and king-fishers among the more than 380 bird species found here.

HIKING THE NYUNGWE RAINFOREST

Nyungwe sports a diversity of flora and fauna, from brilliant butterflies to nearly 300 bird species, 50 mammal species and a number of tree varieties. Parts of the forest are still under threat, but steady progress is being made by the Nyungwe Forest Conservation Project. Butare and Cyangugu are departure points for hikes and gorilla treks, but offer little beyond basic requirements. Some tours into the forests (such as the one starting from the forest station at Uwinka) take only an hour or two and cover only the periphery, while others – such as that to the marshes of Kamiranzovu to see the forest elephants – are longer, taking you into the deepest sections. There are also self-guided trails that vary in difficulty.

RWANDA IN A NUTSHELL

Climate: Hot and humid year-round. The best (but most uncomfortable) times are during the rainy season (Mar–May).
Risk factor: Parts of the country are still considered a security risk and land mines may still be found.
Health: AIDS and malaria are rampant. Tap water is not safe, and bilharzia is a problem in slow-moving waters.
Pack: Take all equipment and gear you need for walks and hikes.
Facilities: Good accommodation is expensive and few operators cater for budget travellers. Forest camps offer the basics.

Top to bottom: Lake Tanganyika; hippos in the Nile below the Murchison Falls; local girl of the Lake Kivu region.

Indian Ocean Islands

QUICK FACTS

COUNTRY	CAPITAL	POPULATION	LANGUAGES	CURRENCY
Madagascar	Antananarivo	21,9 million	Malagasy, French	Malagasy ariary
Seychelles	Victoria	84,000	Creole, French	Seychelles rupee
Réunion	St-Dénis	839,500	French, Creole	Euro
Comoros	Moroni	798,000	Comorian, French	Comorian franc
Rodrigues	Port Mathurin	40,000	English, French	Mauritian rupee
Mauritius	Port Louis	1,3 million	English, French	Mauritian rupee

IN THIS CHAPTER

View of Île Hermitage from Rodrigues Island.

Under the Indian Ocean.

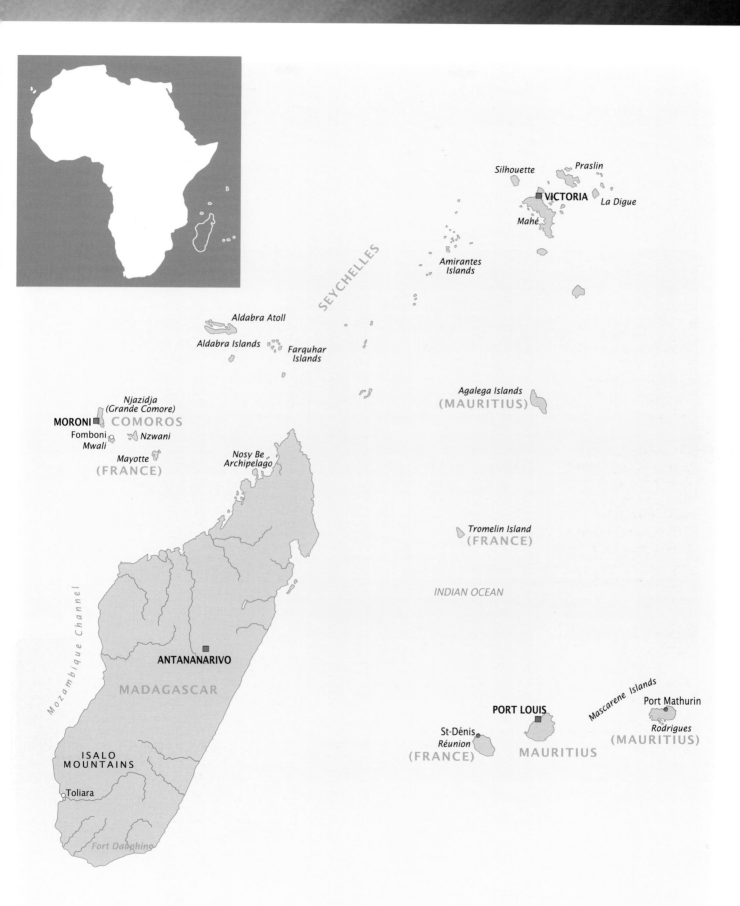

Praslin

Silhouette

VICTORIA

La Digue

Mahé

Amirantes
Islands

SEYCHELLES

Aldabra Atoll

Aldabra Islands

Farquhar
Islands

Agalega Islands
(MAURITIUS)

Njazidja
(Grande Comore)

MORONI COMOROS

Fomboni   Nzwani
Mwali

Mayotte
(FRANCE)

Nosy Be
Archipelago

Tromelin Island
(FRANCE)

INDIAN OCEAN

Mozambique Channel

ANTANANARIVO

MADAGASCAR

Mascarene Islands

Port Mathurin

PORT LOUIS

St-Dénis
Réunion
(FRANCE)

MAURITIUS

Rodrigues
(MAURITIUS)

ISALO
MOUNTAINS

Toliara

Fort Dauphin

Each activity is rated as 'To do', Mild or Wild based on intensity

TO DO   MILD   WILD

0   **3**   **1**

10 TOP ADVENTURES

1. Canyoning (kloofing)
2. Lemur tracking
3. Mountain biking
4. Scuba diving and snorkelling
5. Big-game fishing
6. Kitesurfing
7. Marine safaris
8. Sailing and cruising
9. Submarine tours
10. Paragliding

Canyoning.

ON LAND

Canyoning (kloofing)

 WILD

Journeying down Réunion's steep watercourses involves long abseils, scrambling and some swimming. Though there are canyons to suit all levels of fitness, it's not for the faint-hearted.

Alpanes
www.alpanes.com
+262 692 777 530
Austral Aventure
www.australaventure.fr

+262 262 324 029
Cilaos Aventure
www.cilaosaventure.com
+262 692 667 342

Lemur tracking

 MILD

Lemurs – cute, agile little primates that are unique to Madagascar – are found all over the island, but top spots for sighting them include Antringitra, Ranomafana and Ankaran national parks.

Animaltracks Islandventures
www.animaltracks.co.za
+27 11 454 0543

Mountain biking

 MILD

Mauritius, Réunion and Madagascar are top islands for serious mountain bikers, with a range of exciting downhill trails and guided trips that introduce you to the unique flora and fauna, the friendly people and the tasty cuisine of the islands. Trips are often combined with hiking in the national parks.

Mauritius – Yemaya Adventures
www.yemayaadventures.com
adventure@yemayaadventures.com
Réunion – Maison de la Montagne de la Réunion
www.reunion-nature.com
+262 262 907 878
Madagascar – African Bikers
www.africanbikers.com
+27 21 465 2018
Bike & Saddle
www.bikeandsaddle.com
+27 21 813 6433

ON WATER

Scuba diving and snorkelling

 MILD

Warm, crystal-clear water, colourful coral reefs and an abundance of marine life make diving and snorkelling extremely popular throughout the Indian Ocean. There is an abundance of top-notch dive schools, some of which offer unusual adventures like fast drift dives and shark diving safaris for experienced clients.

Mauritius/Rodrigues
Sinbad Diving
www.justdiving.net
+230 262 7913
Bouba Diving Centre
www.boubadiving.com
+230 832 3063
Seychelles
Seychelles Underwater Centre
www.diveseychelles.com.sc
+248 424 7165 or 434 5445
Angel Fish Yacht Charter
www.seychelles-charter.com
+248 434 4644

Octopus Dive Centre
www.octopusdiver.com
+248 423 2602
Madagascar
Sakatia Passions
www.sakartia-passions.com
+261 208 661 462
Island Quest Sailing and Diving
www.islandquest.co.za
+27 12 329 2917
Réunion
Abyss Plongee
www.abyss-plongee.com
+262 262 347 979

Bleu Ocean
www.bleuocean.fr
+262 262 349 749

Rock cod, Aquarium dive site, Mauritius.

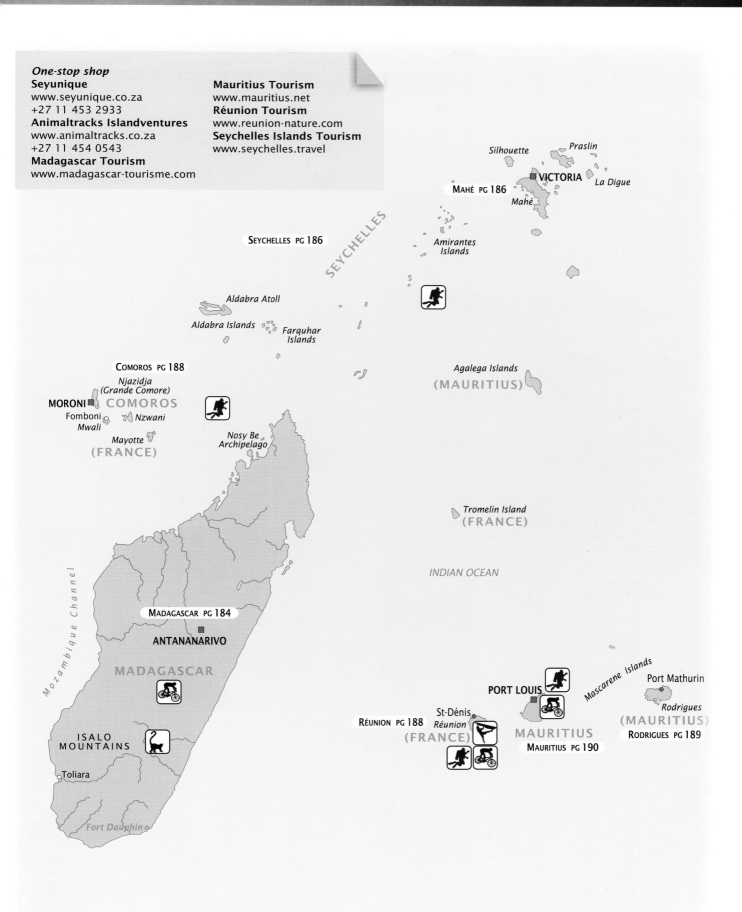

One-stop shop
Seyunique
www.seyunique.co.za
+27 11 453 2933
Animaltracks Islandventures
www.animaltracks.co.za
+27 11 454 0543
Madagascar Tourism
www.madagascar-tourisme.com

Mauritius Tourism
www.mauritius.net
Réunion Tourism
www.reunion-nature.com
Seychelles Islands Tourism
www.seychelles.travel

Silhouette
Praslin

VICTORIA
MAHÉ PG 186
La Digue
Mahé

SEYCHELLES

SEYCHELLES PG 186

Amirantes
Islands

Aldabra Atoll

Aldabra Islands
Farquhar
Islands

Agalega Islands
(MAURITIUS)

COMOROS PG 188

Njazidja
(Grande Comore)

MORONI COMOROS
Fomboni Nzwani
Mwali
Mayotte
(FRANCE)

Nosy Be
Archipelago

Tromelin Island
(FRANCE)

INDIAN OCEAN

Mozambique Channel

MADAGASCAR PG 184

ANTANANARIVO

MADAGASCAR

PORT LOUIS

Mascarene Islands
Port Mathurin

St-Dénis
Réunion
RÉUNION PG 188
(FRANCE)

Rodrigues
(MAURITIUS)
RODRIGUES PG 189

MAURITIUS
MAURITIUS PG 190

ISALO
MOUNTAINS

Toliara

Fort Dauphin

ON WATER

Big-game fishing

WILD

The waters off Réunion, Mauritius, Madagascar and Seychelles are home to marlin, shark and tuna, which attract big-game fishermen from all over the world as well as first-timers and adrenalin junkies trying to land the big one.

Madagascar
Sakatia Passions
www.sakatia-passions.com
+261 324 132 549
Mauritius
JP Henry Charters
www.blackriver-mauritius.com
+230 729 0901

Réunion
Réunion Fishing Club
www.reunionfishingclub.com
+262 262 243 610
Seychelles
Island Charters
www.islandcharters.sc
+248 467 6000

Kitesurfing

WILD

Wherever there's wind you'll find kitesurfers performing death-defying jumps and tricks, but the north and south coasts of Mauritius, the southeast coast of Rodrigues and the west coast of Réunion are very popular spots.

Mauritius/Rodrigues
Kuxville Kitesurfing
www.kuxville.de
+230 262 7913/8836
Kite for Fun
www.kiteforfun-rodrigues.com/
+230 724 1741

Réunion
Kiteboarding Kitezone Réunion
http://www.kitezone-reunion.com
+262 693 042 680

Marine safaris

MILD

You don't have to be a scuba diver to swim with whale sharks. Trips from Mahé in the Seychelles allow snorkellers and boat-based viewers to appreciate the gentle giants.

Seychelles Underwater Centre
www.diveseychelles.com.sc
+248 247 357

IN THE AIR

Paragliding

MILD

The steep slopes of Réunion make this a paragliding hotspot. A tandem flight is an exhilarating way to view the rugged island and the azure waters of the Indian Ocean – and if you're really lucky you might even catch sight of a lava flow from the active volcano.

Parapente Réunion
www.parapente-reunion.fr
+262 692 829 292
Azurtech
www.azurtech.com
+262 692 653 765

Sailing and cruising

TO DO

There are few things to beat sailing out over the turquoise waters of the Indian Ocean, the wind in your hair and a glass of wine in your hand! With 115 coral and granite islands to explore, the Seychelles is a sailor's paradise, and the full range of sailing opportunities – from sunset cruises to bare boat charter – is on offer throughout the region.

Seychelles
Angel Fish Yacht Charter
www.seychelles-charter.com
+248 434 4644
The Moorings
www.moorings.com
+248 434 6120

Madagascar
Island Quest Sailing and Diving
www.islandquest.co.za
+27 12 329 2917
Mauritius
JP Henry Charters
www.blackriver-mauritius.com
+230 729 0901

Submarine tours

TO DO

Now this is really special. Plunge into the waters of Mauritius, checking out the fish and the reefs either in a submarine or on an underwater scooter.

Blue Safari Submarine
www.blue-safari.com
+230 263 3333

Inside a submarine.

Kitesurfing.

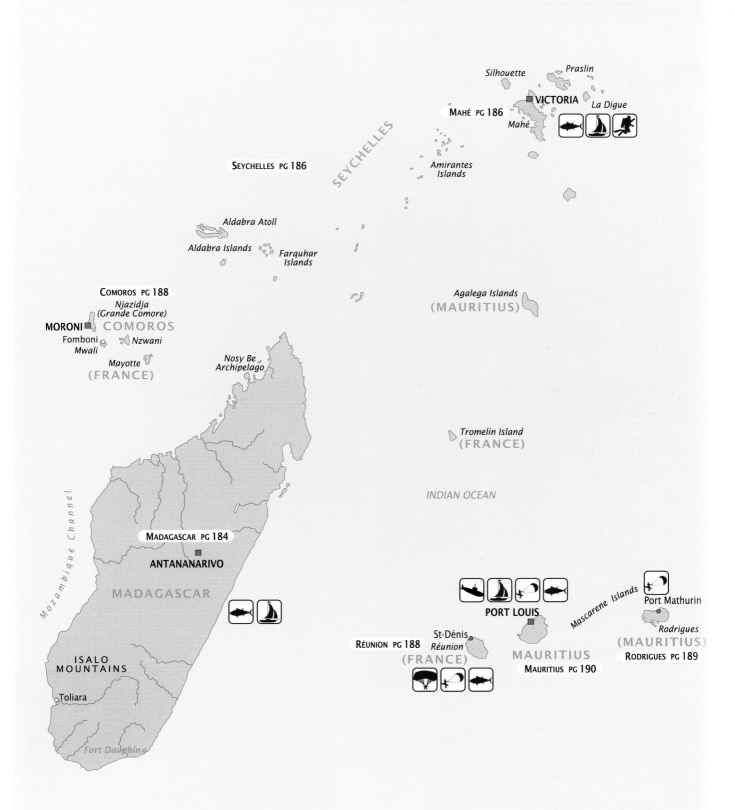

Silhouette

Praslin

MAHÉ PG 186

VICTORIA

La Digue

Mahé

SEYCHELLES

SEYCHELLES PG 186

Amirantes
Islands

Aldabra Atoll

Aldabra Islands

Farquhar
Islands

Agalega Islands
(MAURITIUS)

COMOROS PG 188

Njazidja
(Grande Comore)

MORONI

COMOROS

Fomboni

Nzwani

Mwali

Mayotte
(FRANCE)

Nosy Be
Archipelago

Tromelin Island
(FRANCE)

INDIAN OCEAN

MADAGASCAR PG 184

ANTANANARIVO

MADAGASCAR

Mascarene Islands

Port Mathurin

PORT LOUIS

Mozambique Channel

St-Dénis

Rodrigues

RÉUNION PG 188

Réunion

(MAURITIUS)

(FRANCE)

MAURITIUS

RODRIGUES PG 189

ISALO
MOUNTAINS

MAURITIUS PG 190

Toliara

Fort Dauphin

OTHER ADVENTURES

1. 4x4ing
2. Hiking
3. Sea kayaking
4. Stand-up paddle boarding
5. Surfing

4x4ing

Explore the lunar landscapes of the Plan de Sables and the barren volcanic flanks of the Piton de Fournaise volcano or the lush, remote cirques of central Réunion. Self-sufficient adventurers will also enjoy heading out on the dirt roads to remote spots in Madagascar.

Réunion
Kreolie 4x4
www.kreolie4x4.com
+262 262 395 087
Madagascar
Animaltracks Islandventures
www.animaltracks.co.za
+27 11 454 0543

ON LAND

Hiking

Wild and often bizarre scenery, and the chance of seeing lemurs, means that if you don't mind roughing it a bit, Madagascar is a great place to go trekking. The cirques and high peaks of Réunion, only accessible by foot or donkey paths, offer wonderful multi-day hikes (including the famous G1 and G2 trails which traverse the country) on which you can overnight in comfortable *gîtes*. The hike to Piton de la Fournaise, a live volcano, is very exciting, as is the opportunity to explore the lava tunnels of the volcanic island. There are lovely short trails on most islands of the Seychelles, but hiking the Vallée de Mai on Praslin is a must-do. A UNESCO World Heritage Site, this dense primeval forest is home to some 6000 coco de mer trees and other palms.

Madagascar
Animaltracks Islandventures
www.animaltracks.co.za
+27 11 454 0543
Réunion
Maison de la Montagne de la Réunion
www.reunion-nature.com
+262 262 907 878

Alpanes
www.alpanes.com
+262 692 777 530
Austral Aventure
www.australaventure.fr
+262 262 324 029
Seychelles
Vasco Tours
www.vascotours.com
+248 271 1500

ON WATER

Sea kayaking

Explore the mangroves in the north of Mauritius, or paddle out with dolphins at Tamarin Bay in the south of the island.

Yemaya Adventures
www.yemayaadventures.com
+230 283 8187

Stand-up paddle boarding (SUP)

Beginners can hone their skills in this exciting new sport in sheltered lagoons while the more experienced can try their luck on the waves.

Réunion
Extreme Sud
http://extreme-sud.infoconnect.re
+262 262 266 702

Sea kayaking.

Surfing

The famous break at St-Leu on Réunion attracts surfers from all over the world, but there are numerous other great spots for surfing and body boarding in the region, with professional schools offering board hire and lessons.

Ecole de Surf St-Leu
www.surf-reunion.com
+262 262 496 601

Surfing.

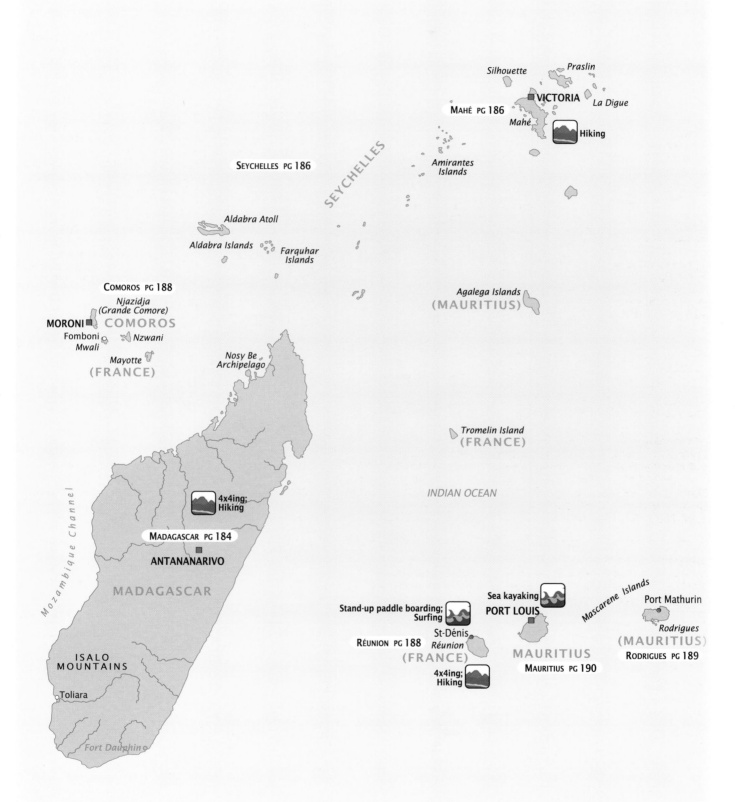

Silhouette

Praslin

VICTORIA

La Digue

MAHÉ PG 186

Mahé

Hiking

SEYCHELLES PG 186

SEYCHELLES

Amirantes
Islands

Aldabra Atoll

Aldabra Islands

Farquhar
Islands

Agalega Islands
(MAURITIUS)

COMOROS PG 188

Njazidja
(Grande Comore)

MORONI

COMOROS

Fomboni

Nzwani

Mwali

Tromelin Island
(FRANCE)

Mayotte
(FRANCE)

Nosy Be
Archipelago

INDIAN OCEAN

4x4ing;
Hiking

MADAGASCAR PG 184

ANTANANARIVO

Mozambique Channel

MADAGASCAR

Sea kayaking

Stand-up paddle boarding;
Surfing

PORT LOUIS

Mascarene Islands

Port Mathurin

St-Dénis

RÉUNION PG 188

Réunion
(FRANCE)

Rodrigues
(MAURITIUS)

MAURITIUS

RODRIGUES PG 189

MAURITIUS PG 190

ISALO
MOUNTAINS

Toliara

4x4ing;
Hiking

Fort Dauphin

Njazidja
(Grande Comore)
Mitsamiouli
MORONI
Foumbouni
Hoani
Mwali
Mutsamudu
Nzwani
COMOROS
Mayotte
(FRANCE)
Mamoudzou

Îles
Glorieuses
(RÉUNION, FR.)
Banc du
Geyser

Lighthouse   Cap d' Ambre
Cap Saint Sébastien
Antsiranana
Mount
Ambre NP
Analamerana
Special
Reserve
Ankarana SR
Antsohimbondrona
Nosy Be
Andoany (Hell-Ville)
Ambanja
MASSIF DU
TSARA TANA
Inharana
(Vohemar)
2876m
Sambava
Bealanana
Analalava
Andapa
Antalaha
Marine NP
Antsohihy
Cap Est
Anataka
Maroantsetra
Boriziny
Corniche de
Farakaraina
Mahajanga
Mandritsara
Lighthouse
Lighthouse
Mitsinjo
Ankaratantsika
NR
Vilanandro
Soalala
Mananara
Besalampy
Soanierana-
Ivongo
Nosy Sainte Marie
Île Juan
de Nova
(FRANCE)
Andilamena
Ambodifotatra
Zahamena
NR
Tamborano
Telomita
Nosy Vao
Mahatsinjo
Ambatondrazaka
Tsingy de Bemaraha
NR (WHS)
Toamasina
Nosy Barren
Antsalova
Tsiroanomandidy
Moramanga
Garge
Bekopaka
ANTANANARIVO
Belo-Tsiribih
ina
Miandrivazo
Ambatolampy
Mahanoro
Antsirabe
Morondava
Malaimbandy
Fandriana
Belo
Ambositra
Mandabe
Ambohimanga Atsimo
Thermal Spring
Mananjary
Fianarantsoa
Ambohinihaonana
Morombe
Tanandava
Beroroha
Cap Saint
Vincent
Ambalavao
Tenika
Caves
Ihosy
Manakara
Isalo
NP
Andringitra
NR
Sakaraha
Ranohira
Farafangana
Ranotsara
Ava
Toliara
Vangaindrano
Sarodrano
Caves
Manambondro
Zombitse
Forest
ISALO MTS
Manantenina
Andavaka
Caves
Mahafaly
Tombs
Andohalela
NR
Ampanihy
Berenty
Reserve
Pic St
Louis
Fort Dauphin
Androka
Andalatanosy
529m
Lighthouse
Ambovombe
Tôlanaro (Fort Dauphin)
Betanty (Faux Cap)
Cap Sainte
Marie

INDIAN OCEAN

Mozambique Channel

Km   100
Miles   50

ANTANANARIVO

Charmingly dishevelled in appearance, 'Tana's' cobbled roads are trod by rickety ox-drawn carts and packed with French colonial-style buildings housing anything from souvenir shops to family-owned produce stores. Many visitors are wildlife enthusiasts – the uniqueness of Madagascar's indigenous flora and fauna is the main attraction. Tana's zoological gardens provide fascinating insights into the island's wildlife.

NOSY BE ARCHIPELAGO

The heart of Madagascar's hospitality industry, the island of Nosy Be is at the centre of the archipelago off the northwest shore that takes its name. Dotted with tourist hotels and amenities, the hilly 280km² (110-sq.-mile) island is easily accessible from the capital and offers open-air markets, a vibrant nightlife and boat trips to neighbouring islands. Walking through the luxuriant vegetation that covers much of Nosy Be (or a visit to the rainforest stand on the Lokobe Peninsula) offers a window into Madagascar's abundant and diverse natural heritage.

FORT DAUPHIN

A bit isolated by unforgiving terrain and an underdeveloped infrastructure, Fort Dauphin was the landing site of the first European travellers in the 16th century and is the centre of Madagascar's lobster industry. The scrubland and relatively high rainfall make it inhospitable to the casual tourist, although naturalists will find the reef-protected beaches, most notably at Libanona, the rugged slopes of Pic St Louis and the protected splendour of the nearby Berenty reserve a great adventure.

TOURIST TREASURES

The continent-in-miniature is blessed with a unique community of plant and animal life that slowly evolved in a protected environment that was effectively isolated from the rest of the world. Perhaps most famed for its chameleons and more than 30 species of lemur, Madagascar is covered with singular habitats spread over numerous parks and conservation areas. Although a regulated tourism industry contributes enormously to conservation, it also tends to put it at risk: take great care when walking this landscape.

ISALO MOUNTAINS

The sandstone mountains of Isalo offer a different view to the conventional image of lush Madagascar. Small patches of grassland break the rather bleak landscape, and the occasional green belts are interspersed with strange rock configurations. Punctuated with ancient burial sites held sacred by locals, the upgraded network of roads affords access to splendid views of the high-lying landscape. The region is largely the domain of hikers, campers and wildlife enthusiasts.

HIKING AROUND ISALO

Isalo is one of the best of Madagascar's many great hiking destinations, and is accessed via nearby Ranohira. The superb walks vary from simple one-day excursions to more extended trips. The guides (based at the hotels in Ranohira) are skilled and informed, yet other facilities are simple at best. Isalo is one of the few areas on the island that may be affected by petty crime. Compared to most other parks, animals are generally scarce here, but its Monkey Canyon Trail remains popular with hikers, taking in lemur sightings and the gentle pools of l'Oasis and Piscine Naturelle, both of which have pleasant camp sites.

OTHER HIKING AREAS

Equally untamed, Zombitse has no demarcated trails, camp sites or guides, yet offers a relatively hassle-free stroll through thick woods. The variety of mammals, birds, reptiles and amphibians is unparalleled and, with trained locals acting as guides, the experience is unmatched. Some of the best opportunities are at dusk and nightfall, when nocturnal creatures emerge to hunt and forage. These excursions are best from October to March, when the hibernating inhabitants venture out after the cooler winter months. Some have become quite accustomed to human presence, but direct contact with them is discouraged.

Top to bottom: Avenue du Baobabs; relaxing on Nosy Komba; the white-footed sportive lemur.

MAHÉ

The largest of the 40 islands and 75 low-lying atolls that make up the Seychelles, Mahé is home to 90% of the population, the seat of the nation's capital, Victoria, and the nucleus of the tourism industry. Visitors are drawn by the exceptional beaches such as Beau Vallon, and the unique plant and animal life. Victoria acts as a base for most excursions into the island wilderness of sea and sand. Blessed with an old-world charm, the capital has rapidly developed a sound infrastructure geared toward the hospitality industry.

SEYCHELLES

Nearly half of Seychelles' land area has been set aside as national park or protected reserve, with some 40% of its seascape a marine conservation area. Morne Seychellois National Park, the most impressive, is laced with hiking trails. Praslin – home to Vallée de Mai, the 18ha (45-acre) World Heritage Site – boasts no fewer than six endemic palms and many other indigenous trees and plants. Even the smaller isles have their treasures, and significant measures have been put in place to help regulate tourist traffic and preserve the balance of unique ecosystems. Despite all these laudable efforts, the Seychelles have seen their fair share of ecological disasters. Tortoise populations have dwindled to alarmingly low numbers, as have fish and bird species, with several now either endangered or extinct – often because of competition from introduced species. All four of the indigenous turtle species – green, hawksbill, loggerhead and giant leatherback – remain at risk. At the same time, concerted efforts to protect the Aldabra giant tortoise (both Arnold's and Marion's tortoises have long been extinct) have meant that further populations have been reintroduced on islands such as Cousin, Frégate and Curieuse. The Aldabra Atoll has been declared a World Heritage Site and is administered by the Seychelles Islands Foundation, in turn sponsored by the Royal Society at the Smithsonian Institute. Tourism to the 34km (21-mile) long atoll is extremely limited, and the relatively insignificant human population on islands such as this one may account for the island-specific ecologies having been little affected by human intervention. Where there is constant human activity on these 'paradise' islands, regulations have been established to help preserve the region's natural heritage: on nine of the islands the sea birds may not be disturbed, while spear fishing is forbidden throughout the island group, with fishing and the collection of seashells and corals prohibited in the marine parks. At the same time, meticulously planned reforestation schemes have been established on those islands already disturbed by indiscriminate plantations.

SURFING THE SEYCHELLES
The waters off the Seychelles are supreme for surfing, and prove most popular when the southeast trade winds blow. At unspoilt coastlines, such as those at Beau Vallon and particularly Grand 'Anse, the wind and waves should be enough to get any surfer pumped. You won't need technical support crews critical in other adrenalin sports; all you need is the wind and the waves. Despite the increasing number of visitors, there are no desperate attempts to find a lift on a wave. Boards most typically seen plying these waters rely on function more than on fashion, and many locals have resigned themselves to the fact that any board is better than none at all. You still see the big, rather ungainly boards that helped pioneer the sport, but the smaller ones (which rely less on volume and more on control and skill) are increasingly common among beach users, as they are far easier to carry to and from the beach.

SEYCHELLES SUB-WONDERLAND
The reefs off Seychelles teem with fish of every colour and size, and the islands – from the corals and coves that circle Praslin to tiny Dénis – offer opportunities to dive and snorkel among a dazzling diversity of marine life and geological structures. Every island seems to be entirely different to the next, making for spectacular diving. The creatures that make the Seychelles such a memorable scuba destination are a diversion from the coral reef's profusion of colour and texture. The fish are used to onlookers and pay little attention to divers. Unfortunately, bleaching has discoloured corals in some areas. In places, powerful sea currents have been known to stir up murky waters, which creates the ideal home for reclusive nurse sharks and feathertail stingrays sheltering in niches, crevices and caves.

SCUBA OFF THE SEYCHELLES
On Aldabra, the world's largest raised coral atoll, schools of black-tipped reef sharks hunt the shallows of the lagoon for small fish, while anemones litter the sea bed and little angelfish dash in and out of the crevices as the tides recede. In the deeper waters, schools of triggerfish and parrotfish feed placidly as scuba divers skirt the reefs, drifting over some of the most colourful expanses ever to be experienced in the Indian Ocean. The trick here is to take your time as you make your way across the undulating seascape, watching for skittish marine creatures and dodging currents so strong that they can suck you in toward the mouths of small caves that punctuate the rock face.

SECRETS OF THE DEEP
Off Astove, one of the four islands in the Aldabra group, the steep inclines of the Astove Wall stretch some 5km (3 miles), dropping abruptly to awesome depths, to a dark and forbidding realm of rough terrain. The wall itself is pleasantly unblemished by human interference, and this silent world is the home of silver-tipped and hammerhead sharks. Most of the more prominent hotels that dot the islands will provide scuba instruction and are well connected to private operators based here. Even the smaller islands, such as Dénis, boast good diving schools with highly qualified dive masters and reliable equipment. There's no excuse for not enjoying the natural diving facilities!

Top to bottom: coco de mer forest; sea turtle.

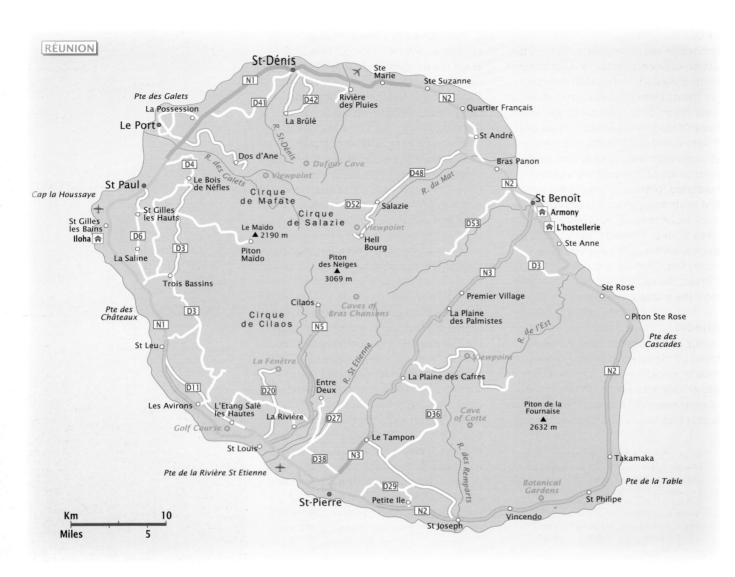

RÉUNION

St-Dénis
Ste Marie
Ste Suzanne
Pte des Galets
La Possession
Rivière des Pluies
Quartier Français
Le Port
La Brûlé
St André
Dos d'Ane
Dufour Cave
Bras Panon
St Paul
Le Bois de Nèfles
Cirque de Mafate
Salazie
St Benoît
Cap la Houssaye
St Gilles les Hauts
Cirque de Salazie
Armony
L'hostellerie
St Gilles les Bains
Iloha
Le Maïdo ▲ 2190 m
Hell Bourg
Ste Anne
La Saline
Piton Maïdo
Piton des Neiges ▲ 3069 m
Ste Rose
Trois Bassins
Cilaos
Caves of Bras Chansons
Premier Village
Piton Ste Rose
Pte des Châteaux
Cirque de Cilaos
La Plaine des Palmistes
Pte des Cascades
St Leu
La Fenêtre
Viewpoint
La Plaine des Cafres
Les Avirons
L'Etang Salé les Hautes
Entre Deux
Piton de la Fournaise ▲ 2632 m
La Rivière
Golf Course
Cave of Cotte
St Louis
Le Tampon
Takamaka
Pte de la Rivière St Etienne
Pte de la Table
St-Pierre
Petite Ile
Botanical Gardens
St Philipe
Vincendo
St Joseph

Km 10
Miles 5

KENYA
ZANZIBAR
DAR ES SALAAM
SEYCHELLES
TANZANIA
COMOROS
MOZAMBIQUE
RODRIGUES
BEIRA
ANTANANARIVO
PORT LOUIS
RÉUNION
MAURITIUS
MADAGASCAR
INDIAN OCEAN

RÉUNION BY AIR

This tiny island is surprisingly sophisticated in its infrastructure, and the knowledge and skill of the few adventure specialists based on Réunion has resulted in a plethora of top-flight outdoor pursuits. Yet, the most memorable is what you see from the air: gloriously rugged mountain faces cracking through the highlands, dormant or extinct volcanoes brooding alongside massive amphitheatres, and cirques carved into the magnificent landscape. The land is crowned by the 3069m (10,069ft) peak of Piton des Neiges, the highest point in the Indian Ocean, and the 2632m (8635ft) Piton de la Fournaise, one of the world's most active volcanoes. The hardy interior of plains and gorges is crowned by cirques and mountains, and Réunion's natural heritage is that much more fascinating from an adrenalin-pumping helicopter flip that takes in the magical beauty from a bird's-eye view. Virtually all the natural arenas and other out-of-the-way spots sprinkled across the land are inaccessible by vehicle, and may only be reached on foot – often arduous and time-consuming. Excursions by helicopter and other aircraft take off at St Gilles les Bains. The skill (and daring) of your pilot will take your breath away as you flit across this remote part of the Indian Ocean, accompanied by the pilot's running commentary: skimming the water, flipping across vast amphitheatres, diving from dizzying heights, or gently drifting on the sea breeze. Light aircraft in particular can cruise at low speeds. The flip across the entire island lasts less than an hour, but takes in everything there is to see: waterfalls and rivers, cirques and mountains, beaches and sea, the gorges of Maïdo as well as the craters of the Plaine des Sables. You can even lunch in the heart of the great Mafate Cirque.

ST-DÉNIS

Located on the scenic north coast of the island, Réunion's capital is most admired for its mountain and volatile volcano, yet boasts picturesque beaches and is a lively centre of social activity. The Indian Ocean's highest mountain is Piton des Neiges (3069m/10,068ft), separating St-Dénis from the urban hub of south-coast St-Pierre. A trendy resort town bordering foothills of rugged hinterland and skirted by cultivated lands of grapevines and crops, St-Dénis' varied climate lends itself to a diverse landscape, from tropical lushness to more temperate vegetation. Most travellers visit the three cirques, the natural amphitheatres that form the island's heart.

MORONI

Capital of the Comoros, Moroni can be found on the island of Grande Comore, the most prominent of the three main volcanic islands that are surrounded by a number of picturesque coral atolls. These atolls are best known for the fantastic diving opportunities offered by their unusual geological formations. Moroni is scenically beautiful, as are the surrounding islands – heavily wooded and cultivated with aromatic crops such as cloves and vanilla, which perfume the Comoros. Although tourism is a burgeoning industry – as well as a vital earner of foreign exchange – most of the 25,000 impoverished citizens of Moroni are in some way involved with the farming of cash crops. The capital is rustic in appearance and there is little by way of an urban lifestyle, yet it is lively and colourful. Moroni's primary attractions make it a true 'island paradise', with magnificent scenery and an unspoiled island wilderness.

RODRIGUES

Mauritius' little sister, the volcanic island of Rodrigues is still in a time warp, close to what Mauritius was like 30 years ago before the tourist explosion. With its mountainous central ridge and deep valleys and ravines, it seems larger than its dimensions – 18km (11 miles) long and 8km (5 miles) wide. A coral reef surrounds the island, enclosing a wide, shallow lagoon twice its size. The lagoon is a scuba diver's and water-sports lover's paradise. Strung in the turquoise water around Rodrigues is a necklace of 17 tiny islets, overgrown with rare flora and inhabited by endangered sea birds.

> **ST GILLES LES BAINS IN A NUTSHELL**
> Climate: Balmy to hot with seasonal rains and warm sea temperatures.
> Best time to visit: May–Oct.
> Risk factor: Buckle up and avoid the cyclone season (Jan–Mar).
> Pack: Light summer clothing; take some rain gear if travelling in the warm wet period (Nov–Apr).

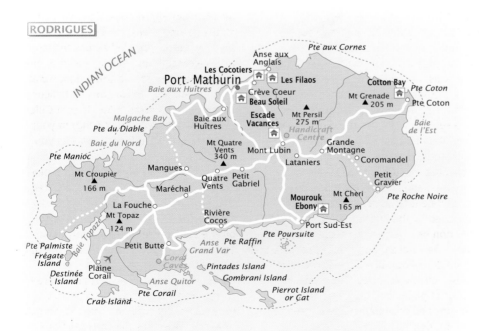

Top to bottom: Réunion's rocky coast; waterfall in Langevin River valley; paragliding.

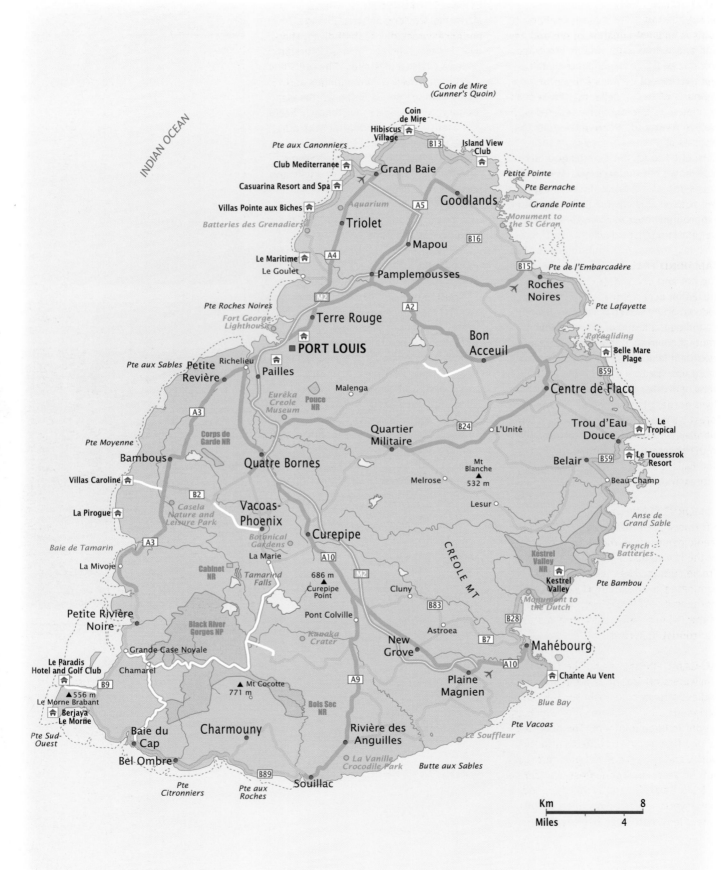

Coin de Mire
(Gunner's Quoin)

INDIAN OCEAN

Coin
de Mire

Hibiscus
Village

B13

Island View
Club

Pte aux Canonniers

Club Mediterranee

Grand Baie

Petite Pointe

Pte Bernache

Casuarina Resort and Spa

Goodlands

Grande Pointe

Monument to
the St Géran

Villas Pointe aux Biches

Aquarium

A5

Batteries des Grenadiers

Triolet

Mapou

B16

Le Maritime

A4

Pamplemousses

B15

Pte de l'Embarcadère

Le Goulet

Roches
Noires

Pte Roches Noires

M2

A2

Pte Lafayette

Fort George
Lighthouse

Terre Rouge

Bon
Acceuil

Paragliding

PORT LOUIS

Belle Mare
Plage

Pte aux Sables

Petite
Rivière

Richelieu

Pailles

B59

Centre de Flacq

Malenga

Eurêka
Creole
Museum

Pouce
NR

A3

Corps de
Garde NR

B24

L'Unité

Trou d'Eau
Douce

Le
Tropical

Quartier
Militaire

Pte Moyenne

Mt
Blanche
532 m

Le Touessrok
Resort

B59

Bambous

Quatre Bornes

Melrose

Belair

Villas Caroline

Beau Champ

B2

Lesur

Anse de
Grand Sable

La Pirogue

Casela
Nature and
Leisure Park

Vacoas-
Phoenix

French
Batteries

Baie de Tamarin

A3

Botanical
Gardens

Curepipe

CREOLE MT

Kestrel
Valley
NR

La Mivoie

La Marie

A10

Kestrel
Valley

Pte Bambou

Cabinet
NR

686 m

Curepipe
Point

Cluny

Monument to
the Dutch

Tamarind
Falls

Petite Rivière
Noire

M2

Astroea

B28

Pont Colville

B83

Black River
Gorges NP

Kanaka
Crater

New
Grove

B7

Mahébourg

Grande Case Noyale

Le Paradis
Hotel and Golf Club

A10

Chamarel

A9

Plaine
Magnien

Chante Au Vent

B9

556 m

Mt Cocotte
771 m

Le Morne Brabant

Bois Sec
NR

Blue Bay

Berjaya
Le Morne

Charmouny

Rivière des
Anguilles

Pte Vacoas

Pte Sud-
Ouest

Baie du
Cap

Le Souffleur

Bel Ombre

La Vanille
Crocodile Park

Butte aux Sables

B89

Souillac

Pte
Citronniers

Pte aux
Roches

Km		8
Miles		4

PORT LOUIS

As the heart of idyllic Mauritius, Port Louis is an amalgamation of old and new, wild and sedate. Encircled by the craggy volcanic peaks of the Moka Mountains and overlooked by the 19th-century ramparts of La Citadelle, the few remaining clearings and gardens are lined with banyan trees and old colonial buildings, legacies of Victoria's empire.

The city has retained a village atmosphere, yet the increasingly modern skyline is dotted with ever-popular fast-food and souvenir shops. Caudan Waterfront is a thoroughly contemporary and impressive tourist hotspot.

TAMARIND FALLS

The hot and dry Sunset Coast is pummelled on occasion by tropical storms and lashed by waves that lure surfers of all abilities. Inland lie the decidedly more tranquil environs of Mare aux Vacoas, a mountain lake encircled by forests of pine and palm, green woods and tea plantations, with stunning views of the Black River gorges. The sometimes demanding forest trails are the domain of deer and monkey, and many visitors go on a hike to the spectacular 295m (968ft) Tamarind Falls, the island's biggest and most impressive waterfall.

LE MORNE PENINSULA

A former haven for runaway slaves, the scenic peninsula is widely considered to be the last remaining outpost of African-Creole culture. The rocky landscape, dominated by the 556m (1824ft) Le Morne Brabant, offers spectacular views of the 14km (9-mile) coast and is a popular tourist drawcard.

BIG-GAME FISHING IN MAURITIUS

The waters off Mauritius are home to an endless stream of sailfish, tuna, kingfish, barracuda and marlin, most of which are caught in huge numbers. The deep-sea fishing here is some of the best in the world, and the season extends throughout the year. La Pirogue hosts the annual 555 Big Game Fishing World Cup, and many world records have been set in waters less than a kilometre (half a mile) off the west coast.

DIVING OFF MAURITIUS

Mauritius provides a varied diving experience: wreck dives, shelf dives, shark dives, night dives and diving excursions to nearby island dive sites. The reefs and wrecks are covered with sponges and corals, and are home to fan worms, sea urchins and anemones. Visibility is best in winter, but the summer months attract the fish and marine life.

Nowhere in Mauritius are spear guns permitted, and the removal of shells and corals is forbidden.

MAURITIUS IN A NUTSHELL

Climate: Weather is generally good all year. The west coast fishing grounds are dry and hot, especially from Jan–Mar (Feb–Mar the wettest).

Risk factor: Big-game fishing is a specialised activity that demands both expertise and strength – novices should be accompanied by a skilled angler. Deep-sea diving can be a very dangerous pastime; obey the rules of safety and etiquette – even in Mauritius' idyllic waters – and employ the services of professional dive masters.

Health: Sunburn can cause considerable discomfort.

Pack: If travelling on a deep-sea fishing trip in a private capacity, make sure you are fully prepared and well equipped, although such diving trips are not recommended. The services of a professional operator are highly recommended, and they will provide all the gear you need. All diving equipment and accessories are provided by the more established dive schools and dive operators, especially for those who are not seasoned divers.

Top to bottom: aerial view of Île aux Cerfs; local hawker on the beach; sugar cane fields.

Imprint

First edition published in 2013
by MapStudio™ South Africa

ISBN 978-1-77026-457-1 (Print)
ISBN 978-1-77026-458-8 (ePub)
ISBN 978-1-77026-459-5 (ePDF)

Production Manager John Loubser
Project Manager Genené Hart
Editors Thea Grobbelaar, Claudia dos Santos
Designer Nicole Bannister
Cartographer Genené Hart
Researcher Abbygail Greybe
Proofreader Roelien Theron
Reproduction Hirt & Carter, Cape Town
Marketing marketing@mapstudio.co.za
Feedback research@mapstudio.co.za
Photo credits © 2013 Individual photographers as credited
(right)
Printed and bound by CTP Book Printers,
Cape Town, South Africa

Special thanks to Mariëlle Renssen and Sean Fraser for their
contributions

MapStudio™
Wembley Square, First Floor,
Solan Road, Cape Town
PO Box 1144, Cape Town, 8000
Tel: 0860 10 50 50
www.mapstudio.co.za

Maps © 2013 MapStudio™
© MapStudio™ 2013

Photographic credits

Abseil Zambia, 107c
Shaen Adey, 6, 7, 8, 9, 10, 11, 40a, 40b, 42, 43, 44a, 46, 47, 51b,
55a, 61a, 62b, 65, 75b, 76, 77, 80a, 81a, 88, 92, 94, 107b, 112,
113 132b, 134, 155, 176, 178b, 180, 182a, 187a
Shaen Adey/IOA, 17c, 19a, 19b, 19c, 21a, 21c, 27c, 31b, 31c, 33a,
39a
Adrift, 170
Daryl and Sharna Balfour/IOA, 151a, 138a, 163a, 165c
Andrew Bannister/IOA, 161a, 161b, 163b, 165a, 165b
Keith Begg/IOA, 85b, 85c
Peter Blackwell/IOA, 141a, 143a, 147, 149a, 149b, 151c, 173c,
175a
Tony Camacho/IOA, 73b, 173a
Ed Cardwell, 91
Children in the Wilderness, 61b
Colour Library/IOA, 29b, 64
Danforth Yachting, 120a, 124
David Foot Safaris, 60
Roger de la Harpe/IOA, 75a, 83, 85a
Nigel Dennis/IOA, 25b, 37, 73a, 73c
Gerhard Dreyer/IOA, 23b
East African Whale Shark Trust, 152a
Eco Resorts, 154
Martin Harvey/IOA, 44b, 49c, 51a, 51c, 53b, 55b, 57a, 57c, 59a,
59b, 67, 71, 185
Leonard Hoffman/IOA, 25a
Hot Air Safaris, 157
Karisia Walking Safaris, 158a
Walter Knirr/IOA, 5, 23a, 33b
Fiona McIntosh, title page, 107a, 108, 110, 111, 120b, 126b, 132a,
136, 138, 145c, 156a, 158b, 166a, 167, 168, 178a, 187b, 189c
Ian Michler/IOA, 49a, 62a, 69, 97, 99, 101, 103, 105, 115c, 117a
Mozambique Dhow Safaris, 93
Peter Pickford/IOA, 27a, 27b, 49b, 59c
Alain Proust/IOA, 191
Peter Ribton/IOA, 131a, 145a, 145b, 151b, 161c
Ryno/IOA, 21b
Semonkong Lodge, 13
Shearwater Adventures, 79
Mark Skinner/IOA, 75c
Swazi Trails, cover (bottom), 14, 15, 156b
Erhardt Thiel/IOA, 17a
Transfrontier Parks Destinations, 90, 95
Vincent van Olphen, 182b
Ariadne van Zandbergen/IOA, 35b, 35c, 39b, 39c, 78b, 87, 109,
115a, 115b, 117b, 117c, 119, 129, 131b, 141b, 149c, 163c, 166b,
171, 173b, 175b, 175c, 189a, 189b
Hein von Horsten/IOA, 25c, 31a
Lanz von Horsten/IOA, 4, 141c
Chanan Weiss/IOA, 29c, 53a, 53c, 55c, 57b, 131c, 143b, 143c,
152b
Wilderness Safaris/Dana Allen, cover (top), 63, 122, 123, 126a
Wild Horizons, 78a, 81b
Keith Young/IOA, 17b, 23c